D0349651

American River College Library
4700 College Oak Drive
Sacramento, California 95841

AMERICAN RIVER COLLEGE

3 3204 01429 3939

Defining the Family

Janet L. Dolgin

DEFINING
THE FAMILY

LAW, TECHNOLOGY,

AND REPRODUCTION

IN AN UNEASY AGE

New York University Press

New York and London

NEW YORK UNIVERSITY PRESS
New York and London

Copyright © 1997 by New York University

All rights reserved

Library of Congress Cataloging-in-Publication Data
Dolgin, Janet L., 1947–
Defining the family : law, technology, and reproduction in an
uneasy age / Janet L. Dolgin.
p. cm.
Includes bibliographical references and index.
Contents: The transformation of the family—Family law in
transition—Status and contract in surrogate motherhood—Unwed
fathers and surrogate mothers—Social implications of biological
transformations—The "intent" of reproduction—Suffer the
children.
ISBN 0-8147-1859-0 (alk. paper)
1. Human reproductive technology—Law and legislation—United
States.   2. Human reproduction—Law and legislation—United States.
3. Domestic relations—United States.   4. Family—United States.
5. Human reproductive technology—Social aspects—United States.
I. Title.
KF3830.D65   1997
346.7301'7—dc40   96-35617
[347.30617]   CIP

New York University Press books are printed on acid-free paper,
and their binding materials are chosen for strength and durability.

Manufactured in the United States of America

10   9   8   7   6   5   4   3   2   1

To Aaron

and our children, Ahuva,

Shoshana, and Nava

CONTENTS

This book examines a subject central to almost all of my academic career. That subject is the anatomy of culture: the investigation of the basic assumptions that underlie culture in general, and that provide the foundation upon which, in particular cultures, institutions, and patterns of thought and feeling, are based.

The study of law has been central to this investigation. The legal system of any culture reflects, and is reflected in, the culture's broader system of meanings and beliefs, and thus the law, properly understood, provides an invaluable aid to understanding social order. As a student of anthropology, as well as of the American legal system, I have asked, for two decades, and continue to ask, the same set of basic questions: upon what cultural assumptions do lawmakers and judges rely as they enact and interpret law? How closely do these assumptions reflect the explanations and justifications the law provides as disputes are adjudicated and rules established? When, and why, does an essentially conservative legal system change? And how accurately does law, as it shifts and adjusts in response to changing social conundrums, reflect and direct the larger culture?

I search for answers to such questions in order to locate and analyze the basic assumptions about people and the world that constitute the cultural bedrock of society.

From time to time in the life of societies, central assumptions about life and thought are challenged openly, and become the subject of debate and ideological controversy. That is happening in the United States now, as assumptions about the scope and meaning of family and of familial relationships are challenged, defended, modified, or rejected. Long-standing assumptions about what families are, and about the differences between familial and other sorts of relationships, are being challenged vociferously and widely. As a result, society faces dramatic shifts in the contours and significance of what has for centuries been among its central institutions—the family.

This process, although not initiated by the advent and development of reproductive technology (including in vitro fertilization, the cryopreservation of embryonic and gametic material, and posthumous conception), has been accelerated by those technologies and by the related phenomenon of surrogate motherhood. New forms of assisted reproduction, which appear with startling rapidity, challenge not only the social dimensions of family, but the biological substrate in terms of which familial relationships have long been understood within Western culture.

Detailed study of the law's responses to the disputes and dilemmas occasioned by the use of assisted reproduction in the creation of familial relationships enables the trained observer to anatomize not only particular law, but a seismic shift in American culture. At stake in the debate surrounding assisted reproduction are many of the central conundrums of the period, including those associated with apparent choices about community and autonomy, about tradition and modernity, and, most concretely, about the dimensions and meaning of actual relationships between parents and their children. In this debate, advocacy is everywhere evident. It is absent, by design, from the present book, whose aim is not to support a position, but instead to analyze the debate, the assumptions—often remarkably similar—that undergird competing views, and the implications of those assumptions for the emerging meaning of family within contemporary American society.

As I thought about and wrote this book, I was aided by a number of people. I am indebted to all of them.

Many of the concepts central to the book developed under the tutelage of Professor David M. Schneider, with whom I studied as a postdoctoral student in anthropology at the University of Chicago in the mid-1970s. Professor Schneider's seminal insights into American kinship during the middle decades of the twentieth century have helped me to assess transformations in the American family in recent decades.

Various sections of the book were read in draft by Professors Robert A. Baruch Bush, Robin Charlow, Eric Freedman, John DeWitt Gregory, Wendy Rogovin, and Carol Donovan, Esq.

Professor Charles A. Wood, The Daniel Webster Professor of History at Dartmouth College, shared with me his remarkable knowledge of medieval history and of the feudal family.

Mr. Daniel May, Esq., Assistant Director of the Hofstra University Law Library, provided scholarly and bibliographic assistance. Ms. Mena

Sieber, Documents Librarian at the Library, researched various government documents.

Professor Stuart Rabinowitz, Dean of the Hofstra Law School, generously encouraged my research and writing.

Mr. Niko Pfund, editor in chief of the New York University Press, was unfailingly insightful and supportive.

ACKNOWLEDGMENTS

An earlier version of parts of chapters 1 and 2 appeared in the *Georgetown Law Journal*, vol. 82, number 4, pp. 1519–1571.

An earlier version of chapter 3 appeared in the *Buffalo Law Review*, vol. 38, number 2, pp. 515–550.

An earlier version of chapter 4 appeared in the *UCLA Law Review*, vol. 40, number 3, pp. 637–694.

An earlier version of chapter 5 appeared in the *Yale Journal of Law and Feminism*, vol. 7, number 1, pp. 37–86.

An earlier version of chapter 6 appeared in the *Connecticut Law Review*, vol. 26, number 4, pp. 1261–1314.

Earlier versions of chapter 7 appeared in the *Arizona State Law Journal*, vol. 28, number 2, pp. 473–542, and in the *Children's Legal Rights Journal*, vol. 16, number 1, pp. 1–10.

Introduction

Cultures depend for stability upon axioms: self-evident truths upon which institutions prone to gain civic allegiance may with confidence be built. When such axioms are transformed into suppositions, a rare occurrence, cultures become unstable.

Among the axioms central to Western culture has been the conviction that the family is rooted in the very nature of things. Definitions of "family" and of "nature" vary. In the Western world, however, consensus has existed that family was as natural as the turning of the sun, as immutable, subject as strictly to intrinsic law, as indispensable to the conduct of life.

Upon that consensus the stability of much of Western society was founded. When it has faltered—when the structure of the family and its essential meaning—has been called into question, society has been faced with unrest.

Throughout most of Western history, the meaning of family was assumed. During the past two centuries, however, as the consequence primarily of major economic transformations in the West, the bedrock axioms by which family was defined have been transformed into mere suppositions. During the past several decades, this transformation has accelerated in a revolutionary fashion.

As a result, the scope and meaning of family are now subject to intense, self-conscious debate, not only in public media, art, law, politics, science, but also among ordinary people. More than the social parameters and fate of family are at stake in this debate, for it encompasses many of the central social concerns of the period. At issue as well are differences over the comparative value of modernity and tradition, freedom and constraint, individualism and community.

This debate has been furthered and complicated by the advent and development within the past few decades of assisted reproduction, including the new reproductive technologies and surrogate motherhood. Since 1978, with the birth of the first child conceived in vitro, reproductive technology has developed at an astonishing pace, altering the means and meaning of human reproduction, and inevitably, the meaning and scope of family. As novel options for reproduction accumulate and multiply, they enter the debate about family. Almost everyone has an opinion, and almost everyone's opinion stems from and, in turn, connects back to, sometimes revising, more familiar understandings of family and of relationships within families.

In less than two decades, it has become possible completely to separate reproduction from sexuality, to distribute the tasks of biological maternity among different women, and to manipulate the spatial and temporal dimensions of reproduction. Moreover, an entire industry—brokers, agents, lawyers, psychologists, and doctors—has developed around surrogacy arrangements.

Today, as a result of reproductive technology, conception need not involve sexual intercourse and need not begin in a woman's body. After conception, the embryo may be divided into two, four, or more identical embryos; it may be tested for genetic disease and discarded if defective; it may be frozen and stored for months, or even years, and then thawed for implantation and gestation. The woman who provides the egg need not be the woman who gestates the embryo. Two different women can give birth to "identical twins," or one woman may give birth to "twins" years apart; babies may be born years after the deaths of their genetic "parents"; men without active sperm can become genetic fathers; and soon eggs for the production of human children may be retrieved from aborted fetuses.

These possibilities are unsettling, even astonishing, to a society that has long understood human reproduction as the inevitable consequence of *natural*, and thus unchanging, biological process and that, further, has understood family relationships through reference to the fixed certainties of biological reproduction. Within such a world, the appearance and expansion of reproductive technology has done much more than present infertile people with a set of new options for having children. This technology, which seems almost daily to present new possibilities for creating, and thus for defining, families, simultaneously disrupts familiar assumptions about the biological correlates of human reproduction.

Previously, society could rely on a set of unquestioned assumptions about biological reproduction to assess the changing parameters of family life. That measuring point has now begun to shift position as rapidly as have the social contours of family life. So, for example, the speculation

about the meaning of motherhood common in twentieth-century society can no longer presume the certainty of biological truth. Until recently, the inexorability of biological maternity anchored considerations of the transforming character of motherhood as a social, cultural, psychological, and economic matter. Now, society's understanding of biological maternity is itself being challenged by phenomena such as in vitro fertilization, embryo transfer (which permits one woman to gestate a fetus formed from another woman's fertilized ovum) cryopreservation (which permits fertilized eggs to be frozen for years, even decades, before implantation and gestation), and the fertilization of eggs from aborted fetuses for gestation in the bodies of women who do not themselves produce ova that can be fertilized. As a result, identification of *the* biological mother is no longer obvious. The social and biological dimensions of maternity being questioned simultaneously, it is no longer possible to judge questions about the social dimensions of motherhood against the unchanging parameters of biological maternity. The complicated shifts in meaning that result are deeply disruptive to social expectations about the relations that do, or should, pertain among family members.

Reproductive technology is unsettling to society in other ways as well. In a society accustomed to individualism, at least in the marketplace, and practically obsessed with consumer choice, it was perhaps inevitable that the possibility of separating gametes and embryos from the bodies that produce them would lead to the sale and purchase of gametic and embryonic material, and that the possibilities of separating conception from sexual intercourse and of dividing biological maternity into genetic and gestational components would lead to surrogacy contracts and paid surrogate mothers. But, still, such options, expressly presented as creative of family life, have seriously disquieted a society conditioned for almost two centuries to understand the family as a domain of life separate and protected from the world of work. To allow the parent-child relation to be created through monetary exchange has seemed antithetical and deeply threatening to the notion of family, developed during the early years of the Industrial Revolution, as a domain of life characterized by love and enduring commitment.

The social and economic choices characteristic of surrogate motherhood, gamete purchase, and embryo transfer do not provide the only instances in contemporary society of familial relationships created and effected through forms once understood as appropriate to the market-

place but not to the home. For several decades before the advent of reproductive technology, the creation and operation of family relations were increasingly recognized as open to the free choices of autonomous individuals. Society reacted with intense ambivalence to that recognition, at once fearing and enjoying the proliferation of choice. The development of assisted reproduction intensified that ambivalence, not simply because assisted reproduction compels society to redefine the family but because it accelerates a redefinition that was proceeding at a rate the society already found hard to accommodate.

Certainly, before the appearance of "test-tube babies" and surrogate mothers, families were becoming increasingly individualistic and the parameters of family life were increasingly seen as open to choice rather than dictated by the nature of unchanging biological and social truths. Indeed, for at least 150 years before the advent of the new reproductive technologies, the family in the United States had been evolving consistently, though not always obviously, toward greater individuality, transiency, and choice. The impact of reproductive technology on contemporary American society must, of course, be understood in that larger context.

In short, although reproductive technology has revolutionized traditional understandings of the family, the advent of reproductive technology did not initiate the process of change. The new technological options for human reproduction did not become widely available until after the family (and family law) had accepted a wide set of changes, including no-fault divorce, nonmarital cohabitation, and prenuptial agreements in contemplation of divorce, that challenge traditional understandings of proper family relationships. Perhaps the appearance of assisted reproduction awaited, because its use depended on, broader social changes that had prepared the way for new understandings of family, relative, parent, and child. Specific questions about the causal links between the development of assisted reproduction and the development of a vision of family that could encompass the consequences of assisted reproduction must be referred to historians of science. Whatever the causal links, the availability and use of assisted reproduction has intensified a set of questions about the dimensions of family life that were already being actively debated within the society in the several decades before babies could be conceived in vitro and before frozen gametic and embryonic matter could be purchased to create human life.

Reproductive technology and surrogacy are doing more than accelerating the rate of change in the contemporary family. In addition, these phenomena provide new, rather startling, contexts within which society must deal with and consider the transformation of the American family. The questions raised by reproductive technology and surrogacy, and the answers being suggested in response, have become part of the wider debate about family. Social responses to reproductive technology and surrogacy almost immediately also became responses in the larger social debate about the shape and fate of the American family. Conclusions about reproduction are used, sometimes self-consciously, sometimes less so, to control, or simply to understand, the fate of the family more generally.

Since the mid-nineteenth century, American society has been openly concerned with the preservation and transformation of the family. The beginnings of this self-consciousness about family coincided with the development of the nineteenth-century market and the consequent understanding of the family as a refuge from the pressures of the world of the marketplace. Before that time, society did not see the world of home and family in express contrast to the world of work. Moreover, home and work were not as likely, in fact, to have been separate in earlier centuries as they were after the Industrial Revolution began.

As vast technological and economic changes transformed life in the nineteenth century, a new ideology of family emerged.[1] This new ideology which developed with the Industrial Revolution included a new awareness of family as a central social unit. The self-consciousness about family that evolved during the nineteenth century suggested that families can be altered—that they have histories—and that, in consequence, the family faced increasing jeopardy as broad changes in the rest of life would come eventually to invade, and then to alter, life within the family. Especially among urban, middle-class Americans, the fear that families would be undermined by larger social forces was understood in counterpoint to a new conceptualization of family life during the nineteenth century as affectionate, selfless, and childcentered.[2]

During the course of the following century, this understanding of family was endorsed and consistently refashioned. Looking back nostalgically toward a past that never was and forward toward a future that seemed increasingly uncertain, the nineteenth century understanding of family was carried into the next century and institutionalized most firmly, but briefly, during the years immediately following World War II in the middle decades of the twentieth century.

By the latter part of the twentieth century, the family more openly reflected, and family law more fully endorsed, aspects of the nineteenth-century family that were feared rather than celebrated—especially autonomous individuality and expanding choice. However, the ideology of family that developed at the start of the nineteenth century continued, and still continues, to inform reactions to, and choices about, family life. During this long period, from the beginning of the nineteenth century into the second half of the twentieth, social understandings of family became increasingly self-conscious as well as increasingly doctrinal. Social images of decent family life continued to be modeled on, and actual families were condemned for departing from, a notion of family and home that contrasted almost completely with the world of the marketplace.

Reproductive technology and surrogacy emerged and developed almost instantaneously at the end of this period, just as society began to acknowledge and openly accept changes that departed from traditional understandings of family. The options introduced by this technology—options about how and when to create children, about which gamete should be used to create them, about which woman should gestate them, and about the contours of the relationship that should connect a child's progenitors to each other and to the child—dramatically complicate society's ongoing debate about family. Assisted reproduction questions the moral limits of individualism—as women sign contracts to produce and surrender children for money. And assisted reproduction also suggests the creative potential of the choice to employ technology in the service of family—as infertile couples become parents with the participation of third-party doctors, gestators, and gamete donors.

To a society already overburdened with choice (and with the illusion of choice), reproductive technology has brought more choices, not just reproductive choices but ideological choices as well. People can design their own reproductive lives in ways very recently unimaginable, limited however by cost and the success rates of reproductive technology, still poor. The fact that such choice exists has become almost as unsettling as the actualization of particular choices. Moreover, the apparent choices often disguise other choices, and as a result the implications of each set of choices are blurred. For example, choices presented by assisted reproduction can be defined as conforming to traditional models of family, as when technology is used to create children (and therefore families) for desperate, infertile couples. The choices presented by reproductive technology can also be defined as destroying traditional families and everything those families represent, as when the technology is seen to turn women and children into commodities and parents into business partners.

Assisted reproduction has provided a new context within which to consider the moral and social parameters of family. But it is a context so confusing that it is less likely to provide direct answers than to expand the terms of, and excite interest in, the society's larger debate about family. In large part, social responses from the society to assisted reproductive technology assimilate the uses and consequences of the technology to familiar things. But there is wide disagreement about how to do that and even wider disagreement about concrete conclusions to be drawn from the analogies. So, for instance, extracorporeal gametic material can be, and has been, equated with a child, a human organ, a special sort of human organ, or a commodity. As a result, conclusions about the proper fate of gametic material become conclusions about babies, human organs, special sorts of human organs, and commodities. The options for defining gametes and embryos multiply, but a shared social frame of reference seems simultaneously to vanish.

Society has reached almost no consistent, generally accepted decisions about how to understand or regulate assisted reproduction. Television personalities, philosophers, and theologians disagree among themselves, and state legislatures have not responded uniformly or comprehensively to the conundrums presented by reproductive technology and surrogacy. When the National Conference of Commissioners on Uniform State Laws devised a model statute for recommendation to state legislatures anxious to regulate the status of children produced from assisted conception, they provided two alternatives. One alternative mandates that all surrogacy arrangements be void. The other permits surrogacy and identifies the parents of any resulting child as the couple who entered into an agreement to produce that child rather than the surrogate with whom the "intending parents" entered into the agreement.[3] Some states have enacted statutes regulating various aspects of reproductive technology and surrogacy, but the response has been neither widespread nor comprehensive.

Courts, unlike legislatures, cannot delay or limit responses to reproductive technology and surrogacy until a social consensus emerges or until the absence of regulation becomes disastrous for the society. Parties to specific, unresolved disputes occasioned by assisted reproduction seek judicial resolution, and the judiciary must respond. Some of the assisted reproduction cases considered by courts arose as part of larger divorce actions. Others presented various sorts of disagreements, including disputes among surrogate mothers and intending parents over the parentage and custody of children they agreed to produce together, disputes between a woman anxious to use her dead lover's frozen sperm to produce a child and the dead man's children, or disputes between gamete donors and the fertility clinics storing their gametes.

Courts have listened to these people's claims, analyzed the implications of their choices, and determined rights and obligations of family members and contract partners to gametes and to babies. Taken as a set of responses, judicial decisions in these cases are characterized by bewilderment and inconsistency. That is indicated, even before particular decisions are examined, by the frequency with which trial courts' rulings in such cases are overturned on appeal or are affirmed but on the basis of an analysis entirely at odds with that of the court that first heard and decided the case.

In general, law provides a powerful commentary on the life it regulates. That commentary is provided differently by legislatures and by courts. Legislative regulation, especially in the United States, signals social agreement far more often than do court opinions. Legislation suggests the resolution of debate. Judicial response, especially to issues not yet subject to widespread and consistent legislative regulation, may suggest only the terms of debate. Certainly, this is the case with regard to reproductive technology and surrogacy. Because courts are compelled to make specific decisions in order to resolve actual disputes, they must make decisions quickly, without the benefit of prolonged consideration. Thus the texts of judicial decisions reflect with comparative transparency the confusions and uncertainties being engendered by surrogacy and by the new reproductive technologies, as well as society's inability to provide any broad, consistent response.

Historically, the law's response to artificial insemination, a form of reproductive control that does not require sophisticated technology and that has been available for application to human reproduction for over a century, provides an illuminating illustration of the process through which the law assimilates, and then comes consistently to regulate, unsettling changes in the possibilities for human reproduction. In the first half of the twentieth century, disputes occasioned by artificial insemination, especially when the procedure was accomplished using the sperm of a donor rather than the sperm of the husband of the woman to be inseminated, involved questions about the paternity of the donor and of the mother's husband. Courts, almost always relying on one or another familiar understanding of family matters, responded variously and usually with intensity. Some equated artificial insemination with adultery[4] and defined the child as illegitimate.[5] Others defined the relation between the mother's husband and the child produced from artificial insemination as one of semi-adoption or potential adoption.[6] Others refused to entertain a divorcing mother's claim that her children were conceived through artificial insemination because that claim suggested the children should be defined as bastards.[7] No legislation specifically guided courts in these cases until the mid-1960s. At about that time, family law was becoming generally responsive to changes in the family that suggested a new place for individualism and choice within families.

In 1964 Georgia enacted the first statute directly responsive to the questions raised by artificial insemination. The statute declared children born through artificial insemination using donor sperm to be the legitimate children of their mother's husbands.[8] Within a short period of time, a majority of the states promulgated statutes that regulated artificial insemination and that provided for the legitimacy of the resulting children. By the 1970s social consensus had emerged.

With regard to both the new reproductive technologies and to surrogacy arrangements, which both appeared over a century after artificial insemination was first used in human reproduction, a similar consensus has not yet appeared in the society or in the law. However, the judicial decisions that have been occasioned by reproductive technology and by surrogacy, and which seem to agree about little beyond the importance of the questions asked, provide a remarkably fruitful context within which to decipher and understand society's developing response to assisted reproduction, and by implication to broader changes in the family. Decisions in these cases provide invaluable texts for the social analyst. In part, this follows inevitably from the fact that judges live within the culture they help order. But even more, judicial decisions, in telling litigant's tales, aim specifically at resolving disagreements in a form approved and institutionalized by the society. When society has not provided, or has not yet provided, a generally appropriate response to a set of disputes being litigated, that, too, is reflected in courts' decisions. Such judicial decisions indicate society's yearnings and fears, its hesitations and confusions, and its assumptions and expectations.

Cases about surrogacy and reproductive technology reveal, for instance, that courts apparently at utter odds over the resolution of disputes involving assisted reproduction may predicate their conflicting decisions on a shared vision of family. In fact, the great majority of courts that have entertained such cases have justified their decisions by linking those decisions to an ideology of family that values tradition and that is, at best, cautious about the benefits of granting family members expanded choice and of defining family members as autonomous individuals.

Thus, the judiciary, faced with cases occasioned by assisted reproduction, has in large part mounted a defense of tradition. However, the defenders are often apparently unaware that they are mounting a defense at all, and when aware, are unclear about precisely what they are defending, and even about why they are mounting the defense at all.

So, for instance, even courts that have validated surrogacy contracts, and have thereby apparently sided with choice and individualism, have done so in the name of the pluperfect, traditional family created, or likely to be created, as a result of the contract in question. In this, courts have accepted surrogacy contracts and recognized intending parents, not because tradition should withdraw in the face of modernity but because, for these courts, the correlates of contract seemed to ensure the preservation of tradition, at least within specific families. In these cases, as in the larger society, the terms of the debate about family are murky. In consequence, central concepts come to seem substitutable for their apparent antagonists.

The confusions underlying judicial decisions in such cases reflect, and also encourage, similar confusions in the larger society. Litigated cases occasioned by assisted reproduction often become news. As such, judicial stories are retold by journalists, newscasters, and even writers of fiction, and are then, in turn, read by judges, lawyers, and future litigants.

For the society as a whole, the confusions engendered by reproductive technology center around a general, social ambivalence regarding the expansion of individual choice in the creation and operation of families.

The society imagines itself to thrive on the expansion of choice in almost all domains of life and acts out that belief daily in selecting among an apparently unending variety of consumer choices. Yet, at the same time, the society continues to limit choice, or at least to mask its interest in expanding choice, within the domain of family life. That the explosion of consumer society in the United States has bred a deep, though curiously illusive, faith in choice-as-salvation is not surprising, nor is it surprising that faith has come openly to ground visions of family life as well as life in the marketplace.

More surprising perhaps is the tenacity of the resistance and of the strength with which society continues to value more traditional visions of family in which relatives are connected through ties that limit individual choice, and in which families are expected to endure as committed units of social interaction because that is what families *are*. Whether society will continue to value such families, and whether "old-fashioned" families will survive, and if so, in what form, is for the future to determine. But responses by the society and the law to the conundrums created by reproductive technology may provide a glimpse of that future.

This book, in looking toward that future, begins by examining the past. Changes in the family and in images of the family in the past two centuries, and more particularly in the past few decades, are examined, as are the shifting responses of the legal system to those changes. Chapters 1 and 2 describe the emergence in the early nineteenth century of an ideology of family which developed in response to the pressures of the Industrial Revolution and which glorified the home as an escape from the tensions of the marketplace. This ideology of family, which today remains important though not unopposed, is referred to in this book as "traditional." Although regnant for almost two centuries, this traditional ideology of family was never as pervasively actualized as people believe it to have been.[9] Throughout the nineteenth century, for example, divorce, although difficult, was far from unknown. In the first half of the twentieth century, a significantly lower percentage of children lived with at least one parent than did so in the last decades of the century.[10] And, in 1835, Alexis de Tocqueville described American children to be largely free of paternal authority even before the teenage years.[11]

Ironically, the traditional ideology of family came closest to being reflected in social fact, and was most extensively articulated, in the 1950s, just before that ideology started to crumble. In the 1960s and 1970s people began for the first time openly to question, and thereby to challenge, the traditional view of family. That challenge is reflected clearly in the law—in legislatures which provided for no-fault divorce, in courts which recognized prenuptial agreements and cohabitation contracts, and in the United States Supreme Court which clearly described the family in the mid-1970s as a collection of independent, autonomous individuals.[12]

Chapters 3, 4, and 5 discuss surrogate motherhood and the new reproductive technologies as these developments are reflecting, and becoming part of the ongoing, and increasingly intense, debate within the society about the permissible scope and meaning of familial relationships.

Chapter 3 describes a singular, traditional vision of family that lay behind, and ultimately unified, a set of apparently conflicting responses to one case involving a failed surrogacy agreement during the late 1980s. Chapter 4 considers a set of cases decided by the United States Supreme Court involving the rights of unwed fathers to exercise their paternity. Assumptions about fathers and mothers underlying those cases are then compared with other assumptions about mothers, in particular, underlying cases occasioned by surrogacy and by reproductive technology. Chapter 5 looks directly at the changing "facts" of human reproduction and considers developing social and legal responses to these new facts. This chapter then examines the remarkable disruption created by the simultaneous transformation of the social and biological correlates of family.

The last two chapters (6 and 7) consider in detail two quite different legal responses to the problems raised by assisted reproduction. One response (reliance on the notion of intent), considered in chapter 6, clearly reflects the laws of the marketplace and thus suggests that family law, which for almost two centuries has defined and regulated the family as a domain apart and different from the world of work, is becoming increasingly similar to the laws that regulate contracts, torts, and property. The second response, considered in chapter 7—reliance on the best interests of the child—has been widely institutionalized within family law for almost a century. Each response shows courts struggling to mediate contradictions between the correlates of tradition and the correlates of modernity in the construction of families—struggling, more specifically, to preserve the illusion of tradition but to accept the correlates of modernity. Neither resolves the dilemmas presented by assisted reproduction.

Each, however, reveals the concerns and confusions that assisted reproduction is engendering.

In sum, this book examines the response of the law as surrogacy and the new reproductive technologies threaten or challenge (depending on perspective) traditional family values and structures. As the law responds, it reconsiders a set of fundamental assumptions about the family that for over a century were accepted, internalized, and only infrequently challenged openly.

The choices the law is now making flow from a set of assumptions about the family that favors holism, fixed relationships, and enduring connection as well as from a set of assumptions that favors autonomy, negotiated bargains, and fungible choice. This book focuses on the development of, and connections among, these assumptions about family, recognizing that, in practice, the incidents of tradition and of modernity have long since become substitutable for each other.

In examining the choices that the law is making about how the family is, and should be, defined, this book makes its own assumption: that the law, in responding to the dilemmas created by assisted reproduction, will be only as fair, just, and equitable as its underlying assumptions allow.

ONE

The Transformation
of the Family

Contemporary changes in the family have become a subject of intense moral and sociological concern in the United States in the past several decades. The value of alterations in the form and meaning of family life is being debated widely, as are the apparent consequences of those changes for social and political life generally.

Both surrogate motherhood and the new reproductive technologies challenge traditional understandings of family and have thus entered the debate about family with great force. However, neither development engendered that debate. Thus, understanding social responses to surrogacy and reproductive technology (that is, to assisted reproduction in general) and the role that assisted reproduction now plays in shaping contemporary visions of the family in the United States depends on understanding the larger debate about family and its history before the advent of surrogate motherhood and of the new reproductive technologies. Therefore, this chapter and the next describe the social and historic context within which the contemporary debate about the family—and thus about assisted reproduction—has developed. This chapter outlines the social and intellectual history of the family; the next chapter considers a basic set of changes in the ideology of family as those changes are reflected in changing responses of the law to the family.

Since the 1960s alternative visions of family have begun to compete openly with the "traditional" ideology of family, developed at the start of the Industrial Revolution. Increasingly, society recognizes, and at least partially accepts, a variety of family forms. More specifically, however, at the same time, society began to categorize families as comparatively traditional or comparatively modern.

Modern families, understood as less dependent on biogenetic relations than traditional families, are further described, especially by their proponents, as ideally egalitarian. Within these families, family members are described as individuals who *choose* to join together as relatives. Although these families-through-choice are sometimes presented as an alternative to traditional families, they can be, and often are, also described in terms that seem as old-fashioned as any. Moreover, some families that might appear to be families-through-choice would appreciate and appropriate the description. Many such families are described in Kath Weston's ethnographic study of lesbian and gay kinship. Others would reject the term or understand it as applicable, but largely irrelevant.

The two notions of traditional (or old-fashioned) families and modern families suggest a developmental process. Such a process has occurred and continues to occur. However, the two notions of traditional and modern families are also presented as ideological antagonists in a contest for the future of the family. As such, the two notions represent contrasting options and are actually used in ways that variously ignore, subvert, elaborate, or reconstruct the history of families.

The English anthropologist Marilyn Strathern makes a similar point in commenting on another anthropologist's analysis of surrogate motherhood. That other anthropologist, Robin Fox, argued in his book *Reproduction and Succession* that surrogacy plays havoc with "biological reality" and therefore must be condemned.[1] Strathern responded:

> Fox situates his battle in a culture that values kinship as some ancient or traditional form that has given away before modernity. But there are times when the *same* culture would also like to entertain both, and technology makes both possible. In truth, the new reproductive technologies enable moderns to choose between "traditional" and "modern" forms of relating, or to choose to facilitate both at the same time for that matter ("artificial assistance" to produce a baby genetically, biologically and psychologically "us", in the words of one father).[2]

When tradition and modernity are posed as ideological antagonists in the characterization of family matters, two contrasting visions of family emerge. The first sees families as ideally hierarchical, holistic, and immune from, or at least unlikely to welcome, the manipulations of choice. It is presented as reflecting a long, moral history in which family relations were always predicated on natural and supernatural truths, and were *therefore* good. The second vision sees families as ideally egalitarian. In such families relationships are understood as grounded in the exercise of autonomy. These families are portrayed by their proponents as heralding an age that tolerantly provides for practically unlimited choice in the creation and ongoing actualization of human connection.

These descriptions of two contrasting sorts of families are stark, too stark to describe the actual process through which people of all persuasions are discussing and constructing families. However, the descriptions do present contrasting possibilities for imagining families. And these possibilities undergird the complicated debate about family that engrosses much of contemporary society.

This debate has a history, and the many actual families around which the debate twirls have histories as well. Those histories are connected but are certainly not identical, and must therefore be disentangled. For the social analyst, neither the ideological debate nor the parameters of family life can be understand apart from the larger social and intellectual history of family. Although this book does not presume to present that history, its outlines can be suggested.

That outline will focus around two periods—medieval times and the period since the start of the Industrial Revolution. Each of these periods is especially significant for understanding the development of the contemporary family today and the development of the contemporary debate about the family.

An ideology of relationship that prize hierarchy and holism is far more characteristic of the medieval, than of the modern, world. That ideology indicates the source of the hierarchical, holistic frame within which families and images of families were structured for many centuries after the demise of the feudal world itself.

The form of feudal relations, understood through an ideology that valued hierarchy rather than equality, and holism rather than individualism, has in the succeeding centuries been more fully preserved and more accurately reflected in family relations than elsewhere in the developing societies of the West. But beyond that, within the past one hundred years especially, the medieval world has provided a model against which contemporary relations, both inside and outside families, have been expressly assessed. In this regard, the feudal model has been interpreted variously and served more than one ideological end. It has been taken to represent an intolerant and hierarchical past best forgotten. But it has also been taken to represent a universe of loving interconnection that should be preserved where possible and resurrected where not. Thus, the medieval world, as viewed by the nineteenth and twentieth centuries in establishing their own understandings of family, may appear more committed to hierarchy and holism than was, in fact, the case. Moreover, the medieval family itself, though embedded in a world that generally prized hierarchy and holism, left significant room for individual choices and thus for structural variety.[3]

The second period of particular importance for understanding the current debate about the family, that from the start of the Industrial Revolution to the present, shows an unsteady, though apparent, transition away from the feudal model, toward individualism and choice as the defining characteristics of familial connections, even though the most pervasive ideology of family during most of the same period seemed to reject individualism and choice.

During most of this period, the family was described as a unique domain of interaction that contrasted with interactions in the marketplace. That notion of separation was reflected in a legal system that regulated the family through a distinct set of rules. These rules contrasted—as "home" contrasted with "work"—with the rules that regulated interactions in the marketplace.

Until the past few decades, society and the law understood the family as a universe distinct from almost every other arena of social life—as a realm of private interactions grounded in natural and supernatural truths. On those truths were predicated the hierarchical structure of the family unit as well as the enduring inevitability of family relationships. During this period, the family was almost unique within the society as a hierarchical social unit grounded in a notion of natural truth.

However, other, older societies, both within the West and elsewhere, did function, far more broadly, with hierarchy and holism as their governing principles. Within the West, the feudal period provides the best example of a society that valued hierarchy and holism and anchored the social whole in a sense of inexorable (supernatural) truth. In that world hierarchy and holism as ideological principles were not relegated to the domain of home and family, but rather broadly defined relations within the society. The medieval world, as a whole, suggested to later centuries a model for understanding the family *in contrast* to the model of interaction in the marketplace.

The present debate about family challenges an ideology of family that developed during the nineteenth century and that was further embellished during the twentieth century. However, the intellectual roots of that ideology took hold centuries earlier, during feudal times, when most social relations were defined in terms that, in the nineteenth century, came to distinguish the family from the world of the marketplace.

I. Hierarchy and Holism: Feudal Models and Feudal Roots

Louis Dumont and Steven A. Barnett,[4] both anthropologists and students of Indian culture, compare the ideology of medieval Europe with that of traditional caste India. Their analyses provide insights about the differences between a world such as the nineteenth- and twentieth-century United States that has come increasingly to value equality (as an ideological matter) and a world such as feudal Europe or caste India that prizes hierarchy at least in significant part. In medieval Europe and in caste India people thought their world was, and should be, hierarchical far more generally than in later centuries. In the West, in comparison, inequalities (such as that represented by patriarchy or those represented by racism) conflict with a more general egalitarian ideology and are thus constantly being explained away (often the response to racism) or justified as appropriate within, though only within, a particular domain of interaction (the family). In fact, choice and equality often competed with hierarchy and holism in defining the medieval world. But that world, because it did value hierarchy and holism, provided later centuries with a useful model of social relations not premised on the valuation of equality and individualism.

This difference between an ideology of hierarchy in medieval Europe and in the modern world with regard to definitions of the family, fundamentally distinguishes the two. However, a closer look at the medieval world and its notions of hierarchy and holism—not so much within the family, as within the society more generally—allows us better to comprehend the development of those notions in application to the family within the transformed world of the modern West.

The medieval world was organized around two interconnected hierarchies, that of the laity, culminating in feudal kings, and that of the Catholic church.[5] Hierarchy and a principle of inequality were central for each. The Church and the nobility, the latter including titular and generally weak kings quite unlike those who emerged later in European history, were antagonists and compatriots. The bishop and the noble each viewed the other as a potential usurper of his own rightful power. Yet the two groups shared a vision of reality that ultimately united them in opposition to the shifts that shook feudal Europe at the end of the medieval period.

Each group relied on, and was organized into, a hierarchical system grounded in sacred or natural fact. The medieval historian Georges Duby refers to the "principle of necessary inequality" that organized the feudal world, and argues that the understanding and structure of that world developed out of

> the conjunction of two kinds of dissimilarity, that instituted by the *ordo*—there were the priests and the others—conjoined with that instituted by *natura*—there were nobles and serfs. The source of disorder was not that nature changed, but that the order was breached. This occurred, for instance, when "rustics" were included in the deliberations of the peace assemblies (or when a man not born into the nobility acceded to the episcopal dignity), when nobles were required to pray, or *oratores* to fight.[6]

Those who labored, called variously peasants or serfs, were supported and exploited by the nobles and the clergy. Their exploitation, however, was not understood as *unnecessarily* exploitative. Rather, oppression was hereditary. Adalbero, bishop of Laon and member of a tenth-century noble family described peasants as those who were fit to serve. "[T]heir blood was not the blood of kings, and because they were not ordained, [they] were compelled to alienate their strength in the service of others."[7] Within the medieval world hierarchy was a fact—indeed the preeminent fact—of life, both everyday and sacred. The fact of hierarchy was considered as inevitable as the fact of social life itself.

Again, hierarchy in the medieval world must be distinguished from inequality in contemporary society. The first reflected society's understanding of what should be; the second contravenes an ideology of equality. So, for instance, Americans may describe a group defined in terms of race or gender as inferior and then proceed to disclaim the implication of that inferiority's inevitability. In contrast, in medieval Europe hierarchy did not need to be excused. Inequalities were taken to reflect an inexorable reality and therefore did not require justification.

Moreover, the medieval world understood hierarchy as a structure with reciprocity and mutuality at its center. Medieval hierarchy, in both its religious and secular forms, constituted a structured *unity*. The whole was defined by a notion of "mutual interchange."[8] When Charlemagne ordered that "every man shall keep to his own life's purpose and his own profession, *unanimously*," he captured the fact of hierarchy and the reciprocity embedded in it.[9] In the world of medieval hierarchy, those at each end of the social order were understood to exist only in dependence on each other. There was little room for autonomous individuality.

Christian metaphors spawned and nourished the mutuality of medieval hierarchy. Georges Duby explained:

> To make discipline bearable, and inequality tolerable, it was prudent to accredit the notion that in Christian society—much as between parents and children, old and young, or as in any community, in monastery and palace alike, in villages as among soldiers—hearts were bound by ties of affection.[10]

In metaphors characterizing the unity and reciprocity of social and ecclesiastical hierarchy in the medieval world, references to the corporal unity of Christ were transformed into references to the domestic unit and relations within it.

To the extent that the medieval family operated as a hierarchical unit, defined by respect and deference, that family reflected the larger society. In this, the family was an extension of the rest of feudal life and was not defined, as modern families have been, in contrast with much of the rest of ongoing social life.

The family metaphor can be applied to the larger feudal society because the society as a whole was seen as a hierarchical unit, each part of which was understood in light of the larger whole. In the medieval world, the structured relations that defined a social whole provided the unit of ideological value.

In the feudal world, the hierarchical and holistic character of social life precluded the sort of extreme individuality and individual privacy later attached to the individual in the West as a fact and then, expressly, as a right. The comparative absence of individual privacy further distinguishes medieval families from those of today. Ideological constraints on the development of individual privacy were paralleled by physical constraints that made personal, physical privacy, as it is understood today, a virtual impossibility within the medieval household. Certainly forms of privacy existed in the feudal period, but that privacy was significantly different from the individual privacy that developed later in Europe and the United States. Even family privacy, so important in social and legal approaches to family matters from the nineteenth century on, was not framed as distinct from other forms of privacy in the feudal world.

Privacy, like almost all other social aspects of the medieval world, was defined and regulated by the reality of a hierarchical universe. *Within* any unit of that hierarchy (e.g., a feudal manor, a *domus*, or a family residence), relations were "private" in the sense that they were not, or were only minimally, regulated by outside powers. Indeed, one of the key developments in the second part of the feudal period was the "privatiza-tion of power." This so-called "feudal revolution" involved a dramatic evisceration of public law and power. It did not, however, involve the sort of autonomous individuality that provided the ideological context for the development of privacy (including, in particular, the development of private property) that occurred in the West in the nineteenth century.

The person in feudal Europe was never private, as presently under-stood. The person was always, and of necessity, defined as *part of* some larger unit. Obviously, individual people existed as physically distinct agents of action, but each person was defined as separate only in the context of some larger, hierarchically organized group.

Medieval society valued the group, not the individual. Individual privacy was an ideological impossibility in a world that did not recognize *individuals* as the ultimately valuable unit of social life. Accordingly, privacy attached to groups and not to individual persons. Within the society's hierarchically structured subgroups (e.g., domestic groups, how-ever widely defined), bonds of connection, grounded in heredity, linked people together. The resulting whole was organized hierarchically. The word *prive* in courtly French referred to "the people and things included within the family circle . . . over which the master of the house exercised his power."[11] Thus privacy in feudal Europe, like privacy in the modern world, could imply intimacy with those inside and distance from those outside. However, the locus for understanding intimacy and distance alike was not the person, but some hierarchically organized, larger, social whole.

The emergence of modern understandings of the person in the West depended on the transformation and demise of feudal society. The notion of personal privacy, defined as an attribute and right of individuals could, and did, develop only after the almost total decline of feudal forms. Privacy in the modern sense depends on defining the individual person apart from larger social forms. The firm institutionalization of the sort of individualism that provided for and encouraged individual privacy came with the Industrial Revolution and the French Enlightenment. Each depended on and promoted the replacement of the notion of privilege with the notion of equality, and of holism with individualism.

Obviously, the decline of privilege and the development of individualism and of the notion of individual equality did not signal the actual end of social inequality. However, as R. H. Tawney, among others, has made clear, the form and meaning of the inequalities that survived differed significantly from the form and meaning of feudal inequality.

The erosion of feudalism and the appearance of modern individualism involved the decline of the feudal world's religious and secular hierarchies. In feudal Europe those forms directed all aspects of life, including the relations among people and the relations between people and God. The person's relation to God was inevitably mediated by an elaborate Church hierarchy; similarly, before the development of the modern state, the person's relation to secular power was mediated by the complicated secular hierarchy composed of nobles and knights, serfs and kings. In the system of belief that undergirded feudal society, unmediated access to the king or to God could hardly be imagined. This description, of course, is at the level of ideology. In fact, every society seems to witness and support various exceptions to preferred and institutionalized forms. But as a matter of belief and value, the feudal world did not acknowledge the possibility of individual people enjoying direct access to king or God.

The emergence of unmediated access to ruling powers—in the sociopolitical world with the establishment of nationalism and in the religious world with the establishment of Protestantism—provided a context within which late eighteenth- and nineteenth-century individualism, along with the individual's right to privacy and to private property, could develop.

Perhaps nowhere are the social implications, if not the concrete history, of feudalism's decline more forcefully suggested than in *Saint Joan*, George Bernard Shaw's play about Joan of Arc. The Earl of Warwick, Shaw's principal representative of feudalism's declining nobility, explained why it was imperative that Joan's voice be stilled. He said of Joan: "It is the protest of the individual soul against the interference of priest or peer between the private man and his God. I should call it Protestantism if I had to find a name for it." [12] Shaw elaborated on the theme in his long preface to the play:

> [Joan's] prayers were wonderful conversations with her three saints. Her piety seemed superhuman to the formally dutiful people whose religion was only a task to them. But when the Church was not offering her favorite luxuries, but calling on her to accept its interpretation of God's will, and to sacrifice her own, she flatly refused, and made it clear that her notion of a Catholic Church was one in which the Pope was Pope Joan. How could the Church tolerate that, when it had just destroyed Hus, and had watched the career of Wycliffe with a growing anger that would have brought him, too, to the stake, had he not died a natural death before the wrath fell on him in his grave? Neither Hus nor Wycliffe was as bluntly defiant as Joan: both were reformers of the Church like Luther; whilst Joan, like Mrs. Eddy, was quite prepared to supersede St. Peter as the rock on which the Church was built, and like Mahomet, was always ready with a private revelation from God to settle every question and fit every occasion.

In Shaw's presentation, Joan foreshadowed Protestantism one hundred years before Martin Luther by effecting a religious stance that afforded the individual direct access to God, thereby precluding need for the mediation of the clerical hierarchy. Joan's relation to God was in that sense individualistic, and for that reason, could become widespread only centuries later.

The hierarchical and holistic bonds of relationship that anchored medieval hierarchy and imbued it with meaning and power have largely disappeared from the modern world. They have been replaced by other forms of connection in the contemporary West. There is no ideological constraint preventing direct connection between the individual and sources of ultimate power. That is, nothing at the level of belief or value now precludes the individual from approaching forms of ultimate power (whether or not those are still defined as "God" and "king") without mediators. Obviously, there may be a host of practical reasons that make it impossible or unlikely that any individual could obtain direct access to the sources of political or religious power. Yet, it is not *unimaginable* that mediation be eliminated. [13]

The obvious demise of the feudal world notwithstanding, pockets of social interaction that might have seemed vaguely familiar to the medieval person have survived into the present century. The family was primary among these pockets of social life that remained hierarchical and that was understood as a social whole rather than as a collection of autonomous individuals long after equality replaced hierarchy as the dominant ideology of the time.

II. The Preservation and Transformation of Feudal Forms in the Modern Family

Connection is no longer inevitably embedded in community. Rather, the ideology of autonomous individuality defines people as free to select their own partners, design their own communities, and act out their own dramas. The most obvious arena for this individualistic focus has been the world of work, the world of the marketplace. There, the connections between people are neither enduring nor deeply rooted. They are not expected to be. The complete person is by definition the person entitled to negotiate and enter contracts. As contracts begin and end, so do the connections they effect. An essential aspect of contractual links is that they are not understood as necessarily enduring nor solidary. Such connections do not generally, and are not expected to, evolve into ties that last beyond the period that the parties bargained for. With these new forms of interaction comes a new form of privacy as well. This is the privacy of the individual apart from any groups to which he or she may belong.

Until recently, in the modern world the family almost alone seemed to stand apart from the encompassing ideology of the market with its stress on autonomous individuality. No longer deeply embedded in a larger world that prized hierarchy and determined worth as an inevitable correlate of social position, the family emerged into the modern world as a lonely reminder of a very different social order. As such, the family became a symbol, as well perhaps as a historic repository, for a world that contrasts with the marketplace. In this sense, beginning with the start of the Industrial Revolution, the family in the modern world distinctively began to represent an older universe in which social relations were hierarchical and holistic and which reflected equality and individuality only fleetingly and only incidentally.

The character of the family began to appear noticeably unique in society by the late eighteenth and early nineteenth centuries because at that time other social institutions had almost completely shed their medieval roots. Indeed, the family—practically alone among Western institutions, and despite significant transformations during the course of the past several hundred years—preserved well into the twentieth century significant aspects of the holistic, hierarchical structure of social relationships that characterized most of feudal life. By this time, the ideological distinction between home and work encouraged the elaboration of an ideology of family that sharply differentiated the family (and the world of women and children) from the world of work (and of men). Obviously, however, the family of the Industrial Revolution and the subsequent century, precisely because it was increasingly distinguished from the rest of social life, differed dramatically from the feudal family which reflected, and formed an integral part of, the larger social world.

In contrast with the family that developed at the start of the Industrial Revolution, families of the colonial period in the United States were distinctly premodern. During the seventeenth and much of the next century, families were joined in ties of mutuality with the larger colonial community. No ideological contrasts, and no distinct social patterns, yet separated families from the larger world. Families during this period resembled those of the following centuries in being composed basically of married couples and their children. However, more than in the next century, families in the colonial period often included boarders, trade apprentices, and servants. Moreover, no separation stood between these nuclear families and the world of work. Each participated in, and was clearly part of, the other. As John Demos describes the colonial family "it was not simply that the family and the community ran together at so many points; the one was, in the words of the preacher, 'a lively representation' of the other. Their structure, their guiding values, their inner purposes, were essentially the same."[14]

By the very end of the eighteenth century, the shift toward family structures now described as modern began to develop. At this time, a sense of impending doom—one still felt and actively discussed—began to develop with regard to family matters. To a significant extent during this period, the society maintained a view of family resembling that of the medieval world with regard to social life generally. Within the family, for instance, the locus of value remained, at least until quite recently, the family unit as a whole—not any particular person. However, even during the nineteenth and early twentieth centuries real changes obviously began to emerge, changes that ultimately transformed the family and the understanding of family away from the medieval model.

Although the traditional ideology of family was rarely contested expressly until recent decades, the sociological contours of family that are so often associated with unprecedented developments during the last half of the twentieth century began to appear clearly a century earlier. In the nineteenth century, paternal authority weakened, marriage became increasingly a matter of individual choice, and the family, no longer unaided in providing for the educational and welfare needs of its members, was more often expected to "provide romance, sexual fulfillment, companionship, and emotional satisfaction."[15] Moreover, the divorce rate rose noticeably in the nineteenth century. Mintz and Kellogg report that in San Francisco in the first part of the twentieth century, one-quarter of all marriages ended in divorce. And divorce at that time was not unknown elsewhere. Twenty percent of marriages in Los Angeles, and 14 percent of those in Chicago terminated in divorce.[16] At the same time, birthrates decreased, especially within middle-class families. Moreover, women began to work for wages in larger numbers.[17]

Ironically, during the nineteenth century, as relations among family members, especially adult family members, began increasingly to resemble relations outside the family, even relations within the market—relations built on free choice rather than on inexorable bonds of connection—an image of the family that depended on, and embodied a contrast between family and work was elaborated and was rarely contradicted by alternative ideological visions. This traditional ideology of family, founded on differences between relationships at home and relationships at work, was most fully developed and was widely, almost universally, embraced in the United States in the middle years of the twentieth century, just before the developing threat to the traditional family became obvious.

Thus, in responding initially to the astonishing changes in culture and family that coincided with the full development of the Industrial Revolution, the society constructed a vision of old-fashioned, decent families that played on and romanticized, but did not really accurately reflect, families as they had existed before the early nineteenth century. Ironically, nineteenth-century, romanticized images of loving, committed, eternally enduring, and deeply affectionate families were embraced most intensely and pervasively in the middle years of the twentieth century.

In the 1950s especially, the society widely endorsed the ideology of family developed during the nineteenth century. Although not all families followed the rules, those rules were clearly defined and vigilantly defended in the middle years of the twentieth century. The family of that period, as described by the anthropologist David M. Schneider, constituted a unit of life, characterized by "enduring, diffuse solidarity." [18]

In an ethnography of American kinship, first published in 1968, Schneider explained:

> The set of features which distinguishes home and work is one expression of the general paradigm for how kinship relations should be conducted and to what end. These features form a closely interconnected cluster.
>
> The contrast between love and money in American culture summarizes this cluster of distinctive features. Money is material, it is power, it is impersonal and unqualified by considerations of sentiment or morality. Relations of work, centering on money, are a temporary, transitory sort. They are contingent, depending entirely on the specific goal—money.
>
> . . . [T]he opposition between money and love is not simply that money is material and love is not. Money is material, but love is *spiritual*. The spiritual quality of love is closely linked with the fact that in love it is personal considerations which are the crucial ones. Personal considerations are a question of who it is, not of how well they perform their task or how efficient they are. Love is a relationship between persons. Morality and sentiment in turn are the essence of the spiritual quality of love, for they transcend small and petty considerations of private gain or advantage or mere gratification. [19]

In analyzing the family of the mid-twentieth century, Schneider described the symbol of love to bridge two culturally distinct domains. He characterized these two domains to involve, respectively. relationships based on shared "substance" (e.g., blood, genes) and relations defined through a particular "code for conduct" (the conduct of kin toward and among each other). Thus Schneider described the family of the period to involve a biological dimension and a social dimension. Much of the contemporary debate about family revolves around consideration of these two dimensions of familial relationships. In the 1960s, however, these terms were more often assumed than actively debated.

Schneider described Americans as envisioning the family of the period as a special, almost sacred domain, distinct spatially, and in almost every other way, from work (the world of money and of the "office"). Schneider portrayed the family as a domain in which relationships were ordered, enduring, and inexorable. In contrast, at work, people could at least in theory negotiate the terms of their own realities and relationships. A bargain was *intended* to last only as long as the parties planned. Not so at home. Relationships endured, and the terms of those relationships were not freely negotiable. Mothers were understood as mothers, fathers as fathers, and children as children because nature harmonized with history to make them so. As home stood to love, so work stood to money.

Thus, well into the twentieth century, the ideology of family, despite significant transformations in the demography of family life during the course of the preceding several centuries, valued both holism and hierarchy, traits that characterized social relations throughout the feudal world.

Moreover family relations, ideally characterized by relations of affection and intimacy, were understood as cemented by the fact of biological inevitability. Similarly, the obligations owed, and rights accorded, to people within families were understood as predicated upon the *substantial* (biological) links among those people. These links were consistently understood to make families families. This understanding of families was held widely in the United States until the late 1960s. Then, with astonishing speed, large segments of the society recognized and accepted alterative visions of family, which conflicted in important regards with the traditional ideology of family.

III. Families of the Present

Within only a decade or two after Schneider so forcefully described the shape of the American family at mid-century, people in almost every walk of life became increasingly self-conscious about the meaning of familial relationships and about alternatives for creating and living in families. The comparatively homogenous ideology of family described by Schneider for the society as a whole just after mid-century seemed suddenly challenged by alternative understandings. As a result, old-fashioned families have increasingly become subject to criticism and even contempt by some within the society. For others, they represent a hallowed past that should be preserved at almost any cost.

The demographics of family life changed more rapidly and more dramatically in the last half of the twentieth century than in the previous century and a half. Elaine Tyler May defined 1960 as a "demographic watershed" in the character of the American family.[20] By the 1970s, 50 percent of American marriages terminated in divorce; 25 percent of households consisted of one individual; and only 33 percent of families contained two parents and their minor children. By the mid-1980s less than 15 percent of American families contained a working father, a stay-at-home mother, and their children. Further, while 12 percent of mothers of preschool children worked in 1950, by 1980 45 percent worked, and by the late 1980s more than 66 percent of three- and four-year-old children were in day care or nursery school. Between the early 1960s and the early 1990s the percentage of children born to unmarried parents increased 500 percent, from 5 percent of all births to 25 percent.

Reactions to these changes differ from those of previous decades in that now significant segments of the society accept, or at least justify, such changes. Certainly, many people within the society see such changes in the family as signaling a disastrous breakdown in the social order, with the "disintegration of the family" at the center of that phenomenon.[21] However, others focus on different aspects of the transforming family, especially the increased choices open to people creating and living in families, and see change as more valuable than disruptive. Only within the last three or four decades has the transformation of the family away from the traditional ideal been widely applauded as well as disparaged. Alternative understandings of family—understandings that value equality and autonomy at least as much as permanence—vie publicly with more traditional understandings.

The resulting debate has engaged wide segments of the society. Self-consciousness about the family has grown throughout the society; the consequent proliferation of widely divergent, often contradictory, responses is occurring with much strength of feeling. This debate, which followed almost inevitably as the gap between images of family and the reality of actual families became almost impossible to ignore, has itself become an important factor in the developing transformation of families and familial relationships.

Still, to some extent, the traditional ideology of family, that seemed to reign almost entirely unopposed during the middle years of the twentieth century, and that today is clearly challenged by alternative visions, continues to inform legal and social choices. However, to a remarkable extent, the family has been and is being redefined in terms much closer to those that only three or four decades ago were associated almost exclusively with the marketplace. As a result, visions of old-fashioned families now compete with visions of families-through-choice.

However, the presentation of these visions as contrasting options belies the reality of contemporary family life. Actually, families viewed as traditional and others viewed as "modern" reflect and resemble each other more often than not, even as they are contrasted with each other. Neither seems clearly to be displacing or replacing the other. Or, more accurately, in a world in which society interprets the "politics of family" to define what is generally valuable, traditional families become more "traditional" and modern families more "modern," each by express comparison with the other. Each depends on, and develops in response to, the other. As the English anthropologist Marilyn Strathern has observed, there are times when our society wants to entertain tradition and modernity at once. She writes:

> [F]or contemporary Euro-American culture, we could say that there is both more status and more contract around—more appeal to genetic essentialism and more openness to optive kinship. And if there seems to be "more," it is because Euro-Americans imagine they are able to do more things with their ideas, implement them in more situations. We can point to one source of enablement, "technology".... In truth, the new reproductive technologies enable moderns to choose between "traditional" and "modern" forms of relating, or to choose to facilitate both at the same time for that matter.[22]

The nineteenth century valued tradition but constructed "traditional" families to suit the needs and desires of the time rather than to reflect accurately what had been. The twentieth century preserved, and broadened that approach to family but complexified it with intensified self-consciousness, with open approval and elaboration of families defined through autonomous individuality, and with the acceptance, however ambivalent, of a technological approach to human reproduction that challenges completely the assumption, so crucial to the nineteenth century, that natural processes of biological connection undergird family relationships.

For these reasons, the dilemmas and disputes occasioned by reproductive technology and surrogacy provide a remarkably fruitful arena within which to examine social responses to the changing family. Assisted reproduction involves incredible, new forms of choice for people both within and outside of traditional family structures. It questions the biological underpinnings of traditional conceptions of family; moreover, it encourages people to create families in contexts that depend upon the assistance of third parties (including doctors, lawyers, brokers, surrogates, and gamete donors) and that usually involve money exchange. As a result, assisted reproduction, much as the families it promises (or threatens) to create, can be, and is, acclaimed for enabling the creation of enduring, affectionate families; equally it can be, and is, condemned for manipulating the dimensions of human reproduction and thereby contributing to the breakdown of traditional family life.

Family Law in Transition

The social and ideological changes examined in the last chapter are reflected in the responses of the law to family matters. In the final decades of the twentieth century, family law changed dramatically. After more than a century of opposition to increased choice and individualism within the family, legislators in every state quickly amended old laws and promulgated new ones in the last four decades of the twentieth century. These new rules clearly acknowledge and reflect the demographic and ideological changes that had been altering the scope and meaning of the family for many decades.

Reproductive technology and surrogacy severely test the law's limits as courts and legislators slowly abandon, or at least reconstruct, the family law system fashioned during the past century and a half. Faced with the startling consequences of surrogacy and the new reproductive technologies, legislators have been slow in responding, and courts, uncertain about how to react but compelled to do so anyway, have as a group behaved with confusion and ambivalence.

For the most part, the law's developing recognition of individualism and choice in the creation and operation of families has limited itself to relationships between adults (especially spouses and cohabitants) within families. With regard to the parent-child connection, the law has been much slower to accept change. But disputes occasioned by reproductive technology often involve questions about parentage and custody and are therefore proving especially difficult for courts to resolve with certainty and consistency.

For this reason, this chapter considers changes in family law during the last decades of the twentieth century that acknowledge choice and that extend the opportunity to negotiate the terms of familial relationships but with regard primarily to relationships involving adults. Subsequent chapters explore the law's far more hesitant and ambivalent response to the consequences of assisted reproduction (which affects the parent-child relationship directly).

This chapter first outlines a widespread set of shifts in the concrete responses of the law in the United States as a whole during the past few decades to relationships among adults within families. These shifts all indicate increasing acceptance by the law of the ideological shift toward individualism within families. The force and implications of that acceptance are then considered through comparison of two decisions of the United States Supreme Court—*Griswold v. Connecticut,* decided in 1965 and *Eisenstadt v. Baird,* decided in 1972. Each invalidated on constitutional grounds a state statute that limited the availability of contraception. Each strengthened legal arguments for protecting procreational autonomy. And thus each holds implications for cases involving the new reproductive technologies and surrogacy.

However, a significant ideological difference separates *Griswold* from *Eisenstadt* in that the first reflects traditional understandings of family and home. The second does not. This contrast between the two otherwise quite similar cases indicates the law's developing acceptance of a vision of family, especially with regard to relations among adults, that values choice and individualism.

I. The Transforming Response of the Law to Family Matters

During the nineteenth century, an interest in stemming social changes in traditional patterns of domestic life provided one encouragement to the growth of family law as a discrete area of American civil law. Even so, the response of the law in the United States to changing family patterns has not been without deviations and regional differences. However, during the nineteenth century the appearance within the family of similarities to forms of interaction in the marketplace threatened a society that more and more defined the family through contrasts with the world of work, and the explicit separation of family law from all forms of commercial law provided one defense against the possibility that the form of relationships in the marketplace could be imported into the home and could begin to affect relationships there.

Thus, one important response of the law to changes in family patterns during the nineteenth century involved the imposition of harsh new definitions and prohibitions. For instance, acknowledging and responding to a rise in the rate of divorce by the late nineteenth century, state legislatures widely reduced the grounds and toughened the procedures by which people could divorce. At the same time and for similar reasons, states widely restricted the availability of contraception and forbade abortion at any point during a pregnancy. Abortion had been made a statutory crime in the United States about fifty years earlier, but the early anti-abortion statutes generally preserved the common-law rule that had no quarrel with termination of a pregnancy before "quickening" (the mother's first recognition of fetal movement).[1]

In 1873, the U.S. Congress passed the Comstock Law (named after New York's "purity campaigner," Anthony Comstock). This law severely punished the transmission or importation of material providing information about contraception or abortion.[2] Thus, for many decades lawmakers refused to endorse the new realities emerging in social and domestic life in the United States. However, the harsh statutes promulgated during the nineteenth century were somewhat less rigidly applied in practice because courts, though generally following legislative direction, were reluctant in particular cases to enforce the stringent new laws. Ultimately, such legislative restrictions and prohibitions failed to contain the processes of change. Despite the promulgation of laws that prohibited contraception and abortion, family size continued to decline; actual husbands and wives noted the new, stiff laws that expressly prohibited contraception and abortion, but spoke in opposition through "silent practice."[3]

Faced with a growing gap between legal rules and life, the law eventually relented, and especially by the second half of the twentieth century began to tolerate, and often actively to endorse, changes in the family that reflected individualism and that valued choice over tradition. By this time, more than half of American marriages ended in divorce, and only about one-third of families consisted of two parents and their minor children.

With astonishing rapidity, beginning in the late 1960s the legislative bulwark, erected in the previous century to thwart changes in the family and represented especially by prohibitions against divorce, contraception, and abortion, collapsed. Within a decade family law reversed course almost completely. By the late 1970s family law, at least as regards adults and the relation between adults within families, provided for broadened understandings of familial relationships. Moreover, family law began, if hesitantly and only partially, to amalgamate with contract, tort, and property law. The process occurred rapidly, though not without lingering ambivalence.

With regard to children and the parent-child relationship in particular, the law has been slower to sanction shifts away from tradition. That process is occurring as well but is more obviously riddled with deep ambivalence, and consequently with contradiction. This process can be seen perhaps most clearly in the responses of the law to disputes involving reproductive technology because there the parent-child bond is being created in transparently new ways, socially and biologically. If this relationship can be *created* in contractual terms and on commercial grounds, perhaps it can, and will, become indistinguishable from commercial relationships in its actualization as well as in its creation. The consequent fear that babies, and the women who produce them, will be commodified is only the most frequently voiced lament about the development of assisted reproduction to surrogacy and the new reproductive technologies.

At present, the law remains reluctant to allow the parent-child bond to be created in terms of the marketplace. But with regard to adults, family law, beginning in the late 1960s, expressly approved the creation — and to some, though a lesser, extent, the operation — of families governed by the predicates of contract (individualism and choice).

The shift in family law toward the acceptance of nontraditional forms of interaction appeared dramatically in the so-called "divorce revolution." In the late 1960s state legislators began to permit divorce upon agreement of the parties: no-fault divorce. California was the first state to recognize no-fault divorce. In less than a decade, almost every state provided for some sort of divorce that at least lessened the need for accusations of fault between the parties.[4] Previously, divorce was never available simply because the parties chose to separate, but only in cases in which the state deemed the actions of one party to the marriage so aberrant as to render the relationship nonexistent. Under laws that permitted divorce only upon accusations of fault, grounds included acts such as adultery, willful desertion, and absence long enough to lead to a presumption of death.[5] Along with the shift from fault to no-fault divorce came a set of procedural changes making it far easier for couples to divorce. A few states even began to provide for summary dissolution proceedings that can be used in cases involving no minor children and that require no divorce hearing at all.

So, within a decade the law transferred a great part of the responsibility for regulating marriage and divorce from the state to the parties involved. In consequence, no-fault divorce, as Mary Ann Glendon notes, is also "no-responsibility" divorce—at least no responsibilities enforced by legal sanction.[6] As with business partners, spouses can design the terms of their relationships' beginnings and endings, and the law will enforce the agreements they reach.

Legal acknowledgement that the spousal relationship is no longer uniquely defined by an encompassing and fixed set of rights and obligations is further indicated by the increasing willingness of courts and legislatures to recognize cohabitation agreements between parties never formally married. These agreements suggest that couples who choose not to marry may enjoy the benefits of cohabitation and may determine, and ask the law to ensure, the financial and other consequences of a potential separation, much as business partners may determine the consequences of their firm's dissolution. *Marvin v. Marvin*, decided in California in 1976, was the first case to recognize and agree to enforce cohabitation contracts in contemplation of the cohabitation's termination. Other states followed the *Marvin* example and thereby gave unmarried cohabitants some of the protection that the law had already provided to couples upon the termination of marital relationships.

A further example of the process of defining and treating the family as a collection of separate individuals rather than as a unit of social value beyond the individuals involved, appears in antenuptial agreements in contemplation of divorce. Dismissed by courts everywhere only a few decades ago as violative of state public policy, such agreements are now widely recognized and enforced. Moreover, several of the courts that first recognized antenuptial agreements in contemplation of divorce justified their decisions with reference to shifts in the character of the family and increases in the frequency of divorce. In *Posner v. Posner*, for example, a Florida court in 1970 took judicial notice of the increase in the ratio of divorce to marriage within the society. In these cases, courts enforcing premarital agreements largely relied on principles of standard contract law. As one review of changes in family law published in 1988 explained, states generally enforce antenuptial agreements if they are "(1) free from fraud and overreaching, (2) reflect a full and fair disclosure by and between the parties of their respective assets, and in some states, (3) not unconscionable as to property division or spousal support."[7] This account could refer to almost any unexceptional contract case.

The law has further begun to consider contracts between couples that define the character and terms of ongoing relationships as well as the terms of the creation or termination of relationships. The Uniform Premarital Agreement Act allows couples to establish certain aspects of an ongoing marriage in an antenuptial agreement.[8] This possibility provides expressly for the contractualization of the terms of marriage as a continuing relationship and represents a change at least as unsettling to traditional understandings of family as that permitting premarital negotiations providing for the terms of a marriage's dissolution. Legal recognition of bargained negotiations between parties to a marriage over the terms of their relationship completely contradicts a long-standing assumption, deeply embedded in nineteenth-century liberalism, that family relationships, unlike almost all other relationships, were not to be regulated by consent but by the natural subordination of one kind of person (wives) to another (husbands).[9]

A further upheaval in assumptions about the nature of families is indicated by a decision of the Hawaii Supreme Court in 1993 which provided that under the state's constitution even the definition of marriage, traditionally understood as a bond between one man and one woman, must be open to revisions based on choice. In *Baehr v. Lewin*, Hawaii's highest court agreed with a group of six litigants protesting the state's prohibition against same-sex marriage, that the definition of marriage can no longer be limited by traditional understandings of the marital relationship. The court held the state's marriage statute presumptively unconstitutional in restricting marriage to opposite-sex parties because the statute violated the equal protection clause of the state's constitution. In earlier cases, decided in other states, courts had always concluded that marriage *by definition* includes a man and a woman.

Thus, more and more the American legal system has come to view adult family members as it views business associates—as autonomous individuals free to negotiate the terms of their relationships and the terms of their relationships' demise. With regard to children and to the parent-child tie, the legal system has been less ready to sanction the amalgamation of family law with the laws of the market. But even here change is occurring.

The pressure to redefine the essence of the parent-child connection is nowhere stronger than in cases involving reproductive technology. But other examples exist as well. Cases of relatively young children attempting to initiate the termination of their relationships with their parents illustrate dramatically the scope of potential shifts in the meaning of the parent-child tie and in the status of children. In *In re Kingsley*, a ten-year-old boy in Florida hired a lawyer (actually his foster father) to help him terminate his biological mother's parental rights and to effect his adoption by the family that had been housing him as a foster child. The trial court decision, although overturned on appeal, is significant because in the decision the legal system recognized the child and his relation to his parents in terms of contract, rather than biological status. Despite the way that the media framed the case, it did not actually involve the creation of a "divorce" action between parents and their children. Rather, the importance of the case lay in the standing given the young boy, Gregory Kingsley, to argue that his biological mother's parental rights should be terminated because she was unfit to be a parent. In one sense, the case can be described as nothing more than a minor transformation of a far more familiar abuse or neglect action. However, the trial court's decision for the boy, which provided for the termination of the biological mother's rights and for the child's adoption by his foster parents, was significant because it suggested that in the future children could initiate termination and adoption actions.[10] The trial court's decision rested on its recognition of the child as an autonomous actor able to engage an attorney and to initiate the legal process that would determine his own parentage.

An older example of choice, rather than biology, determining the parent-child bond is that of adoption. Legal approaches to adoption during most of this century were designed to reflect the model of the nuclear family composed of married parents and their biological children.[11] Present changes in adoption law, and even more, proposals to reform adoption law in ways that would differentiate adoptive families from biological families, suggest widespread confusion about the essence of the bond between parents and their children in general.

For the common law, the significance of biology in the definition of family precluded the recognition of adoptive families. By the late nineteenth century, statutory law provided for adoptive families in the United States and Great Britain, and only in the twentieth century were such families afforded real protection by the law. To some extent, the legal recognition of adoptive families represented an early acknowledgment that the love and intimacy that are supposed to characterize the parent-child relationship need not be anchored in biology. For decades, however, the law continued to insist that adoption be structured "in imitation of biology." [12]

Now, open adoptions in which biological and adoptive parents join together in parenting a child have become increasingly acceptable. [13] The move toward unsealing adoption records represents a similar trend. However, both open adoptions and the so-called "search movement," which advocates unsealing adoption records, can be, and are being, read to support contradictory conclusions about the essence of the family and therefore suggest that society and the law are not consistently embracing negotiations and choice in family matters. These recent changes in approaches to adoption are variously interpreted to suggest that no one model need dictate how family members are related to one another and to suggest that relations founded in biological connections *are* more real than other relations. Generally, controversies about how the law should define and regulate adoption dramatically illustrate the society's ambivalence and confusion about changing understandings of children in families and of the parent-child bond.

Thus, it appears that for the law even the once inviolate core of the family unit, the parent-child connection, has become subject to the pressures of individualism in ways that would have been unimaginable three or four decades ago. The process of change in the parent-child tie is occurring more slowly and amidst much stronger emotion, confusion, and opposition than the parallel process regarding relations among adults. But even here, at the core of the family unit, at least as that unit has been understood for the past century and a half, a new vision, or rather a variety of new visions, of family are being recognized and actualized. This process is occurring, but amidst considerable confusion and uncertainty.

II. From Family Autonomy to Autonomous Individuality: From *Griswold* to *Eisenstadt*

The acceptance by the law of the ideological underpinnings for these shifts in family law (the acceptance of choice, consent, and autonomous individuality in the construction of family matters) emerged clearly—although this was little noted at the time—in a United States Supreme Court decision in 1972. In *Eisenstadt v. Baird* the Court held unconstitutional a Massachusetts statute that prohibited the distribution of contraception to unmarried adults. In *Eisenstadt*, the Court declared unhesitatingly, almost as if it were merely reiterating a familiar, unchallenged assumption, that families can only be comprehended, and therefore regulated, through protection of the autonomous individuality of each family member.

The full significance of *Eisenstadt* is framed through comparison with another case, *Griswold v. Connecticut*, decided only seven years earlier and generally presented as the immediate precursor of *Eisenstadt* and a number of other cases, including *Roe v. Wade*, in which the Court granted women a limited constitutional right to abortion. As a group these cases created a constitutional right to various sorts of procreational autonomy.

In fact, *Griswold*, though innovative from the perspective of constitutional jurisprudence, reflects a rather traditional view of family relationships. *Eisenstadt* does not. The difference is especially revealing since it was precisely in the years between the two cases that state legislatures began widely to revise family law statutes and courts began to overturn long-standing precedents in order to acknowledge and provide for individual choice in family matters.

Comparison of *Griswold* and *Eisenstadt* dramatically reveals the character and deep significance of the shift occurring in family law at the time. The implications of *Eisenstadt* for changing understandings of the family can best be appreciated by first considering *Griswold* and the limits of that decisions's rhetoric, and then examining *Eisenstadt*, and finally, the distinctions between the two.

The appellants in *Griswold* were Estelle T. Griswold, the executive director of the Planned Parenthood League of Connecticut and C. Lee Buxton, a doctor and professor at Yale Medical School who had served as a medical director at the New Haven center of Planned Parenthood of Connecticut. Both were found guilty of having been accessories to violations of a Connecticut birth control law that forbade them from giving "information, instruction, and medical advice" to married people in order to help them avoid conception.[14] The statute in question provided: "Any person who uses any drug, medicinal article or instrument for the purpose of preventing conception shall be fined not less than fifty dollars or imprisoned not less than sixty days nor more than one year or be both fined and imprisoned."[15]

In *Griswold* the Court justified its decision to declare Connecticut's birth control statute unconstitutional by reference to a certain view of the family. The text of the Court's decision clearly limits the holding to cases involving married couples. The Court in *Griswold* declared that the state cannot invade the "zone of privacy" that surrounds the marital relationship.

Griswold was controversial when it was decided. However, virtually none of the disagreements that surrounded *Griswold* focused on, or were engendered by, the Court's invocation of marriage as a "sacred," "intimate," and "enduring" state.[16] Rather, *Griswold* was controversial largely for relying on a "substantive due process" approach to the Constitution. The right to "privacy" that the decision protected was not found in the clear language of the Constitution but was discerned in various "penumbras" surrounding several constitutional provisions. The jurisprudential altercations that followed the decision related primarily to the absence of any specific constitutional referents for the right defined in, and protected by, *Griswold.*

In contrast, virtually no controversy surrounded the Court's understanding of marriage as a sacred, enduring state. As a cultural, social, and political matter, that claim was almost incontrovertible in the United States in 1965. Within less than a decade after *Griswold,* however, the law challenged and quickly revised statutes protecting the traditional view of marriage reflected in Justice Douglas's majority opinion in *Griswold.*

The clear language of *Griswold* suggests that the Court extended privacy rights to married couples because family relationships, unlike other relationships in which individuals may engage, should partake of sacred privilege. That position is explicit in the Court's emotional conclusion, which makes stirring reference to the family unit as explanation and justification for the decision. The Court wrote:

We deal with a right of privacy older than the Bill of Rights—older than our political parties, older than our school system. Marriage is a coming together for better or for worse, hopefully enduring, and intimate to the degree of being sacred. It is an association that promotes a way of life, not causes; a harmony in living, not political faiths; a bilateral loyalty, not commercial or social projects. Yet it is an association for as noble a purpose as any involved in our prior decisions.[17]

Thus, without question, the express language of *Griswold* provides constitutional protection to relations between spouses *within* families, and any extension of that protection to people outside families relies on a mode of reasoning not even implied by the text of *Griswold.* Moreover, *Griswold* suggests protection is afforded to the marital couple, as such, and not to the individuals who compose the marital union.

The language of the opinion reflected accurately the larger society's view of families, a view long echoed in the law. The Constitution makes no reference to any privacy rights that protect relationships between married couples or among family members more generally. However, a long tradition of family case law extols the "autonomous" family unit and presumes to protect it from state intervention, except in the most compelling circumstances.[18] Thus, in fact—though not from the perspective of constitutional theory—the Court's decision in *Griswold* acknowledges and reiterates a long-standing, widely accepted, common-law view that in most cases relations between family members should not be subjected to state regulation or perusal. The controversies surrounding *Griswold* cannot be explained as a response to the notion of "family autonomy," per se. Those controversies focused expressly on the constitutional grounding, but not upon the wisdom or historical accuracy, of the *Griswold* Court's claims about the character of the family. Those who criticized *Griswold* did not question the vision of the family inherent in the opinion's constitutionalization of family autonomy. Rather they questioned the Court's attempt to ground a right to "privacy"—whether familial or individual—on constitutional "penumbras" instead of on the explicit language of the Constitution.

The interpretative debate encouraged by *Griswold* was complicated by other confusions in the Court's opinion. When *Griswold* was decided in the mid-1960s, some commentators read the opinion to protect the private sexual behavior of individual adults, rather than to protect behavior of any kind, including sexual behavior, *within* families alone.[19] But, if that reading reflected the Court's intent and desire, it certainly contradicted the Court's words. The opinion clearly refers to *marital* privacy, and the language of the text makes it abundantly clear that the Court was concerned about safeguarding the family, as a sacred unit, from state intrusion.

That commentators immediately reached alternative readings to any implied by the text was largely testimony to the rhetorical strength of *individual* rights in contemporary understandings of constitutional rights and not to anything implied in *Griswold* itself. American law has steadfastly concerned itself with relations between, or the rights and obligations of, autonomous individuals, and in general cannot or will not seriously address group needs or responsibilities except by focusing on the needs or responsibilities of the individuals that compose such groups. Family law has been a remarkable exception in this regard and one that points dramatically to the power of established family values in the American tradition. Family law was long rooted, and to some extent continues to be rooted, in a social order that understood and provided for group interactions and identity apart from the individuals composing such groups.

It was no accident that family matters were only infrequently the subject of constitutional litigation before the mid-1960s. In practice, constitutional law, at least since the nineteenth century, resembled most of law in the United States in recognizing the invocation of *individual* rights only. In general, for about a century and a half before *Griswold*, the American legal system focused on the individual, not the group, as the unit with regard to which rules were devised and effected. Family law was an exception. Family matters, handled by a separate and distinct body of law and heard in state courts under state law, were largely regulated with reference to the family, not the autonomous individual, as the smallest unit of social relevance and value.

That family law so long remained an exception to the individualistic focus of the society's legal system reflects the strength of the distinction for Americans since at least the early nineteenth century between home and work, between the family and virtually all other associations. Thus, in sum, the *Griswold* opinion, though open to honest debate for its invocation of rights not expressly stated in the Constitution, reflected a mainstream view of the American family and its special place in the culture.

However, since many of the commentators focus on individual rights in interpreting *Griswold*, an explanation of that focus is in order. Several can be found. It is possible that the Court clothed its message in traditional rhetoric in an attempt to preclude, or at least dull, the controversy that would likely have developed in 1965 in response to a decision that, at least by implication, protected the individual's right to sexual freedom. The very issues at stake in *Griswold*, the availability of contraception and the role of Planned Parenthood in fostering the use of contraception, had long provoked angry debate about the changing mores of the period. The Court, in anticipation of controversy, may have consciously selected family metaphors to describe the privacy right delineated in *Griswold* in order to soften the implications of a more libertarian position, one that implied "the constitutionalization of some contemporary version of John Stuart Mill's principle of liberty."[20] This explanation of the disparity between the text of *Griswold* and its immediate interpretation and use by the larger society suggests that the language of the majority opinion may have been artfully chosen in order to mask the underlying agenda.

More likely, a somewhat different explanation is in order; the justices who wrote *Griswold* may themselves have been ambivalent or confused about the implications of the case. *Griswold* came to the Court at a moment of startling transition in the life of the American family, and just before American law reacted widely and approvingly to changes in family life. When *Griswold* was decided, however, neither the scope nor the intensity of that transition had yet emerged concretely. Thus, it is possible that the Court's invocation of traditional family values and its disruption of those values in the name of the individual's right to privacy and freedom reflected a real, though not necessarily completely obvious, conflict for the justices who decided *Griswold* just as a period of astonishing alteration in family life and family law was beginning.

Comparing an earlier draft of *Griswold* to that finally rendered by the Court, shows that the Court was originally uncertain about grounding the *Griswold* holding in a right to privacy, buttressed by domestic metaphors.[21] In a draft opinion of the Court, Justice Douglas founded the *Griswold* holding on a First Amendment right of spouses to associate freely. Such a right would have stemmed from each spouse's freedom to associate with the other, a subspecies of individual rights, rather than from the collective privacy of the family unit.

Concurring opinions in *Griswold*, written by Justices Goldberg, Harlan, and White,[22] similarly invoked domestic metaphors to describe and legitimate the right to privacy and similarly suggested that that right belonged to individuals within families rather than to families as such. Justice Goldberg declared "that the rights to marital privacy and to its specific guarantees demonstrate that the rights to marital privacy and to marry and raise a family are of similar order and magnitude as the fundamental rights specifically protected [by the Constitution]."[23] Justice Harlan urged protecting the "privacy of the home" *so that* individuals could control information about intimate matters.[24] At home, individuals deserved to be "let alone" by government.[25] Finally, Justice White would have based the decision on respect for the "marriage relationship," but he did not explain why.[26]

All of these justices preserved traditional understandings of the family. That notwithstanding, it might be argued that today, when constitutional rights are clearly interpreted as *individual* rights, the constitutionalization of privacy in the family context must assume the individualization of the once holistic family. Such an argument suggests further that in a world of traditional families regulated by a traditional family law system, there was no need to constitutionalize family privacy because family law assumed, and therefore protected, privacy within families. To the extent that that is so, *Griswold* foreshadowed later cases including *Eisenstadt* in heralding the individualization of the family, and thereby the erosion of the family as a unit mediating between the individual and the state.

However that may be, the explicit theme in *Griswold* assumed a holistic family unit, not a collection of autonomous individuals. In this regard, *Eisenstadt v. Baird* carried a different message. *Eisenstadt* presents exactly the position that commentators attributed to *Griswold*. Decided seven years after *Griswold*, *Eisenstadt* declares unconstitutional a Massachusetts statute that prohibited the distribution of contraception to unmarried adults.

At issue in the case was a state statute that provided a maximum five-year prison term for "whoever . . . gives away . . . any drug, medicine, instrument or article whatever for the prevention of conception." The statute made exceptions for "[a] registered physician" prescribing "for any married person drugs or articles intended for the prevention of pregnancy or conception."

William Baird was convicted at trial in Massachusetts for exhibiting contraceptive devices during a speech to students at Boston University and for giving a package of Emko vaginal foam to one woman at the end of his lecture. The Massachusetts Supreme Court sustained the conviction for giving contraceptive foam to an unmarried woman. The United States Supreme Court reversed, basing its decision on the equal protection of unmarried, as compared with married, people.

The Court's decision in *Eisenstadt* discards the essential distinction in *Griswold* between home and work and firmly attaches the right of privacy to the individual person. Indeed, *Eisenstadt* expressly and firmly disavows any view of families as more, or other, than the individuals who compose them. The *Eisenstadt* Court explained:

> It is true that in *Griswold* the right of privacy in question inhered in the marital relationship. Yet the marital couple is not an independent entity with a mind and heart of its own, but an association of two individuals each with a separate intellectual and emotional makeup. If the right of privacy means anything, it is the right of the *individual*, married or single, to be free from unwarranted governmental intrusion into matters so fundamentally affecting a person as the decision whether to bear or beget a child.[27]

That explanation was essential to the Court's equal protection analysis in *Eisenstadt*. *Griswold*, decided seven years before, had made it unconstitutional for states to prevent married couples from using birth control. The conclusion in *Eisenstadt*, that a similar rule must apply with regard to unmarried persons, was premised on the conclusion that a state's different treatment of married and unmarried persons in a birth control statute lacked a rational basis, and could therefore not be tolerated.

Massachusetts had delineated various goals the statute served. That the statute was justified as a deterrent against fornication made little sense to the Court, since the statute made contraceptives generally available to prevent the spread of disease and to married persons for use in marital or extramarital relations. The Court further described it as "plainly unreasonable" for the state to punish fornication, a misdemeanor under state law, with pregnancy and the birth of an unwanted child. Moreover, the Court concluded that the statute, originally promulgated as part of a set of statutes dealing with "Crimes Against Chastity, Morality, Decency and Good Order," could not be justified as a health measure. Among other things, if protecting health demanded that contraceptives be prescribed by doctors, that need pertained to married and unmarried persons. In addition, not all contraceptives posed a danger to health. Therefore, the statute, if justified as a health measure, would have been overbroad.

Finally, the Court in *Eisenstadt* stated that if preventing contraception per se formed the state's purpose, then that purpose must apply equally to married and unmarried people. The Court concluded "that by providing dissimilar treatment for married and unmarried persons who are similarly situated, [the Massachusetts statutes in question] violate the Equal Protection Clause."[28] But, in a world in which the bonds that connect family members are viewed as inherently unlike the connections that link autonomous individuals, the dissimilar treatment at issue in *Eisenstadt* would be not only rational it would be inevitable. As long as the family continued unambiguously to enjoy the sacred prerogatives its history implies, it made perfect sense for the law to treat legally married couples differently from other people in other sorts of groupings. In such a world, neither the relationship between spouses nor relationships within families could generally be described as an "association," of "individuals each with a separate intellectual and emotional makeup."[29]

Thus the express claim in *Eisenstadt* is far more startling and far less traditional than that in *Griswold*. The *Eisenstadt* Court's reference to a married couple as an "association of two individuals" and its language affirming the right of the *"individual"* to privacy seem familiar in a world largely defined through, and deeply dependent on, notions of the autonomous individual. In fact, it is revolutionary when applied to the family. Long after the last vestiges of the feudal order were replaced in the marketplace by notions of free contract and autonomous individuality, Western society continued to define spouses—and, even more particularly, parents and their children—as units of relationship with a reality apart from, and encompassing, that of the individuals involved. The Court's straightforward, unapologetic description in *Eisenstadt* of the "marital couple" as nothing other than two people, associated together, signals a fundamental alteration in the society's view of the sort of relationships traditionally associated with families.

Because in later cases decided after the 1970s the Supreme Court moved back from its position in *Eisenstadt*, *Eisenstadt's* ultimate role in the evolution of family or "privacy" law, remains unclear. Whatever that role, the opinion constitutes an important statement from the Supreme Court about the changing character of the American family. Commentators have described *Eisenstadt* as an extension to nontraditional families of the protection the Constitution grants the family (as explicated in *Griswold*). Thus a 1991 family law casebook discusses *Eisenstadt* in a section called, "Constitutional Protection of Nontraditional Families," and explains:

> We begin [our discussion of the topic] with *Griswold v. Connecticut*, the modern source of the constitutional right of intimate association. *Eisenstadt v. Baird* follows because it is the first case to vindicate, if obliquely, the constitutional claims of the unmarried, and is therefore the foundation case in any argument urging protection of nontraditional families.[30]

The notion of a "nontraditional family" has indeed been widely institutionalized in the years following *Eisenstadt*. And it is a notion that reflects the license granted in *Eisenstadt* to define, and thus to form, families as units involving no more than the separate individuals recruited to play familial roles. The family—understood as a whole, and grounded in natural (e.g., "blood" or "genes") or supernatural truths suggesting each member's clear roles and obligations—is thus replaced by a group of people, ultimately unfettered by ties that connect them inexorably. This is the association to which the Court in *Eisenstadt* referred.

The character of that association, as compared with the sort of association protected in *Griswold*, and the far-reaching implications of the transformation in the understanding and place of the family in American society that *Eisenstadt* signals, become even clearer when the case is compared with a much earlier, though equally controversial, case that had nothing directly to do with family matters. That case, *Lochner v. New York*, decided by the Supreme Court in 1905, considered a New York statutory prohibition against bakeries hiring employees to work more than sixty hours in a week or more than ten hours in a day. The Court, describing the statute as an interference with "the liberty of person" and "the right of free contract,"[31] held it unconstitutional as a violation of the Fourteenth Amendment.

The opinion, now almost a century old, portrays clearly and unapologetically the ideology of contract as that ideology was constructed during the development of the Industrial Revolution. *Lochner* thus provides a useful comparison for the later "privacy" cases, in which the Court used a similar interpretive approach in the context not of economics or business, but of relationships between people within families. Justice Peckham, writing for the Court in *Lochner*, understood what was at stake. The statute, he explained, was not concerned with the prohibition of involuntary labor. Rather, its opening words—"no employee shall be required or permitted to work . . ."[32]—revealed the statute's purpose. In Justice Peckham's view, the statute was "equivalent to an enactment that 'no employee shall contract or agree to work,' more than ten hours per day."[33] As such, the statute interfered with the employer's and the employee's equal rights to negotiate the terms of their working relationship, and thereby, violated the Constitution's guarantee that all individuals be at "liberty" to negotiate the terms through which they "purchase" others' labor or "sell" their own.[34]

The notion that the liberty of contract belongs at least as much to the employee as to the employer emerges as a basic assumption in *Lochner.* In terms perfectly reflecting nineteenth-century liberalism's view of individual liberty, the Court referred to the bakery owner and the bakery employee as "persons who are *sui juris,*" and focused on the imbalance in power, not between employer and employee, but between the state and the bakery employees affected by the statute. Thus the Court framed *Lochner* as a dispute between the state and the individual bakery worker. The Court explained:

> [I]t becomes of great importance to determine which shall prevail,—the right of the individual to labor for such time as he may choose, or the right of the state to prevent the individual from laboring, or from entering into any contract to labor, beyond a certain time prescribed by the state.[35]

The Court argued that the health of bakery workers or of bread eaters could not have been the real motivation behind the statue at issue. Bakeries, the Court reported, do not pose particular dangers to health, and there is no "connection between the number of hours a baker may work in the bakery and the healthful quality of the bread made by the workman."[36] Thus, according to the Court, the argument that section 110 of the state's labor law served the health interests of the employees or of the public was mere pretext. The state's motive lay elsewhere. The Court wrote:

> It seems to us that the real object and purpose were simply to regulate the hours of labor between the master and his employees (all being men, *sui juris*) in a private business, not dangerous in any degree to morals, or in any real and substantial degree to the health of the employees.[37]

The state's aim, as the Court viewed it, was simply and conclusively to intervene in the market so as to deprive worker and employer alike of the right to negotiate the terms of their own interactions.

The Court's concerns about state regulation presumed that the worker and the employer entered the negotiation process as equals. Twice, the Court referred to the two as being equal before the law. "The master and his employees," declared the Court, "all being men, *sui juris*," [38] should not be subjected to state intervention in their private affairs. The Court affirmed the equality of the two by noting that the "one has as much right to purchase as the other to sell labor." [39] The Court went further, arguing that New York's labor law impugned the equality and intelligence of bakers, who surely could negotiate their own working conditions without governmental interference. The Court wrote:

> There is no contention that bakers as a class are not equal in intelligence and capacity to men in other trades or manual occupations, or that they are not able to assert their rights and care for themselves without the protecting arm of the state, interfering with their independence of judgment and of action. They are in no sense wards of the state. [40]

Justice Holmes's dissent emphasized the economic underpinnings of the Court's holding. To what extent the Court believed in the accuracy of the factual assumptions beneath its economic theory is less clear. But it is clear, as Justice Holmes declared in his dissent, that the Court was motivated by its preference for a substantive outcome contrary to that of New York's labor law. The Court's preference, in Justice Holmes's view, though arguably reasonable as a view of economic affairs, failed to provide adequate grounds for a decision invalidating the statute as unconstitutional. Justice Holmes explained:

> It is settled by various decisions of this court that state constitutions and state laws may regulate life in many ways which we as legislators might think as injudicious, or if you like as tyrannical, as this, and which, equally with this, interfere with the liberty to contract. . . . Some of these laws embody convictions or prejudices which judges are likely to share. Some may not. But a Constitution is not intended to embody a particular economic theory, whether of paternalism and the organic relation of the citizen to the state or of *laissez faire*. [41]

Justice Holmes's criticisms of the Court's decision in *Lochner* are echoed by the critics of *Griswold* and *Eisenstadt* who suggest that the decisions in those cases were not rooted in the Constitution and were, therefore, the illegitimate products of reading substantive guarantees into the Constitution. Just as the Constitution fails to protect the unfettered right to enter contracts that New York, and other states, perceived as threats to public health and welfare, so too the Constitution fails to assert a general right to privacy, or more specific rights, regarding sexual freedom, marriage, or abortion, protected in privacy cases following *Griswold*. [42]

In this regard, the officially repudiated *Lochner* era,[43] and its use of substantive due process arguments in constitutional interpretation, was revived in another context, at least as a methodological matter, with the *Griswold-Eisenstadt-Roe* line of cases. The later cases use substantive due process to protect not economic interests, but interests related to the family or to decisions that implicate family matters.

Curiously, however, those who deplore substantive due process arguments in the economic context often accept them in the noneconomic context of cases such as *Griswold, Eisenstadt,* and *Roe.* Indeed, in deciding *Griswold,* Justice Douglas expressly and decisively disassociated the Court from *Lochner* and the model for protecting liberty interests offered there. The *Lochner* Court, declared Justice Douglas disapprovingly, served as a "super-legislature to determine . . . laws that touch economic problems, business affairs, or social conditions."[44] In distancing the *Griswold* Court from the *Lochner* precedent, Justice Douglas simply distinguished the two statutes because one was concerned with economics, business, or social conditions while the other "operate[d] directly on an intimate relation of husband and wife."[45] The assumptions on which the Court predicated that distinction between the economic and the intimate or familial were not made clear. However, they can, and should, be delineated.

The *Griswold* Court suggests that, when determining the constitutionality of a state statute, it is the *content* of the legislation under consideration that determines the legitimacy or illegitimacy of a constitutional approach that relies on contemporary perceptions of values. More specifically, the Court's disclaimer suggests that governmental interference with freedom of contract does not compare in seriousness with governmental interference in the "intimate relation between husband and wife." Thus, the Court in *Griswold* suggests that the prior sort of state interference cannot justify the invocation of contemporary values to interpret the Constitution, but that the latter can.

Embedded in that difference—the difference between the contractual connections of the marketplace, and the intimate connections of home and hearth—are the crucial terms that structured American thinking about the family by distinguishing the world of home from the world of work. The Court's decision in *Griswold,* whether consciously or not, used the ideological difference between home and work to justify resurrecting a *Lochner* approach to constitutional interpretation. *Griswold* was written to suggest that a threat to the society's core values, described as the values of the marital tie and the domestic nest, compelled the Court's response. The *Griswold* Court wrote in a way that appeared to reflect and even replicate the wider society's vision of the family as a universe of love and enduring obligation almost entirely set off from the fungible negotiations that defined the market, and attempted thereby to justify the same sort of noninterpretivist reading of the Constitution that allowed an earlier Court to decide *Lochner* as it did. The Court in *Griswold* appeared to suggest that for this hallowed purpose, and for this purpose alone, the Constitution's protection was meant to be extended and its text stretched. Such was Justice Douglas's apparent reading for the Court.

A seemingly similar reading was suggested by Justice Harlan's concurrence. Justice Harlan described the violation of the Constitution as "an intolerable and unjustifiable invasion of privacy in the conduct of the most intimate concerns of an individual's personal life."[46] He found the right of privacy to be contained in the due process clause of the Fourteenth Amendment's guarantee of liberty. Justice Harlan wrote:

> The best that can be said is that through the course of this Court's decisions [due process] has represented the balance which our Nation, built upon postulates of respect for the liberty of the individual, has struck between that liberty and the demands of organized society. If the supplying of content to this Constitutional concept has of necessity been a rational process, it certainly has not been one where judges have felt free to roam where unguided speculation might take them. The balance of which I speak is the balance struck by this country, having regard to what history teaches are the traditions from which it developed as well as the traditions from which it broke.[47]

Justice Harlan's opinion—although not unlike Justice Douglas's in justifying a noninterpretivist approach by reference to the centrality of the values in need of constitutional protection—indicates a serious flaw in the majority's justification for the right of privacy attached to familial units. Justice Harlan described the liberty interests protected by the Fourteenth Amendment as attaching to the individual. He expressly referred to "the liberty of the individual."[48] In this regard he was entirely correct as a matter of constitutional jurisprudence. From at least the early nineteenth century, the individual has been the locus of the interests protected by the Constitution. Traditionally, the interests of the family— long preserved in our society as one of the few units with value beyond that of the individuals involved—were regulated and protected, if at all, by state statutory law and not by the Constitution. Only in the last few decades, since *Griswold*, have courts come rather routinely to consider the constitutional implications of family disputes.

Griswold appeared to justify its form of constitutional interpretation by invoking the inviolability of the family as a whole, separate from the person and the state alike, and thus justly protected from legislative attempts to regulate its most intimate affairs. However, precisely that view of the family—the family as a whole, the family as a unit beyond, but encompassing, its members—had previously played a significant part in placing the family beyond the Constitution's reach. And that fact emerged definitively in *Eisenstadt*, the case in which the implications that commentators read into *Griswold*, as well perhaps as the implications of the *Griswold* subtext, became clear.

Underlying its simple and seemingly inconsequential (because obvious) distinction between "home" and "work," *Griswold's* apparently straightforward attempt to distinguish itself from *Lochner*, obscured a larger process—the process through which the society's understanding of the family was beginning to shift and new understandings of family were beginning to exist alongside more familiar understandings. In the society at large, the family referred to in *Griswold*—a sacred universe, understood as set apart from the world of money and of work—was being joined and transformed by the family implied by *Eisenstadt*—a discrete collection of individuals, associating together as a matter of choice.

Some remarkable implications of that process are present in *Eisenstadt*, which provides at the level of constitutional adjudication one of the first express acknowledgments of the set of changes regarding family matters that were occurring widely in the society. That acknowledgment signals a clear transformation in the traditional ideology of family as well. In the seven years between *Griswold* and *Eisenstadt*, a momentous set of changes that had been developing in the structure and scope of the American family for many decades began to gain widespread acknowledgment and acceptance from the law. Though society remained, and still remains, confused and ambivalent, the strength of the changes is indicated in the law's willingness to define and regulate the family—or at least its adult members—as a collection of discrete individuals connected by a set of temporary choices and unaffected by the eternal dictates of God or blood. In consequence, the ideological distinction between home and work becomes murky, and as that happens, family relations appear less and less different from relations in the marketplace, and further, seem increasingly amenable to regulation by rules resembling those formulated for the regulation of market interactions.

Ironically, in this regard, *Griswold*, but not *Eisenstadt*, can ultimately be harmonized with *Lochner*. Both *Griswold* and *Lochner* (though the second only implicitly) presume a world in which home and work are separate. *Eisenstadt*, in contrast, discards that distinction. This reading depends of course on *Griswold's* express language. The opinion's subtext, as well as an earlier draft[49] prepared by Justice Douglas, but never used, suggest that the Court may have been far more comfortable with a view of the family as a collection of autonomous individuals than the language of the opinion actually states. Whatever the agenda or unresolved confusions underlying *Griswold*, the rhetoric and metaphors that were used by the Court suggest the unprecedented character of the *Eisenstadt* decision, which clearly defines the individual as the unit to which value attaches, even within families.

Over three decades after *Griswold*, it seems clear that families (at least with regard to adults within them) are increasingly understood to be composed of individuals and, that, for a large segment of the society much of the time, families as units of moral value are no more and no less significant than their separate, individual members. As the family is increasingly defined through the terms of the market, it is less often automatically understood as a locus of sacred value, apart from, or rather encompassing, individual family members. To the extent that families deserve protection from the law, that protection increasingly attaches to individual family members and not to the family unit as an undivided, and indivisible whole. That of course was the message of *Eisenstadt*.

Purportedly, *Eisenstadt* grew out of *Griswold*. But that is so only in a limited sense and only if *Griswold's* express language is ignored. Certainly each decision recognized a privacy right to the use of contraceptives. However, in their respective characterizations of family, the two decisions are far more different than similar. In fact, in many regards *Eisenstadt* resembles not *Griswold,* but *Lochner.* The justification that buttressed the *Griswold* decision—that the *family,* surely, had to be free from state intrusion—is present only as allusion in *Eisenstadt.* The *Eisenstadt* Court's equal protection analysis presumes that the protection afforded by *Griswold* applies to individual family members and not to the family or marital unit per se.

Eisenstadt and *Lochner* alike sought to protect the individual from state interference. In both cases it was the individual as the ultimate unit of social value, the individual as a social whole, joined to others only by choice and never absolutely, whose interests the Court protected. The *Lochner* Court accused the New York maximum hours statute of "limiting the hours in which grown and intelligent men may labor to earn their living" and therefore concluded that the law was a "mere meddlesome interference[] with the rights of the individual." [50] The *Eisenstadt* Court took a similar view with regard to adults making sexual and reproductive choices. That Court said that the Massachusetts birth control statute at issue curtailed "the right of the *individual,* married or single, to be free from unwarranted governmental intrusion into matters so fundamentally affecting a person as the decision whether to bear or beget a child." [51]

Differences continue to separate the world at issue in *Lochner* (of employer-employee relations) from the world at issue in *Eisenstadt* (of relations between unmarried lovers). These differences are, however, less absolute than those that once unambiguously separated home from work in American ideology; the earlier differences depended centrally on an understanding of home and family that precluded autonomous individuality. What is remarkable about the similarity between *Lochner* and *Eisenstadt* is that *Lochner's* idealized portrait of the nineteenth-century market—populated by individuals equally free to make their separate choices and to design their unique connections—was transferred with virtually no notice, and therefore with little recognition of the consequences, to *Eisenstadt's* mid-twentieth-century portrait of couples—married or unmarried—described as "an association of two individuals each with a separate intellectual and emotional makeup" [52] who, as such, deserve constitutional protection. In both *Lochner* and *Eisenstadt,* parties involved in a relationship (whether commercial, as in *Lochner*, or familial as in *Eisenstadt*) are considered to possess equal bargaining power.

Despite the similarities between *Lochner* and *Eisenstadt*, however, the two opinions cannot be read to say the same thing. In fact, *Lochner* portrays one pole of a world, whose other pole, as defined in nineteenth- and early to mid-twentieth-century American ideology, is the family, whose members in relating together were understood to contrast almost totally with the unrestrained individuals of the free market. This is the family as portrayed, at least on the face of the text, in *Griswold*, but it is not the family envisioned by *Eisenstadt*.

Certainly the justices who wrote *Lochner* would have been as unsettled by *Eisenstadt* as those who wrote *Eisenstadt* were unsettled by *Lochner*. The explanation of each group's real or presumed disquiet with the other is the same. Between *Lochner* and *Eisenstadt*, as more dramatically, because more suddenly, between *Griswold* and *Eisenstadt*, established truths about the differences between home and work, as well as truths about the people who populated those two worlds, had been torn asunder. For the justices who wrote *Lochner*—and probably for most people who approved of the decision—the world of work and the world of home were understood to be inevitably separate. The family, described by David Schneider in his study of American kinship at mid-century, as a universe of "enduring, diffuse solidarity" defined through ties of natural substance ("blood"), contrasts in almost every regard with the individualism of the marketplace, in which "every man is, in principle, an embodiment of humanity at large, and [where] as such he is equal to every other man, and free."[53]

Both *Lochner* and *Eisenstadt* presume the autonomous individual and protect that individual's freedom from unjustified restraint. In the context of relevance in *Lochner* (the world of work), that presumption is, and since the late eighteenth century has been, familiar and therefore expected. At the time and in the context of relevance in *Eisenstadt* (the world of home), the presumption of autonomous individuality was not generally expected and is still not always expected or entirely acceptable. For over a century, Americans had assumed that the autonomous individual existed in the market, but not in the home. *Eisenstadt* is significant for envisioning the autonomous individual at the center of the domestic unit. In this regard, the opinion suggests forcefully—because it seems almost to assume—that a fundamental change had occurred in the society's understanding of the family. For centuries, the family had provided one of the very few contexts in American life within which the putatively equal, unfettered individual of the marketplace was *not* presumed. *Eisenstadt* represented a new view and acknowledged a new reality.

In *Eisenstadt*, the family was clearly and unmistakenly recognized as a collection of individuals. And even though *Eisenstadt's* express language protected only the right to make a certain kind of procreative, or sexual, decision, there is no express language in the decision that limits the protection delineated only to people engaged in those activities, and in addition, the view of the family suggested in *Eisenstadt* reappeared in a set of later cases, including *Roe v. Wade*. In protecting families, or activities associated with families, *Eisenstadt* protected the right of the individual, alone, to decide how to design his or her life. In this regard, *Eisenstadt* does not reflect *Lochner*. It extends it. However, the extension contends with the ideological underpinnings of the world in which *Lochner* was decided, a world in which home and work were viewed as fundamentally separate. In this regard, *Eisenstadt* can be distinguished from *Lochner* and *Griswold* alike. Of the three opinions, only *Eisenstadt* declares that the differences between the marketplace and the home have become essentially incidental.

The very justification offered by the Court for its approach in *Griswold*—that the family as a world apart from the rest of everyday life deserves special protection—was declared illusory by *Eisenstadt*. *Eisenstadt*, despite citing *Griswold* as its central precedent, differed from *Griswold* in declaring that the family is merely a collection of individuals, no different from individuals who join in other forms of association and that, therefore, individuals in families are deserving of no greater and of no lesser protection than individuals in market associations.

III. Privacy, Liberty, and Procreational Autonomy

The right to privacy, formulated in *Griswold* and reaffirmed in *Eisenstadt*, was extended, and then limited, in future constitutional cases and has been applauded, examined, reinterpreted, and condemned by judges and commentators. Almost nobody has considered the issues and remained entirely neutral, and even people approving the apparent consequences of creating a constitutional right to privacy have questioned the Court's jurisprudence in these cases.

Griswold and *Eisenstadt,* and the privacy cases that followed, including *Roe v. Wade,* in which the court based a limited right to abortion on the right to privacy, as well as cases decided about a decade later such as *Bowers v. Hardwick,* which restricted the right to privacy, reveal the legal concerns and moral puzzles that constitute the law's contemporary response to cases occasioned by reproductive technology. *Eisenstadt,* especially had the implications of that case been furthered rather than circumscribed in later cases, might be read to provide a clear constitutional right to enter surrogacy arrangements, to donate or to buy and sell gestational services or gametic material, and to reproduce using the gametes of deceased spouses or lovers. John A. Robertson in *Children of Choice* recommends such an approach to reproductive technology, one based on a right to "procreative liberty." "There is," proclaims Robertson, "no better alternative than leaving procreative decisions to the individuals whose procreative desires are most directly involved."[54] Robertson's approach flows from *Eisenstadt* more directly than from *Griswold.* He suggests an individual, not a communal, right when he discusses "procreative liberty." In fact, as Robertson recognizes, the ultimate implications of privacy jurisprudence for laws restricting the right to use reproductive technology or to enter into surrogacy arrangements remain uncertain. However, to the extent that the early privacy cases do protect the right to have children through surrogacy, through the use of donated gametes, or with the assistance of other reproductive technologies, that protection stems from the understanding of privacy articulated in *Eisenstadt,* and not from that in *Griswold.*

The sort of privacy protected in *Griswold*—the privacy of the family, as a whole, from those outside the family—reflected, and thereby confirmed, long-standing images of the family as a domain protected from the larger world of work and money. The right to privacy protected in *Eisenstadt* attached to the individual and not the group, and in that important regard, was thereby of a different order than the right protected in *Griswold.* Far more than the familial privacy protected in *Griswold,* the right protected in *Eisenstadt* (the right of the *individual* to reproduce or not) supports the sort of procreational liberty that Robertson recommends, especially because assisted reproduction has come increasingly to require the participation of third parties, including sperm donors, egg donors, and women willing to gestate babies for others. Only unusually are such third parties defined, even by participants, as "family members."

A more explicit consideration of the differences between privacy as defined in *Griswold* and privacy as defined in *Eisenstadt* is in order. Some commentators and judges have suggested that "liberty" might have been a better term than privacy to describe the right protected in both cases. That suggestion provides a good starting point from which to explore the differences between the notions of privacy involved in the two cases. Justice Douglas studiously avoided any mention of the term "liberty" in *Griswold*. His choice of the term privacy to describe the right protected was probably motivated by an interest in avoiding the sort of direct reference to *Lochner* which use of the term "liberty" would undoubtedly have suggested. However, the term "privacy" *does* describe the right extended in *Griswold*, and from a social and historical, though not perhaps from a constitutional, perspective, the term "privacy" was a better choice than liberty would have been for describing that right.

Privacy and liberty do not suggest precisely the same thing. Though the two terms are closely connected in meaning, the tone of each differs from that of the other. In common language, privacy more often connotes "intimate" and "personal" than does liberty. The family had long been the central arena for private relations in Western society. "Private life should be lived behind walls," wrote Littré in his mid-nineteenth-century *Dictionnaire*. "No one," he continued, "is allowed to peer into a private home or to reveal what goes on inside."[55] In contrast, at least since the French Revolution, the individual—not larger units such as the family—has been understood as the agent of "liberty." Thus, *Griswold* protected the right to privacy for family relationships, within families. That right reflected a pervasive perception of family life during the century and a half before *Griswold* as private from those outside the family unit. Family privacy does not, however, depend on, or guarantee, the privacy of family members, each from the others.

Griswold's subtext, as well as Justice Douglas's earlier draft which predicated the decision on a First Amendment right of spouses to associate freely, suggest the Court may at some level have understood the privacy right as attaching to individuals rather than to families as holistic units of social interaction. It would strain credulity to argue that fundamental understandings of personhood and family could have changed as completely in seven years as the differences between *Griswold's* express language and *Eisenstadt* suggest. However, in 1965, the Court still voiced its concern with protecting privacy in language recalling traditional families as wholes. In 1973, the Court did not.

The establishment of individual privacy, suggested perhaps in *Griswold's* subtext, but elaborated expressly in *Eisenstadt* and later privacy cases, depended on, and reflected, the transformation of the predominant ideology of family. In this transformation, the family, once understood to involve inexorable and enduring connections, came to be understood to entail relationships far more similar to those expected in the marketplace. Privacy was valued for centuries, but the notion of privacy as attached exclusively or at least most fittingly to the autonomous individual is a recent innovation in the history of ideas. It is even more recent with regard to people in families. The position that family members are private, or at least have the *right* to be private, one from another, is fundamentally different from the notion that family privacy should be protected from the larger society and the state.

That difference is illuminated by comparing the traditional notion in family law of "family autonomy" with the sort of autonomy right protected in *Eisenstadt*. Courts often justified, and to some extent continue to justify, decisions to avoid state intervention in family matters under the rubric of family autonomy. As traditionally understood, the right of families to enjoy autonomy protected families as social units from state intervention aimed at assisting or controlling *individuals within ongoing families*. The state has regulated the creation of families and, to whatever extent it was willing to do so, the termination of families for centuries. The state defined marriage, determined custody, and made cohabitation criminal. But, the doctrine of family autonomy proclaimed that within operational families—and only there—the family as a whole could, and should, design and create the specific contours of everyday life.

Unstated in most applications of this doctrine—because thoroughly assumed—was a certain understanding of families. Rarely challenged, at least before the latter part of the twentieth century, families in this view were understood as hierarchical units in which men and adults, in the very nature of the case, controlled women and children. So, for example, in a well-known Nebraska case decided in 1953, a state court refused to agree with Lydia McGuire that her husband, Charles McGuire, despite his ample financial resources, should furnish the couple's home with indoor bathroom facilities, a new furnace, and decent furniture. Invoking the doctrine of family autonomy, the court reasoned that these matters were private to each family which should not have to suffer state intrusion because a particular husband was less generous than he might have been. "[T]he living standards of a family," the Nebraska court wrote, "are a matter of concern to the household, and not for the courts to determine." [56] In the court's view, the McGuire family followed the social expectation that husbands, not wives, make major financial decisions for the family. Thus, this family (or rather this family understood inevitably with Mr. McGuire as dominant) could not be disrupted by state interference to protect the wife's interest in decent support.

Family autonomy (the privacy of the family as a structured whole) is more likely to preclude than to provide the sort of protection to individuals involved in family matters that would seem to be assured by *Eisenstadt*. However, once the right to privacy attaches to the individual, rather than to the whole, options for creating and for living everyday life in units definable as "families" multiply exponentially. For this reason, *Eisenstadt*, though not *Griswold*, suggests broad constitutional protection for individuals to form intimate relationships that may or may not resemble traditional understandings of family, including relationships produced from, or necessary for the use of, reproductive technology.

Had the implications of *Eisenstadt* been extended and elaborated, rather than reinterpreted and limited in Supreme Court cases that followed it, some of the most troubling questions presented to family law, including questions raised by reproductive technology, would find readier, though not necessarily better, answers than is the case. That that has not happened seems not surprising, perhaps even inevitable, in light of the wide-scale ambivalence in the society that accompanies the transformation of the family toward the sort of assembly envisioned in *Eisenstadt*. That such a shift could occur without vacillation and disarray is not easily imaginable.

In fact, a little more than a decade after *Eisenstadt*, the Supreme Court expressly limited the right to privacy defined there. In *Bowers v. Hardwick*, decided in 1986, the Court refused to extend the protection based on privacy to sodomy between consenting adults. In other cases, as well, the Court limited the implications of *Eisenstadt*. For instance, in

Webster v. Missouri Reproduction Services, decided in 1989, the Court sharply restricted a woman's right to abortion guaranteed by *Roe v. Wade*, a right that *Roe* located within the right to privacy.

These cases were decided by a different assortment of judges from those who decided the earlier cases, judges with different responses and concerns. However, from the perspective of the social analyst, the confusions and ambivalence that followed *Eisenstadt* and its immediate progeny represent the complicated, but not surprising, responses of a society adjusting to profound changes in a central social institution and to equally consequential changes in the concepts of personhood and of persons in relation to each other.

For similar reasons, society is ambivalent and confused about the increasingly impressive solutions offered by reproductive technology to infertility. This ambivalence and confusion are precisely reflected in the law which seeks both to protect and to discourage such technology. Legislative responses are neither comprehensive nor timely. Courts, in responding to particular cases that demand resolution, seek to preserve the correlates of individuality and expanding choice, while also working to protect families—and especially the parent-child bond—from the consequences of unlimited, often unregulated, choice.

THREE

Status and Contract
in Surrogate Motherhood

The society and the law remain deeply ambivalent and confused about the transformation of the family from a holistic unit, protected by the law as such, to the family as a collectivity of people, protected by the law individually. Social and legal responses to reproductive technology and surrogate motherhood reflect that ambivalence and confusion.

This chapter considers those responses in the context of surrogacy. Even the labels—surrogate, surrogacy, surrogate motherhood—can be viewed ambivalently, since from a certain perspective the surrogate mother is the real mother. In fact, surrogacy is not really an instance of reproductive technology although it is almost always considered and discussed as if it were. Surrogacy—at least what has come, quite remarkably, to be called "traditional" surrogacy—requires no sophisticated technology. Nothing beyond a turkey baster is necessary to perform the artificial (or assisted) insemination of a so-called surrogate mother with the sperm of an "intended" father. The procedure need not involve medical assistance, though for legal and other reasons it often does.

I. "Traditional" Surrogacy

Traditional surrogacy poses no challenge beyond that posed by artificial insemination to familiar notions of biological maternity, though it does upset expectations about the connection between biological and social maternity. In contrast, gestational surrogacy involves the separation of biological maternity into a genetic and a gestational aspect, with each aspect allotted to different women. Gestational surrogacy does thereby unsettle expectations about human reproduction and presents different conundrums from those presented by traditional surrogacy. Gestational surrogacy is considered in later chapters.

Traditional surrogacy has some ancient precedents including the biblical story of the birth of Ishmael to Hagar after Sara pleaded with her husband Abraham to become the father of a child with Sara's servant Hagar. "Come to my slave," Sara told Abraham, "and hopefully I will have sons through her."[1] Biologically, the biblical precedents differ from current practice only in that in the biblical cases conception followed sexual intercourse rather than artificial insemination. As a social matter, however, surrogacy was more acceptable to the world in which Sara, Abraham, Hagar, and Ishmael lived than it is in the contemporary world. But that fact notwithstanding, the consequences of Hagar's "surrogate motherhood" were quite calamitous for everyone involved.

As resurrected in the modern world, surrogacy is classed as a form of reproductive technology for social, rather than technological or biological, reasons. Although now surrogacy arrangements can take many forms, they all involve the participation of a woman who agrees to gestate and give birth to a child whom she further agrees to surrender to other parents. These parents are variously called "contracting," "intending," or "social" parents.

In the most typical surrogacy case, the father who contracts with the potential surrogate is also the sperm donor and is, therefore, the biological father of the child. Just as the name "surrogate" suggests that the biological mother is not a real mother, so the terms contracting, intending, and social parents suggest that these people are not real (in the sense perhaps of complete) parents either. Sometimes, the father, who is usually a biological parent, is referred to simply as "the father," while his wife is called a contracting, intending, or social parent. However, insofar as biological fathers in our culture have traditionally become fathers by marriage to their children's mothers, fathers in surrogacy arrangements may not be considered social fathers until and unless their wives become mothers.

Surrogacy is sometimes considered by infertile couples who, for various reasons such as advanced age, may find it difficult to adopt. Married couples engaging a surrogate mother usually, though not necessarily, include a wife unable to conceive or gestate a baby, and desire a child to whom at least one of them (the husband) will have a genetic connection. Variations on this pattern exist. For instance, if the husband is infertile or has a family history of genetic disease, the sperm of a third-party donor can be used in the insemination. In such a case neither intending parent will be connected through genetics to the resulting child. In addition, the intending parents may not be married to one another; the biological and intending father may be unmarried and may desire to become a single parent, or an unmarried woman may enter into a contract with a surrogate who will then be inseminated with the sperm of a third-party donor.

When surrogacy involves a contract—and it may not, especially when the parties are relatives or close friends—the practice has been for the intending father, but not the intending mother, to sign the agreement. This practice is aimed at mitigating the suggestion that a child is being purchased and sold. In every state, it is illegal to pay for a child. If the surrogate is married, her husband generally enters into the contractual arrangement with the surrogate and the intending father. The husband of the surrogate must expressly refuse to consent to the insemination of his wife; otherwise, under existing law, in most jurisdictions he will be the child's legal father.

Commercial surrogacy generally involves payments of between $10,000 and $15,000 to the surrogate. That price has hardly budged in the past decade. In addition, even larger sums may be paid to brokers, including commercial surrogate mother programs. Helena Ragoné, who did anthropological research with surrogates and intending parents, reported in 1994 that there were eight such programs operating in the United States and that most couples were paying fees between $28,000 and $45,000, including payments to the surrogate.

Surrogacy, as a means for infertile couples to have children, appeared in the 1980s, a few years after an Englishwoman gave birth to the first child conceived in vitro. Thus, in exactly the same period, beginning in the early 1980s, society was faced with a variety of new forms for creating families, and courts were soon being asked to resolve disputes occasioned by surrogate motherhood and others occasioned by the use of the new reproductive technologies. Although surrogacy does not confound expectations about biological reproduction as profoundly as in vitro fertilization, embryo transfer, or the cryopreservation of gametes and embryos, surrogacy and the new reproductive technologies alike challenge traditional understandings about the family. The simultaneous appearance of "modern" surrogacy and the new reproductive technologies was probably not coincidental. By the late 1970s, as the law's increasingly liberal response during the previous decade and a half to other changes in the family suggests, the society was prepared to entertain, however ambivalently, families that conflicted with traditional expectations. Surrogacy and the new reproductive technologies depend on the recognition of choice and variety in the creation, and perhaps in the operation, of families. Each therefore can find acceptance only in a world, such as that assumed in *Eisenstadt*, that views families as collectivities of individuals who join—and dissociate—through *choice*. In such a world, but not in one that imagines families as holistic social units produced and defined through inexorable biological processes, couples can contract to produce children and families can include, or ignore, social parents, genetic parents, and gestational parents. The competing social, moral, and legal claims to which surrogacy and the new reproductive technologies have given rise all derive at bottom from continuing uncertainty about the value of the cultural shift represented—though obviously not generated—by the transition from *Griswold* to *Eisenstadt*.

However, traditional surrogacy differs from the new reproductive technologies in not seriously disrupting familiar assumptions about human reproduction. Therefore, surrogacy provides a comparatively straightforward context within which to begin the analysis of social responses to assisted reproduction, including surrogacy and the new reproductive technologies. These technologies present a more complicated challenge to traditional images of family life than does surrogacy. Surrogacy manipulates, and therefore challenges, the social dimensions of family, but unlike the new reproductive technologies, surrogacy raises few metaphysical questions about the parameters of *biological* maternity or paternity.

Surrogacy does depend on the use of artificial insemination. But today use of that procedure raises few metaphysical or ontological questions about biological parentage. The society and the law were once deeply troubled by the implications of artificial insemination, especially in cases involving the use of sperm from third-party donors rather than from the husband of the mother. However, American law accepted and widely regulated artificial insemination over a decade before the appearance of surrogacy in the early 1980s. With that, earlier concerns about adultery and bastardy resulting from artificial insemination have been replaced with the determination that at least in the case of married couples the consenting husband of a woman who conceives through artificial insemination using donor sperm, and not the sperm donor, is the father of any resulting children.

Surrogacy is problematic for society and the law today, but not because it involves artificial insemination. Rather surrogacy questions traditional understandings of mother and commodifies and commercializes the creation of the parent-child bond. With surrogacy, the biological mother (the surrogate) agrees to participate in the act of reproduction but not in the process of socialization that follows. That has troubled a society which as a whole continues to understand biological mothers, far more than biological fathers, as inexorably conditioned by the processes of biological reproduction to become social parents. In addition, because surrogacy so often involves contractual agreements and financial exchange, it suggests the erosion of traditional understandings of family which have for so long defined the world of family in contrast to the world of work. Thus, although surrogacy does not seriously disrupt familiar expectations about the biological correlates of kinship, it does suggest images of women and of families that contrast with traditional images in important regards.

In the traditional ideology of family, women are distinguished from men—and mothers from fathers—on the basis of biological correlates. Fathers represent culture, whereas mothers represent nature. Fathers stand for contract—for the right to negotiate reality, including relationships; mothers stand for status—for the inevitability of relationships and their structure. But, in the context of surrogacy arrangements, mothers can be opposed to *other kinds* of mothers as well as to fathers. In this opposition, certain mothers represent culture or contract; whereas others represent status or nature. This opposition is more complicated than that between fathers and mothers. Surrogate mothers represent contract and culture in that they enter written agreements that provide for the creation of new forms of relationship and for the termination of maternal ties. But they represent nature in that they are "natural mothers"; their claim to the child is based in biology, more than in law. Intending mothers may also represent contract and culture. They become mothers through agreement, rather than through pregnancy. But intending mothers may be associated with tradition in that they typically hope to replicate traditional family forms, to create families indistinguishable, except in origin, from old-fashioned American families.

Although surrogacy disrupts familiar expectations about, and understandings of, families, it also promises to create *more* traditional, old-fashioned families. It suggests the commodification of women and of their children and the absolute collapse of loving, enduring families. But, it suggests as well, the creation of loving, enduring families that, were it not for surrogacy, could never be.

These differences, and their implications, can be sharply focused through reference to an ideological shift described in the late nineteenth century by the English social theorist, Sir Henry Maine. "[T]he society of our day," wrote Maine in 1861, "is mainly distinguished from that of preceding generations by the largeness of the sphere which is occupied in it by Contract."[2] In contrast to a universe so largely occupied by contract, Maine poses a more ancient world, largely defined through relations of status, relations which "fixed a man's social position irreversibly at his birth."[3]

In a universe based in status, rights and duties are set at birth; moreover, in such a universe, rights and duties are viewed as inexorable because they attend relationships understood as natural. Thus, the relationships between a master and a serf, or between a *pater familias* and his children, are established at birth, follow familiar forms, and determine the rights and duties between the two parties. In a world based on status, laws are not formulated abstractly for application to putatively equal individuals. Rather, they follow the perceived natural order of things, reflecting the inevitability of status and relationship. In such a world, people are who they are because they were born to be that way, and the pretext of abstract equality is absent.

In contrast, in a world based on contract, as Maine describes it, the basic unit of social reality is understood as the individual, equal to other individuals and free to define his or her own life apart from the accidents of birth. Such an individual is defined legally by the ability to contract with other, equally situated individuals. Maine wrote:

> The movement of the progressive societies has been uniform in one respect. Through all its course it has been distinguished by the gradual dissolution of family dependency and the growth of individual obligation in its place. The individual is steadily substituted for the Family, as the unit of which civil laws take account. . . . Nor is it difficult to see what is the tie between man and man which replaces by degrees those forms of reciprocity in rights and duties which have their origin in the Family. It is contract. Starting, as from one terminus of history, from a condition of

society in which all the relations of Persons are summed up in the relations
of Family, we seem to have steadily moved toward a phase of social order
in which all these relations arise from free agreement of individuals.[4]

In theory, in such a world individuals who are putatively equal and
unconstrained by *a priori* characterizations reach their own bargains, act
out their own dramas, and define their own lives. In this social world, the
individual is thought of as "the proprietor of his own person," free from
dependence on the will of other people.[5]

The theory of complete equality was belied in Maine's world and is
belied in our own by the reality of equality only for some—for those who
are defined at any moment as full human beings. Various groups, including women, blacks, and children have been denied that recognition.
Maine did acknowledge that in certain circumstances, women might
be defined as complete people, putatively equal to other autonomous
individuals. Thus, he wrote that the status of the Female, under Tutelage,
"if the tutelage be understood of persons other than her husband, has
also ceased to exist; from her coming of age to her marriage all the
relations she may form are relations of contract."[6] But, for the most part,
Maine defined women as inherently incomplete as people in a world of
contract. For most women of Maine's period, of course, the time between
coming of age and marriage, during which time females could form
relations of contract, was quite short. For the most part, women continued to be defined through relations of status, despite declarations such as
Maine's which suggested that as an ontological, if not a social, matter
women *could* be the sort of people capable of entering into contracts. A
similar recognition of women's incompleteness in a world of contract
underlay the 1872 U.S. Supreme Court decision in *Bradwell v. Illinois*.
There, the Court refused to grant Myra Bradwell the right to practice law
because as a married woman she could not form contractual relations on
her own.

In the language of contemporary sociology, the universe of status is
one in which people's condition is largely ascribed; whereas, the universe
of contract is one in which people's condition is largely achieved. As
Maine wrote:

All the forms of Status taken notice of in the Law of Persons were derived
from, and to some extent are still colored by, the powers and privileges
anciently residing in the Family. If then we employ Status . . . to signify

these personal conditions only, and avoid applying the term to such
conditions as are the immediate or remote result of agreement, we may say
that the movement of the progressive societies has hitherto been a movement from *Status* to *Contract*. [7]

Although intended as a historical and anthropological presentation,
Maine's description of the differences between status and contract is
accurate less as a historical account than as a description of the ideology
of family that developed during his own century and that was elaborated
during the next 150 years. Certainly, Maine's account reflects some
aspects of the transformation that occurred with, and after, feudalism's
demise. However, in the feudal world, the locus of value for the status
relations that Maine describes—was the social order as a whole, not
individuals and not families. The contrast between status and contract in
terms of which Maine proposed and delineated differences between his
own world and that of earlier periods describes in fact a nineteenth-
century solution to the broad disruption in social patterns brought about
by the Industrial Revolution. The separation of family from work, and the
romanticization of family as a domain of love and enduring commitment,
preserved for the nineteenth century the illusion, and to some extent the
reality as well, of stability and tradition despite the vast changes represented by the developing marketplace.

The status/contract contrast provides an especially powerful frame
within which to examine contemporary responses to surrogacy since
those entering into surrogacy arrangements willfully premise the creation
of familial relations, and even more of the parent-child bond, on contractual negotiations and financial exchange. This remains troubling to a
society still concerned to preserve at least the illusion that the family is
a realm apart from the world of work, defined through autonomous
individuality, contract, and choice. [8]

Certainly, in the contemporary world legal relations defined in terms
of contract predominate over those defined in terms of status. Yet, relations based on status are found alongside those based on contract and
often conflict with the general presumption in our society that legal
rights and duties do not depend on "accidents of birth." Family law has
been the most significant exception to the law's general tendency to
define and regulate relationships in contractual terms. In family life, the
law has proclaimed, quite firmly and consistently at least until the last

few decades, that relations of status rather than of contract are *supposed* to predominant. The vision of family on which the law has predicated, and to some extent continues to predicate, its stance toward family matters reflects the nineteenth-century's romanticization of family relationships as loving *because* inexorable. The parent-child relationship became the best illustration of a relationship in which social facts were grounded in biological facts. In this view, the biological foundation of the parent-child relationship constitutes and directs actual relationships between parents and their children. So, for instance, in this vision of the parent-child tie, in which children are supposed to love their parents, and parents their children, parents are supposed to provide a home for their children and care for them because love, not money, is involved. This vision of family reflects David Schneider's description of the culture of family at about the middle of the twentieth century.

That surrogacy has received any public acceptance stands as a testament to the extent that the universe of contract has entered into the law's understanding of family relations. In large part, surrogacy has continued to prove troubling to the society because, even more than relationships between adults within families, the parent-child relationship has been understood conservatively as a status-based relationship characterized by the loyalty and commitment of kinship. The shift away from this understanding, as illustrated in surrogacy cases and in cases involving the new reproductive technologies as well, has been startling and disconcerting. The resulting controversy has been intricate and heated.

This controversy about surrogacy has been public and has frequently been presented and debated in the press and on television. Such public presentations sometimes suggest that families can be categorized into two sorts, one reflecting the parameters of status and the other, the parameters of contract, as if some families have retained traditional forms of interaction and others have evolved with the modern world. In fact, however, as a sociological, if not necessarily as an ideological, matter, most families reflect both images. Moreover, many families that might appear as modern families-through-choice see themselves as happily reflecting traditional forms of familial relationships. Assessments by courts and others of families created through surrogacy arrangements often illustrate a tendency to define such families as either completely at odds with the world of traditional families or as almost paradigmatically illustrative of that world.

In addition, the effort to categorize, and thus make sense of, surrogacy is widely informed by a basic conservatism in the society's and the law's responses to family matters. That conservatism is unavoidably and profoundly challenged by surrogate motherhood. The arrangement directly threatens the biological predicates of the romanticized notion of family developed during the previous century and a half. The particular threat that surrogacy poses to that ideology of family can be observed in detail by substituting for "status" and "contract" two correlative terms, respectively "gift" and "commodity," both understood to refer to children. Just as the predominant ideology of family has assumed that the family is supposed to be created from (and for) love, not money, children may be understood as "gifts of nature." They are valuable but are not to have a monetary value put on them. Every state prohibits the sale of children. Adoption laws specifically prohibit payment to a biological mother for her agreement to allow adoption of her child beyond those necessary to cover medical and other costs incurred as a result of the pregnancy.

The society firmly opposes the self-conscious commodification of children. Children cannot be bought or sold. Their parentage can, however, be transferred from biological parents to others and in making, or accepting, such transfers, parents sometimes imagine the exchange through the metaphor of gift-giving. "A gift," writes Lewis Hyde, "is a thing we do not get by our own efforts. We cannot buy it; we cannot acquire it through an act of will. It is bestowed upon us."[9] A gift creates a bond. It cannot be compared with, or fairly exchanged for, other things. In Hyde's words, a gift has "worth"; it is prized, but we "can't put a price on it." In contrast, a commodity has a "value." It can be compared with, and exchanged for, other things, including money.[10] As Hyde recognized, the distinction between worth and value that he draws correlates with Marx's distinction in *Das Kapital* between use-value and exchange-value.

Contracts are written in order to arrange for the exchange of commodities. In fact, legally, a contract to give a gift is unenforceable for the lack of consideration (quid pro quo). Within the ideology of contract, contracts are entered into and commodities are exchanged between putatively equal individuals who need not, and ideally do not, have other ties to each other. By contrast, gifts are exchanged between people in relationships. Like relationships based in status, and unlike ties based in contract, gifts do not demand that the giver and the receiver be putatively equal. Hyde writes:

We might best picture the difference between gifts and commodities . . . by imagining two territories separated by a boundary. A gift, when it moves across the boundary, either stops being a gift or else abolishes the boundary. A commodity can cross the line without any change in its nature; moreover, its exchange will often establish a boundary where none previously existed (as for example in the sale of a necessity to a good friend).[11]

The home and family still represent a domain of life in which status distinctions—distinctions derived through birth such as age and gender— are transparently important. Members of a family exchange gifts. They do not typically enter into contracts with each other. If they do, they begin to treat familial relationships as if they were market relationships. Hyde tells the story of a girl who agreed to donate a kidney to her ill mother only if the mother promised a fur coat in return. The daughter's consequent agreement to donate her kidney was not a gift but an exchange of one commodity (a kidney) for another (a coat). "As soon as the daughter shifted the category of the exchange and tried to barter," explains Hyde, "all her authority drained away. When either the donor or the recipient begins to treat a gift in terms of obligation, it ceases to be a gift."[12] The marketplace represents a domain of life based on contractual understandings. In the market people exchange commodities. Commodity exchange does not reinforce relations. It is an economic exchange without emotional, spiritual, or aesthetic correlations. Commodity exchange is an exchange between free agents. Gift exchange has the capacity to cement and to commit people to each other.

Surrogacy arrangements can be ordered so that the baby is defined primarily as a commodity, or primarily as a gift. In either case, the results are problematic. The crucial variables affecting the definition of the baby in this regard are whether money is exchanged between the parties, and if so, how and when and whether the parties bind themselves contractually. Surrogacy arrangements involving contracts and the exchange of money become legal business deals, obviously opening the way for the development of adversarial, legal relationships. Such relationships cannot be harmonized with the idea that life is a gift which can be bestowed but not sold, or with the sense of family as an arena of loyalty and commitment, rather than of legal controversy and commercial interaction.

If, however, the child in a surrogacy arrangement is defined as a gift, the limits of what constitutes an appropriate present are superseded. Children are "gifts of nature" but are not considered appropriate objects to be exchanged between people as presents. Although gifts differ from commodities in establishing and reinforcing bonds, they are like commodities in being property. Again, Hyde's organ transplant example is a good one. When organ transplantation developed there were no legally cognizable rights to body parts. Now the Uniform Anatomical Gift Act, enacted in every state, gives an adult the right to bequeath organs at death. In the case of minor children, the right to bequeath body parts falls to the parents.

For the society, commercial surrogacy is questionable because it defines a baby as a commodity, up for sale at the prevailing market price. Such deals can also be interpreted as defining the surrogate as a commodity. Mary Gordon refers to a fear of "some feminists" that surrogacy will lead to "large-scale baby farms where poor women are turned into breeders for the rich who cannot or choose not to bear their own children."[13] Surrogacy arrangements involving no exchange of money are less problematic. Although such arrangements also define a baby as property, the baby exchanged as a gift has a unique worth; whereas the baby exchanged for money is fungible, substitutable for other, equally valuable things.

The difference is not only ideological. The relationships between the parties, including the baby, are likely to develop differently in the two cases. Where the baby is exchanged in the "spirit of a gift" (as between friends or siblings), the transfer is more likely to reinforce existing bonds. Where the baby is exchanged for money, pursuant to a contract, the parties are likely to remain free of one another. Just as people are expected to enter contracts as equal, free agents, so they are expected to complete them and go on to other things. And as Hyde notes, while gifts bind, contracts separate. While gifts transform relationships, contracts leave them untouched, and while gifts bespeak attachment, contracts bespeak freedom.

Thus Helena Ragoné, in her ethnographic study of surrogacy, found many surrogates experienced disappointment after the birth of the child because they, though receiving payment, understood their role as gift-giver more than as contract partner. As a result, the surrogates whom Ragoné studied often expected the relationship with the couple to continue, but the couple, understanding the relationship in contractual terms, expected it to terminate when each side had received the contractual benefits of the arrangement. Ragoné quotes one paid surrogate: "I felt they [the intending parents] had been my friends, but after they got what they wanted, they weren't." [14]

The surrogate's disappointment stemmed from differences between her vision of surrogacy and that of the couple for whom she bore a baby. Ragoné reports that many paid surrogates claim not to be primarily motivated by the financial aspects of surrogacy. She concludes that surrogates as a group see surrogacy as a calling or vocation rather than simply as work for money. She describes many surrogates, when they first heard about institutionalized surrogacy (often through advertisements seeking surrogates or from television programs) to have been "astonished to learn that surrogacy was not merely a privately held fantasy about helping infertile couples but an actual arrangement in which they could have a part." [15] For the intending couples whom Ragoné interviewed, however, surrogacy was a means to an end, understood much more clearly as a business deal, though one that would result in the satisfaction of their deepest desires.

With respect to surrogate motherhood in particular and social institutions in general, such contrasting visions of relationship as those suggested by differences between surrogates' and couples' understandings of their connections with each other—the apparent choice between status and contract or between gift and commodity—represent essentially different conceptions of one reality. Yet each vision—and usually such visions are neither distinct nor perfectly self-conscious—can be defended, or opposed, in language that often echoes, and almost always resonates with some truth for, the other. The vision defined in terms of status relationships promises the advantages of secure familial loyalties and commitments; however, that vision threatens, and often precludes egalitarian relationships. In a universe in which commitments and loyalties are understood to be the consequences of biological inevitabilities, it is easy to justify the unequal treatment of certain groups (e.g., women) by reference to natural or biological differences among groups. A vision of family defined largely in terms of contract relationships understood in contract terms, promises equality, choice, and the freedom to enjoy that choice. However, this vision threatens families with a loss of relational anchors and with the potential commodification of family members, with, for instance, the possibility of purchasing or selling babies. Together these two visions, usually intertwined and constantly referring back and forth to each other, constitute a contemporary ideology of family. From within this ideology are generated the meanings, as well as the confusions and disagreements about the meanings, of family and of familial relationships at present.

Surrogacy, especially commercial surrogacy, forces almost all the confusions and disagreements to the fore because it depends on contracts and bargained negotiations and yet aims to create loving, usually "traditional," families. The response of the law to commercial and contractual surrogacy arrangements reflects these disagreements and confusions. American law concerns itself directly with surrogacy arrangements only when contract, as defined by Maine, is integral to the arrangements made by the parties involved. When contract does not exist, the law is generally silent. The law regulates instances of noncontractual surrogacy, but not as a special case. Existing laws that regulate adoption and artificial insemination provide a noncontroversial vehicle for effecting noncommercial surrogacy arrangements and do not comment on surrogacy per se.

With the introduction of significant commercial and contractual obligations, the luxury of relying on existing statutory schemes, schemes that regulate adoption and artificial insemination in particular, disappears. Prebirth agreements which oblige the surrogate mother, in return for some financial consideration, to revoke her parental rights immediately upon the birth of the baby inescapably entail a wide range of profoundly unsettling questions and dilemmas. With these, people and society must deal. And so, in consequence, must the law.

Not surprisingly, the law is ambivalent. As we shall now see, both in rulings that establish the context of the *Baby M.* case and in that case itself, as adjudicated both at trial and on appeal, two contradictory efforts have been made: to protect the family, as defined by status, from the incursions of surrogacy; and to empower surrogacy, as defined by contract, to effect such incursions.

Thus, for the most part existing law does not adequately regulate contractual surrogacy arrangements. With regard to these arrangements, the law, like the society it reflects, has not yet decided conclusively whom to protect, how completely, and when. Its ambivalence is reflected in the tentative, slow response of legislatures and in the uncertain, conflicting responses of courts.

Legislatures regulating traditional surrogacy have followed a few very different models.[16] One prohibits contractual surrogacy absolutely, sometimes even making participation in surrogacy arrangements a criminal offense. In Michigan, for instance, participation in a surrogacy contract is defined as a misdemeanor. Arranging or mediating such a contract is a felony, punishable by a fine of up to $50,000 and/or a prison term of up to five years. In New York, surrogacy agreements are void and unenforceable; participants are subject to civil penalties and brokers and other mediators receiving payment are subject to a civil penalty for a first offense and to criminal penalties for subsequent offenses.

A second model permits some forms of contractual surrogacy, but without providing a comprehensive regulatory scheme. A number of states, including Alabama, Nevada, and West Virginia, exempt surrogacy from rules that prohibit payments in the context of an adoption. Kansas has made rules prohibiting advertising to effect an adoption inapplicable to surrogacy. Arkansas, one of the first states to permit surrogacy, regulates surrogacy on the model frequently found in statutes regulating artificial insemination. Although Arkansas generally defines the birth mother as the natural and legal mother, in cases of surrogacy "the woman who intended to be the mother" is deemed the legal and natural mother. The provision was added to that part of the state's statute defining the consequences for a child's parentage of artificial insemination.

A third model, found in only a couple of states, permits contractual surrogacy and regulates it comprehensively. New Hampshire, for instance, has established a broad regulatory scheme that permits and monitors surrogacy arrangements. In New Hampshire, all parties to a surrogacy agreement must be evaluated medically and psychologically, and agreements must be authorized judicially before the parties may go ahead with the arrangement.

Thus, the legislative response to surrogacy reflects the ambivalence of the society. Most state legislatures have failed to respond at all, and of those that have responded, the results are extraordinarily varied and generally fail to establish a broad regulatory system for handling surrogacy.

Moreover, beyond the statutes that have been promulgated, and those that have been abandoned or never drafted, constitutional jurisprudence offers little guidance to statute-makers. Both the right to procreate and the right to raise children are encompassed by the more broadly defined constitutional right to privacy, discussed in chapter 2. Yet these two privacy rights hold conflicting implications for surrogacy.

Even if the right to procreate includes noncoital reproduction, the presence of an essential third party (the surrogate) in surrogacy arrangements may defeat a privacy claim. The more surrogacy participants resemble contract parties, the less easily can relationships among them be defined as familial. In most contractual surrogacy arrangements, the intending parents do not expect the surrogate to become a member of the family they want to form, whatever the surrogate's own hopes about this may be. Postbirth contacts between the surrogate and the intending parties or the baby are usually minimal or nonexistent. Thus, the relationships between intending parents and surrogates are not understood as familial or "family-like," and would not, therefore, be protected by the right to privacy, at least insofar as that right protects individuals *in families*.

Beyond the right to procreate, a parent has a right to "the companionship, care, custody and management of his or her children." [17] This right, in contrast to the right to procreate, however, depends, for its effect, on extant definitions of parent, mother, and father. Only to the extent that parents in the context of traditional surrogacy cases are defined as biological parents (therefore including the genetic father and the surrogate), could the right to raise one's children limit the right of a state to enforce surrogacy agreements against a surrogate's wishes. On the other hand, even if parents are so defined, the right to raise one's children does not, alone, prefer surrogates over genetic fathers or genetic fathers over surrogates.

Finally, conflicting or inconclusive answers that follow from analysis of the right to procreate and the right to raise one's children are magnified by the fragility of the privacy right itself. Cases following *Griswold* and *Eisenstadt* make it clear that protections such as the ones afforded in those cases will follow unreservedly only to protect traditional family structures. This became transparent in *Michael H. v. Gerald D.*, a 1989 Supreme Court case involving the constitutionality of a California statute that presumed a child to be the natural child of the mother's husband. Rejecting the claimed "liberty" interests of the biological father, Michael H. (a man not married to his biological child's mother), the Court, in an opinion authored by Justice Scalia, declared that such asserted liberty interests must, in order to receive protection, "be rooted in history and tradition." [18] Michael's was not. "Our traditions," wrote the Court, "have protected the marital family . . . against the sort of claim Michael asserts."[19] With regard to innovative family structures, in most cases the Court is decidedly ambivalent about extending constitutional protection.

In general, a broad constitutional right to privacy (or liberty) in family matters encourages the development of nontraditional relationships and arrangements. That was precisely the concern of those who opposed the privacy decisions in the 1960s and 1970s. Thus, in deciding whether to limit the right to privacy (or liberty), and if so, how, lawmakers are faced with two interrelated questions. First, should individuals be free to effect changes that may entail the transformation of the family in the direction of increased autonomy for its individual members? Second, should individuals be free to choose new rights and duties, or new forms of interaction, within the universe of family? That is, should they be encouraged in celebrating the proliferation of choices about how to create, and even about how to live in, families? Since the acknowledgment that the form and scope of familial relationships are mutable *is* the acknowledgment that such relationships are not inexorably based in nature, the two questions are related. Thus, a decision to permit the unregulated alteration of familial relationships recognizes the family as a domain defined in terms closer to those of the market than to those of the traditional family.

In addition to constitutional considerations relating to family matters, surrogacy arrangements are also arguably protected by a broad right to enter contracts and an expectation that states will enforce those contracts. In the absence of relevant legislation or countervailing public policy concerns—and both may of course, and in some places already do, exist with regard to surrogacy—a potential surrogate and intending parents have the right to enter a contract in which the surrogate agrees to bear a child and forego the companionship, care, and custody of that child. The Supreme Court has held that constitutional rights can be waived in a number of cases.[20] The waiver of a constitutional right requires a demonstration "that there was an 'intentional relinquishment or abandonment' " of the right.[21] If this can be shown, people have a right to enter into a surrogacy agreement, and all else being equal, that agreement should be enforceable.

Yet, the right to enter contracts does not ensure the legality of surrogacy contracts, and in fact, of course, those contracts have been declared illegal or unenforceable in a number of states. Most of the requirements for a valid contract are found in surrogacy contracts, but it can be argued that such contracts are inevitably baby-selling agreements and thus should be void as violative or public policy. Alternatively, it can be argued that such contracts should be neither void nor enforceable—that the state should not intervene between parties to a surrogacy contract but should also not enforce such contracts against unwilling biological mothers.

The confusing and indeterminate results suggested by examining the implications of rights analyses for surrogacy, like the law's more general ambivalence about surrogacy, reflect society's uncertainty about the present form and likely, or hoped for, fate of the family. Identification of relevant legal rights does not resolve the surrogacy issue because legal analysis of those rights contains the same tension generated by the choice between at least two visions of family—one resembling Maine's world of status and one resembling Maine's world of contract—that effects surrogacy. In short, the conflicts that surround and constitute the surrogacy debate are simply replicated at another level in the attempt to resolve questions about surrogacy through rational selection of established legal principles.

II. *Baby M.:* When Is a Family a Family?

All of the ambivalence thus far discussed—the inability or essential unwillingness of contemporary American society, and therefore of its legal system, even a decade after *Baby M.*, to decide whether the family belongs—and should belong—to the universe of status, or to its apparent ideological antagonist, the universe of contract—and all of the tensions, confusions, and perplexities inevitably engendered by that ambivalence, are reflected clearly in the case of *Baby M.* which, therefore, merits detailed analysis.

The case involved the most difficult and unpleasant consequence of a surrogacy arrangement: a custody battle between the intending parents and the surrogate mother. The case, the first involving a surrogate seeking to retain maternal rights to the baby and a biological father seeking to enforce a surrogacy contract in court, was brought by William Stern, the biological father. Stern had entered into a contract with a surrogate, Mary Beth Whitehead, and her husband, Richard Whitehead. Mary Beth Whitehead agreed that she would be artificially inseminated with Stern's sperm, gestate the resulting fetus, and at the baby's birth terminate all parental rights in favor of Stern and his wife, Elizabeth. Elizabeth Stern did not enter into the contract in order to avoid violating state rules that forbid purchasing a baby. After the birth of the child, Whitehead, unwilling to surrender the baby, fled to Florida with her husband and their two children Ryan and Tuesday, respectively about ages thirteen and eleven at the time of the trial. Several months later, the baby, named Melissa by William and Elizabeth Stern and named Sara by Mary Beth Whitehead, was forcibly returned to the Sterns as a result of a court order.

The opinion of Judge Sorkow, before whom the case was heard in the New Jersey Superior Court, proceeded from the assumption that the preservation of the universe of status, as defined by Maine, was and ought to be, the overriding, though not the exclusive, concern of the law. Almost exactly the same assumption underlay both the opinion of the New Jersey Supreme Court (which heard the case on appeal) and a brief presented to that court by the Sterns. An assumption more conservative than any other in the case underlay the brief presented by Mary Beth Whitehead. Thus, though the positions of the interested parties and of the courts differed radically, the consensus as regards ideology was almost total. The superior court held in almost all respects for the Sterns. The court expressly declared void only one provision in the contract that had been entered into among the parties. That clause gave William Stern control over any abortion decision. The trial court upheld the surrogacy contract, framed the case as involving primarily the best interests of the baby—calling all the other issues "commentary"—decided that those interests required terminating the surrogate's parental rights, granted full custody to William Stern, and ordered the adoption of the baby by Elizabeth Stern.

By contrast, the New Jersey Supreme Court invalidated the surrogacy contract, outlawed the payment of money to the surrogate, and voided both the termination of Mary Beth Whitehead's parental rights and the adoption of the baby by Elizabeth Stern. Judicial positions more thoroughly at odds cannot be imagined. The differences between Whitehead and the Sterns were absolute. Yet, astonishingly perhaps to the casual observer, everyone involved argued from essentially the same ideological assumption: that whatever the legitimate demands of the marketplace, they should retire before the sacred prerogatives of institutions and impulses hallowed by fixed, eternal nature.

In almost all respects, the New Jersey Superior Court held for Stern, upholding the surrogacy contract and deciding that the best interests of the baby required terminating the surrogate's parental rights and granting full custody to the contracting father.

The centrality of status to the superior court opinion may not seem at once obvious, since Judge Sorkow focused intently, and at some length, upon the surrogacy contract itself. In fact, however, the contract was only an element of Judge Sorkow's "commentary," and even as such was forced to serve the only concern he described as ultimately of importance: the best interests of the baby. With respect to that concern Judge Sorkow's commitment was almost unreservedly traditional. It was a concern for status.

The judgments that lie at the heart of Judge Sorkow's opinion are very old-fashioned: that families should be traditionally middle-class, consisting of two parents and their children living in a conventional fashion, and that such families should be protected from unstable "outsiders." In defense of these judgments Judge Sorkow was prepared to rule very creatively indeed: by in effect asserting that Baby M. had no mother and therefore no family. One's view of whether or not a "family" existed for this child before the court created one depends on one's view of the family in the United States. If the notion is limited to familiar and mainstream variants, then, as Judge Sorkow suggested, Baby M. had no "real family" before the court's decision created one. Apparently believing so, the trial court found itself obliged to identify a mother, and thereby create a family (to its liking), for Baby M. It did so by invoking, for the act of creation, the presumptions of contract.

That social polar opposites confronted him was self-evident to Judge Sorkow. He depicted William and Elizabeth Stern as a perfect middle-class, professional couple, with a "strong and mutually supportive relationship," "cooperative parenting" skills, and the ability to "initiate and encourage intellectual curiosity and learning for the child."[22] In contrast, Mary Beth and Richard Whitehead were portrayed as financially and emotionally unstable. Mary Beth was characterized as a manipulative wife and mother, unable or unwilling to "recognize and report the truth" and essentially unreliable.[23] As evidence of this last assertion the court referred to Mary Beth Whitehead's breach of the surrogacy contract. Judge Sorkow decided that a woman who balked at fulfilling a contract to terminate maternal rights to her newborn baby, or who defied a court order by "running away with the infant," could not be an impressive mother in general, or in particular, a good mother to Baby M.

That being the case, Judge Sorkow proposed to find a good mother, part of a good family for Baby M. He did so by the remarkable expedient of asserting that in effect, at birth Baby M. had lacked not only a family, but also a mother. "When Melissa was born on March 27, 1986," Judge Sorkow wrote:

> there were no, attendant to the circumstance of her birth [sic] family gatherings, family celebrations or family worship services that usually accompany such a happy family event. . . . In reality, the fact of family was undefined if non-existent [sic]. The mother and father are known but they are not family. The interposition of their spouses will not serve to create family without further court intervention.[24]

The context of these conclusions was the court's consideration of Mary Beth Whitehead's parents' application for visitation rights. In rejecting the application of Mr. and Mrs. Messer for grandparental visitation rights, the court reaffirmed its understanding that Baby M. was not part of their family. The court's depiction here is obviously biased. Whether or not a family existed before Judge Sorkow wrote his opinion depends on one's understanding of family. In this regard, the court had a number of choices. It could, for instance, have approached the case sociologically and asked: What *is* going on here? What definitions of family are suggested by this case? And, of these, which makes most sense legally, culturally, or psychologically? Or, the court could have assumed a definition of family. It did the latter. It assumed that a family is composed of two parents and their children, and failed to consider the possibility that practices such as surrogate motherhood may represent or encourage new kinds of families. Judge Sorkow did not write that he was creating a proper family from an improper family. He wrote that the "fact of family was . . . non-existent" before the court reached its decisions.

In order to create a family from the characters involved in the case, Judge Sorkow slotted the parties into his own model of an ideal American family. For that to be done in this case, one of the biological parents had to be obliterated. Further, the spouse of the other biological parent had to be named *as a parent*. Thus, Baby M.'s family was defined so as to include her biological father and his wife Elizabeth Stern, who was able to adopt the baby immediately after the court's termination of

Whitehead's parental rights. The court's adoption order excused Elizabeth Stern from compliance with state law mandating procedures prerequisite to a successful adoption.

The court symbolized its decision to grant full custody to William Stern and its creation of a family for Baby M. by shifting, at just the point in its decision that it declared the Sterns' parentage, from "Baby M." to "Melissa" in references to the child. Melissa was the name given Baby M. by the Sterns; Whitehead had named her Sara. No longer merely a key character in a complicated legal drama, the child was now *named*. In its view, the court had erased her afamilial past and allowed her to become a *real* baby, identified as part of a family, with a name and two parents. With this, the court attempted to obliterate history and its complications.

That done to its satisfaction, the court was able in good conscience to deprive Mary Beth Whitehead not only of custody but also of parental rights. On the face of the opinion, the termination of Whitehead's maternal rights was simply the result of the court's best-interest determination and its reading of the contract. Mary Beth Whitehead, declared the court, "agreed to terminate [her parental rights]. This Court gives effect to her agreement."[25] Such conclusions did not reflect legal conclusions so much as the court's sense of "good" families, in general, and its sense in this case of the best family that could be created from the parties in the Baby M. drama. Thus, the court concluded that Whitehead's rights could be terminated because, as she had never really been the baby's mother, they had never existed.

The trial court's conclusions about parentage in this case entailed as well a class element that was largely masked, but that was relevant nonetheless, in the court's best-interest analysis. In that analysis, considered in much more detail in chapter 7, the court relied on a set of criteria proposed by psychologist Lee Salk that will usually encourage judicial preference for the more middle-class parent, especially in cases such as that of Baby M. in which one potential parent or custodian seems not to be middle-class with regard either to income or to presentation-of-self while another is. Among other things, Salk's determinants for establishing Baby M.'s best-interests asked whether the child was "wanted and planned for." Salk's criteria further asked the court to look at the "stability" of the home; "familial attitudes toward education"; the "capacity of the adults ... to make rational judgements," to "instill positive attitudes" about health and nutrition, to explain the circumstances of the child's birth to her, and to assist her in becoming "a productive member of society."[26] Relying on these criteria alone, almost any court would almost be compelled to select the Sterns—he a scientist with a Ph.D. in bio-chemistry, and she a pediatrician with a Ph.D. in human genetics and an M.D.—over the Whiteheads. The court made much of the Whiteheads financial and emotional instability as compared to the Sterns. Mary Beth, who dropped out of high school at age fifteen, had been on public assistance during a period of separation from her husband in the late 1970s. Richard, who worked as a driver for a waste collection company at the time of trial, had had seven jobs in the previous thirteen years. Together the couple had moved twelve times in one eight-year period. Moreover, during the period of the marriage Richard had had a constant problem with alcohol. Perhaps the most illuminating aspect of the court's understanding of the Whiteheads' comparative fitness as parents was its apparent conclusion that Mary Beth was not, and was essentially not fit to be, the mother of William Stern's child, but that she was a perfectly adequate mother for her two children with Richard Whitehead.

Further, to demonstrate that this was so Judge Sorkow invoked the universe of contract, but to serve his interests rather than its own. Relying upon the contract in the case, he enforced an agreement which, in a larger context, represents significant alternation in familiar notions of the family. Implicitly, of course, Judge Sorkow recognized this contradiction by defining his contract analysis as "commentary," not law.[27] In addition, the contradiction between Judge Sorkow's view of family and his enforcement of the surrogacy contract was mediated by an association of the contract with Whitehead rather than with the Sterns. This association served to bolster the court's conclusion that Whitehead was not a *mother* to the baby in this case. In contrast, the court portrayed the Sterns as an ideal couple, who exhibited all the virtues associated with a "good" family defined in traditional, status terms. Whitehead was characterized as being *outside* family. In relation to Richard Whitehead and her two children with him, Mary Beth was seen as a wife and mother, even a fit wife and mother. Certainly, the court never suggested that Whitehead was unfit to be a mother to Ryan and Tuesday, her two children with Richard

Whitehead. But in relation to Baby M., Whitehead was seen as someone who had signed a contract, an individual who had undertaken a personal service commitment pursuant to an agreement, and then breached the agreement. She was portrayed not as a mother to Baby M., but as the person who had promised to provide the Sterns with the means to create their family. Therefore she was ordered—legitimately, in the opinion of the court—to honor her part of a business agreement between autonomous, self-interested principals.

Whether or not Judge Sorkow understood the problems inherent in his appeal to contract is not certain. His overriding commitment, however, is beyond doubt. The law of parentage and custody, as he demarcates it, bespeaks a universe defined unmistakably in terms of status.

The New Jersey Supreme Court did precisely the same thing, and although in a unanimous opinion it reversed almost all of the law made by Judge Sorkow, it did so in the name of moral standards more or less identical to his own.

As has been noted, the state supreme court invalidated the surrogacy contract on the grounds that it conflicted with state law and public policy. Further, the court outlawed the payment of money to a surrogate. The court described such payment to have been made in order to affect the adoption of the child by Elizabeth Stern and proceeded to void both the termination of Mary Beth Whitehead's parental rights and the adoption of the baby by Elizabeth Stern.

In particular, the supreme court declared that the promise of money from William Stern to Mary Beth Whitehead constituted payment for an adoption, not for Whitehead's services, and therefore contravened New Jersey law prohibiting the transfer of money in connection with the placement of a child for adoption. A basic argument against the legality of commercial surrogacy contracts in general has been that they violate state laws proscribing adoptions in exchange for payment. The New Jersey Supreme Court stressed this and described such payment of money to a surrogate as "illegal, perhaps criminal, and potentially degrading to women."[28] The trial court, with regard to this issue, had reasoned that the legislature could not have intended adoption statutes to govern surrogacy because surrogacy was unknown when the state's adoption laws were promulgated and therefore held that laws governing adoption were irrelevant to surrogacy.[29]

The supreme court further declared the contract invalid because it provided for the termination of Whitehead's parental rights without satisfying relevant statutory criteria. Termination of parental rights in the state could be effected only pursuant to a voluntary surrender of a child to an agency approved by the state or to the Division of Youth and Family Services along with a document acknowledging termination or pursuant to a showing of parental abandonment or unfitness.[30] Neither had occurred in this case.

Additionally, the supreme court decided that the absence of a revocation right for Mary Beth Whitehead contravened New Jersey law. In short, the court ruled, the central provisions of the contract were "designed to circumvent [state] statutes, and thus the entire contract was unenforceable."[31] The court further declared that the surrogacy contract between the Whiteheads and William Stern conflicted with New Jersey public policy since state policy preferred that children be raised by their "natural" parents, that the rights of a "natural father" be equal to, and not greater than, those of a "natural mother," and that a "natural mother" contemplating surrender of parental rights be evaluated and counseled.[32]

For the New Jersey Supreme Court, the child's parents were, and were to remain, her two biological parents, William Stern and Mary Beth Whitehead. The opinion allowed no legal relationship between the child and either Elizabeth Stern or Richard Whitehead. Although her husband was given custody of the child, Elizabeth Stern was given no legal rights to Baby M., and should her husband die or should she and William Stern divorce at any point during the child's minority, it would be difficult for her to insist upon a continuing relationship with the child. The case was remanded to the trial court for consideration of Mary Beth Whitehead's right to visit her daughter. On remand, the trial court granted Whitehead the immediate right to visit with the child one day each week between 10:30 a.m. and 4:30 p.m. Beginning the following fall, Whitehead was to be given an additional day every other week with the child and by the following spring, the child was to stay with her for two days and overnight every other week. In addition, visitation during specified holidays was ordered. The court expressed the hope that the parties would not need to rely on the specific visitation rights outlined but would be able to work out a mutually agreeable visitation schedule that would be suitable to both sides. That did not happen.[33] Further consideration of the implications of the final resolution of this case—especially with regard to the courts' views of children and childhood—is found in chapter 7.

Thus, in sum, the state supreme court ruled that babies could not be bought or sold, and that contracts could not eliminate motherhood—obvious truths, but only in a universe in which absolute value, utterly unrelated either to commerce or to autonomous self-fulfillment, can be assigned both to babies, and to a clearly defined setting—the traditional family—presumed to give both babies and their parents the best chance to flourish. The supreme court ruled, in short, precisely as Judge Sorkow had ruled: almost unreservedly in favor of the universe of status.

In both opinions, only one concession—though a significant one, productive of significant tension—was granted to the universe of contract. It was granted perhaps unwittingly by Judge Sorkow. When relying upon the expedient of the contract, he in effect empowered the substitution of law for nature in defining the relationship between parent and child. In this regard, the supreme court was far more self-aware and explicit, inviting the legislature to alter surrogacy law in any constitutional manner it chose:

> We have found that our present laws do not permit the surrogacy contract used in this case. Nowhere, however, do we find any legal prohibition against surrogacy when the surrogate mother volunteers, without any payment, to act as a surrogate and is given the right to change her mind and to assert her parental rights. Moreover, the Legislature remains free to deal with this most sensitive issue as it sees fit, subject only to constitutional constraints.[34]

By thus invoking the potential role of the legislature in regulating surrogacy, the court acknowledged, as Judge Sorkow had done far less overtly, that family forms and relationships are mutable. The court cautioned against the danger of such transformations but did not recognize an essential discontinuity between family forms and natural processes. In short, each opinion, though only grudgingly and only in part, opened the way for the transition of family relationships from relationships defined in traditional terms to relationships defined (because created) as the result of bargained negotiations between autonomous individuals.

The parties, in their briefs to the courts, reflected the courts' preference for traditional families. Mary Beth Whitehead's position, however, was far more conservative than the Sterns and than either court. She argued emphatically and without ambiguity of any kind that her claims should be judged *exclusively* against the imperatives of traditional families, defined in terms of the world of status, almost precisely as Maine characterized that world.[35]

Whitehead grounded the mother-child relationship definitively in the inevitabilities of nature, describing her pregnancy not as a *quid pro quo* entitling her to a baby, but as an inexorable process endowed with natural, inalienable value.[36] Her brief to the New Jersey Supreme Court focused upon the biological basis of the mother-child tie, and declared that surrogacy represents a doomed effort to alter natural events and processes. More particularly, Whitehead characterized the mother-child relationship as quintessentially natural, contrasting it in this regard to the relationship between fathers and children. She declared that "[t]he emphasis on relationship found in women will tend to enhance bonding, while the emphasis on separation and independence in men will tend to minimize the importance of bonding."[37] Whitehead's brief founds the tie between mothers and their children on "hormonal balance" during and following pregnancy, and asserts that "the learning responsible for the initial formation of the maternal bond appears to be heavily dependent upon the hormonal conditions normally present for a short time after birth."[38] Moreover, Whitehead, invoked a cross-cultural similarity in maternal behavior as well as a similarity between human and animal parental behavior in support of her position.

In short, Mary Beth Whitehead's position before the court provides an excellent illustration of the argument that surrogacy is evil *because* unnatural, and should be prohibited in light of its effects on the natural operation of familial relationships. In arguing that she was entitled to the child not because she had suffered hardships but because her claim was natural, she asserted that familial relationships are based in nature and cannot be altered or effected by the will of the parties to a contract. They are, in effect, immune from contractual manipulations. Her position represents in its purest form status as defined by Maine and reflects most clearly the romanticized image of family constructed during the late nineteenth century, when, not by coincidence, Maine did his work.

In apparent contrast, the Sterns' brief argues that traditional families can and should be effected by the will of the parties to a contract.[39] But here, as in Judge Sorkow's opinion, appearance can deceive; like Judge

Sorkow the Sterns invoked the universe of their ideological antagonist in their interest, rather than in its own. Upholding the contract, they argued, would serve to strengthen traditional values.

Like Whitehead, the Sterns were concerned with effecting status-based relationships, and neither denied the importance of natural process nor suggested that traditional families should be reexamined and refashioned in modern times. Rather, they asserted that good, old-fashioned American families can be created in a variety of ways and need not be grounded in natural processes:

> Through surrogate parenthood, traditional family values are strengthened. In seeking to create a traditional family structure in the only way available to the commissioning couple, surrogate motherhood insures that the couple who has invested both considerable time and money in the surrogacy process will be dearly dedicated to the child. A surrogate motherhood arrangement actually increases the overall number of family units within society.[40]

"Surrogate parenting agreements," the Sterns' brief continued, "also facilitate the exercise of procreative liberty for women. A women who is unable to have a child can now become a parent regardless of medical limitations."[41] The Sterns' argument here may seem opaque in that surrogate parenting agreements do not extend what the brief calls "procreative liberty" to women like Elizabeth Stern. In vitro fertilization may do that. Gamete transfer from one woman to another may do that. But surrogacy does not. Elizabeth Stern hoped to adopt Baby M. That option was available long before surrogacy.

By defining surrogacy as a case of expanded "procreative liberty" the Sterns' argument connects traditional surrogacy to the new reproductive technologies and thereby blurs the biological reality that Whitehead, not Stern, is the baby's mother according to traditional understandings of "mother." That is, despite the implications of the brief, Elizabeth Stern was neither biologically nor genetically related to Baby M. The brief did not really intend to declare that Elizabeth Stern was Baby M.'s "natural" mother; rather, it intended to suggest that Elizabeth was the baby's "real" mother and that, to be such, she need not demonstrate a genetic or biological link to the child. The Sterns' arguments imply that "blood" or genetic relationship is not essential to the creation and development of a simple, old-fashioned American family. In this regard, the Sterns relied on that aspect of American culture which stressed "code-for-conduct" (culture) as opposed to "blood" (nature), to use the terms David Schneider proposed, as the crucial element of kinship relations. Today, far more than in the 1960s when Schneider wrote, the society and the law recognize kinship connections predicated on patterns different from those represented by the traditional, nuclear family, tied together by bonds of "blood." The Sterns argued in effect that traditional families can be formed and can thrive, even if not created in traditional ways. Their arguments suggest that bonds of kinship traditionally predicated on biological connections can be predicated on love and choice, as in the case of adoption. Such bonds, the Sterns declared in their brief, can be quite as strong and permanent as any familial bonds.

In presenting the case that surrogacy harmonized with traditional family values, the Sterns expressly addressed the counterargument that surrogacy for money is immoral.[42] They responded that the family was already affected by and defined through commercial interactions without ill effects. They referred to fees paid to sperm and ovum donors, to "commercialized social parenting in the form of day care facilities, baby sitting, wet nurses and nannies" and to fosterparenting "subsidized by the state." The Sterns examples were poorly chosen. Even the best day-care facilities, baby-sitters, and nannies do not become kin to the children, or to the parents of the children, to whom care is given. The intent of the Sterns' arguments is, however, clear. They aimed to demonstrate that a proper family, even a traditional family, can be created through relations based on notions of blood (and status) *or* through relations founded on choice and confirmed by law.

In the Sterns' view, the mode through which such a family came into existence was relatively unimportant. That traditional families should be encouraged to exist and to thrive was crucial—to them, to Mary Beth Whitehead, to Judge Sorkow, and to the New Jersey Supreme Court, and to each of these participants in the legal drama for essentially the same ideological reason. In the unmistakable position of each, the family in general, and motherhood in particular, are absolutely valuable and must therefore be safeguarded, even at the cost of tension resulting from the counterclaims of a legitimate and strengthening modernity. Thus the courts that issued the *Baby M.* opinions and the parties themselves all stressed the overriding need to safeguard the family as an arena in which relationships are based on status—which they all understood to mean enduring bonds of loving commitment. However, they disagreed about how that should, and could, be done.

The trial court and the Sterns argued that surrogacy (including surrogate contracts) can preserve relationships based on status because such relationship can stem from biology or from law. The Sterns even suggested that law can create biology when they argued that surrogacy offers "procreative liberty" to (otherwise) infertile women. The trial court was more confused about the significance of the surrogacy contract, viewing it, in the end, as an expedient for guarding status relationships *in this case*. Similarly concerned to protect the family from the incursions of contract in Maine's sense, the state supreme court chose to preserve status *in general* by invalidating the contract in this case. In contrast to both courts and to the Sterns, Mary Beth Whitehead described the mother-child relationship as essentially unavailable except through a biological tie and vilified surrogacy contracts for defying natural processes. Each position represents an instance of society's ambivalence about the perceived move from relationships based on status (on ties that represent enduring commitment and structured bonds) to relationships based on contract (on ties established through the exercise of autonomous choice).

In *Baby M.* the mode of a family's creation was at issue. The Sterns and Judge Sorkow agreed that traditional families can be *created* on the basis of bargained negotiations and contractual agreement. The state supreme court and Mary Beth Whitehead disagreed. However, neither judge nor any of the parties suggested that the parameters of the parent-child relationship should become generally negotiable. On the latter point everyone favored tradition. Whether the contractualization of the creation of the parent-child bond will result ultimately in the contractualization of the incidents of that relationship as well remains unclear. But answers to that question—answers that are far more often assumed than articulated and studied—account for much of the disagreement in society and in law about the consequences of permitting, or of legally enforcing, surrogacy arrangements.

In general, the law's ambivalence about the move from tradition to modernity in the creation—and perhaps finally in the living out—of the parent-child relationship is especially heartfelt because the relationship at stake has constituted one of the last, important preserves of status relationships in modern society.

Thus, the challenge facing family law today, one poignantly represented by *Baby M.*, is to nothing less than a traditional, and extraordinarily influential, conception of the family, in particular, to a traditional conception of fathers and mothers. Confronted with this pressure, the American judiciary, in *Baby M.* and widely in other cases, has responded with steadfast resistance, insisting that the traditional conception be maintained. But, ironically, as *Baby M.* suggests, in the effort to preserve that conception, courts have, without knowing it, empowered the effort to alter and redefine it.

FOUR

Unwed Fathers
and Surrogate Mothers

The irony in *Baby M.* is evident in other cases as well. In these cases, the American judiciary, confronted with a basic challenge to understandings of family assumed at least since the nineteenth century to reflect inexorable truth, has responded with essentially conservative opposition to the challenge of modernity. And yet its response has aided and abetted the challenge. Thus, unwittingly, the judiciary has undermined its own cause and advanced the cause of its avowed antagonists.

Many courts in cases involving potential redefinitions of maternity and paternity fail to see the needs that motivate the decisions they reach, or the extent to which their decisions endanger their own avowed ends. Thus, some courts, such as the two courts that issued decisions in *Baby M.*, work to protect traditional conceptions of the family, but, in attempting to do so, appropriate the language of change. At the same time, other courts approve new forms of family, but in doing that, disguise the results with traditional garb. The net result is the instructive phenomenon of a judiciary operating at cross-purposes to itself, unaware that its ideological conservatism is fostering the evolutionary change it opposes. This phenomenon can be seen in *Baby M.* but becomes even clearer when *Baby M.* (and other cases focusing on the meaning of "mother") are compared with cases raising questions about the limits and implications of paternity.

The law's response to parties involved in surrogate mother agreements as well as its response to fathers never married to the mothers of their biological children reveals some basic changes occurring in the understanding of family that has been predominant for almost two centuries, but also illustrates courts working to preserve traditional understandings of family.

Cases involving unwed fathers and cases involving surrogate mothers provide an illuminating contrast, each with the other. Both sorts of cases defy some aspect of traditional understandings of family. The unwed father cases involve men anxious to be fathers to their biological children but not anxious, or not able, to marry the mothers of those children. Cases such as *Baby M.*, in contrast, defy tradition by involving third parties in the reproductive process and, at least sometimes (as in *Baby M.*), by defining the creation of the parent-child relationship in contractual terms. Gestational surrogacy cases similarly involve third parties and contractual relationships in the process of human reproduction and, beyond this, upset familiar assumptions about the biological facts of reproduction. The disruption posed by that third aspect of gestational surrogacy is examined in greater detail in the next chapter. Here, understandings of "mother" in the context of gestational surrogacy are examined for the comparison presented with understandings of "mother" in cases involving unwed fathers.

Comparison of cases involving unwed fathers and surrogate mothers is illuminating in a number of specific regards. Each set of cases involves *too many*, rather than too few, parents. That phenomena, found as well in many cases occasioned by the new reproductive technologies, contrasts with cases heard earlier in the twentieth century and in the nineteenth century, when courts resolving questions about parentage or custody rarely faced a plethora of ready and willing parents. In addition, these cases as a whole illustrate differences in the way fathers are understood as parents when they are compared with mothers and when they are compared with other fathers, and differences in the way mothers are understood when they are compared with fathers and when they are compared with other mothers. Finally, both sorts of cases reflect, and participate in the erosion of, traditional conceptions of family that depended on maintaining a firm separation between home and work.

Judicial decisions in cases involving unwed fathers and in cases involving surrogate mothers recognize, but often oppose, shifts in society's understanding of family (or "mothers" and "fathers" and their relations to each other and to "children"). As in *Baby M.*, the decisions in these cases more generally represent an attempt to preserve, despite the frequent legitimation of change, a traditional domain of family. The decisions represent an attempt to keep the family separate from and unaffected by the world of money and work, unaffected that is by the market, including its often unremitting view of people as unconnected autonomous individuals. In the effort to preserve traditional families while assimilating patterns and possibilities that seem to constitute genuine change, courts rely on and articulate, but also begin to alter, fundamental assumptions about what makes families "families" and about what makes mothers "mothers," fathers "fathers," and children "children." The result is curious. To safeguard treasured forms in the face of changing values and structures, courts have considered, and then sometimes shifted or defined anew, the key symbols through which families are discussed and understood. But, in consequence, the very effort to preserve traditional families and traditional conceptions of family represents and has been providing new grounds for justifying the changes feared.

Specifically this chapter analyzes a number of assumptions about fatherhood—and by contrast, about motherhood—made by the United States Supreme Court in a set of cases in which unwed fathers have sought paternal rights; then the chapter considers assumptions about motherhood underlying judicial decisions in cases involving surrogacy contracts. The cases reveal the transformation of the family as the force of tradition is increasingly molded by the pressures of modernity to recognize the family as a collectivity of equal, autonomous individuals, connected by choice and by negotiated design.

I. What Makes a Father a "Father"?

Not until 1972 did the United States Supreme Court recognize the constitutional rights of unwed fathers in their relationships with their children. Since that time the Court has decided four additional cases which further delineate the scope of unwed fathers' paternal rights. Commentators heralded, and continue to herald, the unwed father cases as exemplifying a new recognition of the rights of fathers as compared to those of mothers.[1]

Certainly, these cases did effect concrete changes in state laws regulating the authority of unwed fathers to sustain relationships with their biological children. However, the assumptions behind the Supreme Court's unwed father decisions and the theoretical ground on which those cases rest, harmonize with a view of the father constructed over a century and a half earlier, during the early years of the Industrial Revolution. In this view fathers—because male—are defined primarily through their relation to the market economy. The organic bonds, seen to relate fathers to their families in an earlier time, had long been sundered. By the early nineteenth century, fathers, as family members, were largely defined by *choice*, not nature. In the second half of the nineteenth and first half of the twentieth century, paternity was mediated by the biological father's link to his children's mother. More recently, paternity has additionally been recognized on the basis of the father's *behavior* toward his biological children. That recognition, however, was conditioned by an understanding that the requisite relation between a father and his biological child must include the child's mother. Both the view that conditions paternal rights on a marriage (or other similar relationship) between a biological father and his children's mother and a view that conditions paternal rights on a biological father's behavior toward his children assume a father's relationship to his children is a *cultural* creation, and thus a choice,[2] not the automatic correlate of a biological tie.

In 1991 John Hill delineated three dimensions of relevance to the law in identifying paternity. These include "the man's biological relationship with the child, his legal or social relationship with the child's mother, and the extent of his social and psychological commitment to the child."[3] However, these factors do not, as Hill's analysis might suggest, carry equal weight for the society or for its legal system. Rather, they are weighted differently depending on context, and on the essential understanding that fathers, unlike mothers, are not *socially* limited by their biological relation to their children. Fathers are free either to invoke biological fatherhood or to ignore it.

The debate about paternity, however, does not focus around biological questions. Instead, this debate concerns the other two dimensions that Hill delineated by which society and law identify fathers. Although each of these two dimensions predicates paternity on culture and choice and variously assumes, downplays, or ignores a man's biological relation to his child, the implications of the two dimensions differ considerably, each from the other. The debate about paternity has largely become a debate between the decision to predicate paternity on a man's connection to the mother of his child and the decision to predicate paternity on a man's relationship with his children.

The position that presumes a father becomes a father only through the mediation of his child's mother presumes an older century's definition of family than the position that presumes a man can become a father by establishing a social relationship with his child. With the first position, there is far less room for the autonomous individual, for the father, free to create and even recreate relationships as he chooses. Rather, historically, this first position presumed, and to some extent continues to presume, that each familial relationship can only be understood within the context of the larger familial whole. So, for example, the relationship between a father and his child was inevitably understood in the context of the relationship between the father and the child's mother. In this view, men become fathers by marrying women who will be the mothers of their children.

In contrast, the view that allows putative fathers to effect their paternity through the development of a relationship with their children, apart from those children's mothers, erodes traditional forms. From this view, a putative father can *choose* to be a father without regard for a larger network of familial relationships. He can, that is, effect a connection with his child entirely outside the context of a larger family, much as one might choose to establish a relationship with a friend or even a business associate. Thus this second position, which presumes legal paternity to follow from the development of a relationship between a father and his biological child, largely rejects older patterns that embedded every familial relationship in an encompassing network of familial connections and that viewed each relationship as entailing a set of clear rights and obligations.

Confusion about these differences and about what exactly does, and should, make fathers fathers, is apparent in the set of Supreme Court cases decided between 1972 and 1989,[4] that consider the paternal rights of unwed fathers as a constitutional matter. The implications of the cases seem ambiguous exactly because the Court shifted between the position that fathers become fathers because they establish relationships with their children, and the position that fathers become fathers because they are connected to the mothers of their children, without acknowledging that it was doing so.

All five of the recent cases concerned with the legal paternity of unwed fathers say quite clearly, though each with more or less force, that the paternity of biological fathers who have developed social relationships with their children is guaranteed constitutional protection. Yet, underlying all five cases and explicit in the most recent Supreme Court case (*Michael H.*) involving the rights of an unwed biological father, is the suggestion that legal paternity depends on the father's developing a relationship, not with his children, but with their mother. The express language of several of the cases does suggest that legal paternity can be premised on an unwed biological father's establishing a paternal relationship with his children. In fact, the majority of commentators on the unwed father cases have stressed this trend and have read the cases to predicate legal paternity on the presence or absence of a social relationship between a putative father and his child.[5] However, the cases, as a set, make sense only if the apparently sufficient requirement for effecting legal paternity—that a father effect a social relationship with his biological child—is read as a code for the requirement that he effect such a relationship *within the context of family.* And *that* context is most easily identified in cases in which the father has established a marriage or marriage-like relationship, with the child's mother.

Stanley, Quilloin, Caban, and *Lehr:*
The Choice to Be a Father

Stanley v. Illinois, the first Supreme Court case to extend constitutional protection to unwed fathers, involved Peter Stanley, who had lived intermittently with his three children and their mother, Joan Stanley, for eighteen years. Peter and Joan never married. When Joan died, Illinois law presumed unwed fathers were unfit and therefore, required the state to take the children as wards. The Court described Peter Stanley as a member of a family unit, including himself, Joan, and the three children and determined that the statute, by failing to provide Stanley a hearing on his fitness as a parent, deprived him of due process and equal protection. Justice White wrote for the Court: "The private interest here, that of a man in the children he has sired and raised, undeniably warrants deference and, absent a powerful countervailing interest, protection."[6]

The Court's decision in *Stanley* strongly suggests that the rights extended to Stanley depended on his position as a biological *and* a social father to his children. But it was not entirely clear after *Stanley* whether biological paternity outside the context of marriage (or an established family unit) or outside the context of an established social relationship between the biological father and his children would be enough to constitute legal fatherhood.

Nor was it clear from *Stanley* how heavily the Court's decision rested on Peter's having had a relationship with Joan that resembled a traditional marriage. It was not clear, that is, how future courts would interpret the significance of the finding that the Stanleys were a "family." A footnote in the opinion created particular confusion about the implications of biological paternity alone. That footnote read:

> We note in passing that the incremental cost of offering unwed fathers an opportunity for individualized hearings on fitness appears to be minimal. If unwed fathers, in the main, do not care about the disposition of their children, they will not appear to demand hearings. If they do care, under the scheme here held invalid, Illinois would admittedly at some later time have to afford them a properly focused hearing in a custody or adoption proceeding.
>
> Extending opportunity for hearing to unwed fathers who desire and claim competence to care for their children creates no constitutional or procedural obstacle to foreclosing those unwed fathers who are not so inclined. The Illinois law governing procedure in juvenile cases . . . provides for personal service, notice by certified mail, or for notice by publication when personal or certified mail service cannot be had or when notice is directed to unknown respondents under the style of "All whom it may Concern." Unwed fathers who do not promptly respond cannot complain if their children are declared wards of the State. Those who do respond retain the burden of proving their fatherhood.[7]

The footnote created confusion because the Court failed to explain whether the protection afforded Stanley was to be made available to all unwed fathers or only to those, such as Stanley, who had played a part in the socialization of their children or who had lived with those children and the mother of those children as a family.[8]

Chief Justice Burger, dissenting in *Stanley*, was more explicit than the majority about the social and legal consequences of biological fatherhood. Chief Justice Burger disavowed the significance of biological paternity as compared with biological maternity, first, because biological fathers are harder to identify than biological mothers, and, second, and more importantly, because the biological link between mother and child is understood as having *social* significance. Chief Justice Burger wrote:

[T]he biological role of the mother in carrying and nursing an infant creates stronger bonds between her and the child than the bonds resulting from the male's often casual encounter. This view is reinforced by the observable fact that most unwed mothers exhibit a concern for their offspring either permanently or at least until they are safely placed for adoption, while unwed fathers rarely burden either the mother or the child with their attentions or loyalties. Centuries of human experience buttress this view of the realities of human conditions and suggest that unwed mothers of illegitimate children are generally more dependable protectors of their children than are unwed fathers.[9]

In short, for mothers, biology ordains and constitutes a maternal "role"[10] and thus carries social significance; for fathers it is simply a fact of "nature," not necessarily connected in any way to social consequences. Fathers are left free to choose. Although offered in dissent, Chief Justice Burger's commentary on the comparative significance of biological maternity and biological paternity supports and reflects basic assumptions behind the majority opinion. In both opinions, though more expressly in Chief Justice Burger's, maternity is defined through biology and paternity is defined as a matter of choice.

Chief Justice Burger did, however, provide a different version of Stanley's own conduct as a father than did the majority. Chief Justice Burger's rendition of the facts asserted that Stanley was not, in fact, a good father, and he suggested that *that* fact supported the general position that for men, though not for women, biological parenthood should not be read to imply the likely development of a parent-child relationship. As Chief Justice Burger told the story, Peter Stanley was not the attentive father the majority opinion suggested. Rather, after the death of the children's mother, Stanley transferred care of the children to another couple. He made no efforts to be recognized as the father until the state became aware that no adult had any legal obligation for the support of the children. At that time Stanley made himself known but only, according to Chief Justice Burger, because he feared losing welfare payments if others were named guardians of the children.

Obviously, Chief Justice Burger recounted these facts in order to buttress his claim that unwed fathers rarely provide adequate care for their children and, more particularly, to implicate *this* father as one of that purported multitude. The additional facts presented by Chief Justice

Burger about Peter Stanley do not provide logical grounds for questioning the majority's opinion since the majority only required that the state prove, rather than presume, Stanley's unfitness before depriving him of the children. Similarly, the additional facts do not, of course, gainsay the position that biological paternity is no less, or at least not much less, determinative of parental affections than biological maternity, and those facts pose no theoretical objection to the Court's decision that the state cannot presume men like Peter Stanley unfit fathers.

However, in the arena of discourse in which nature and nurture are separated and compared as determinants of human behavior, science offers very few assurances. Conclusions about the contributions of nature and nurture to human behavior are more faddish than certain. Therefore, the telling of a particular story can be a crucial determinant of the weight given each component of the nature/nurture controversy.[11] Moreover, by presenting facts that minimized the significance of Peter Stanley's actual relationship with his children, Chief Justice Burger's account strengthens the significance of Stanley's long-term relationship with his children's mother and of the fact of "family" in the *Stanley* case, as factors crucial to the Court's holding.

Again, in *Quilloin v. Walcott,* decided six years after *Stanley,* the Court assumed—now more explicitly even than in *Stanley*—that biological paternity, unlike biological maternity, offers no assurances about the probable actualization of parental behavior. In *Quilloin* the Court considered a Georgia statute that gave all unwed mothers, but only certain unwed fathers, the right to veto the adoptions of their children. Under the Georgia statute at issue in the case, unwed fathers could acquire the right to veto the adoption of a child if they "legitimized" the child by marrying the mother and acknowledging paternity, or by having the child declared legitimate through a court order.[12] Leon Quilloin, an unwed father, desired to veto the adoption of his child by the child's stepfather, Randall Walcott. The mother, Ardell Williams Walcott, had married Randall Walcott in 1967, almost three years after the birth of her child with Leon Quilloin. Quilloin and Ardell Walcott had never established a home together with the child, who had been in the custody of its mother since birth. Quilloin had offered irregular support to the child and had visited with the child on "many occasions" before the mother, asserting the child's best interests, had ended Quilloin's contacts with the child.[13]

The Court in *Quilloin*, retreating from the more expansive implications of *Stanley*, explicitly refused constitutional protection to unwed fathers on the basis of biological paternity alone; under *Quilloin* constitutional protection is only extended to certain unwed fathers. The Court was not very clear, however, about *who* those unwed fathers are. The opinion (especially when read in concert with *Caban v. Mohammed*, decided the next year), has often been interpreted as defining the fathers who *are* protected as those who *act* like fathers, who "shoulder[] . . . significant responsibility with respect to the daily supervision, education, protection, or care of their child." [14] However, that reading of the opinion offers only a partial rendition of what the opinion actually says.

The Court was at least equally concerned with the absence of a "family unit" including Quilloin, his child, and that child's mother as it was with the absence of a social relationship between Quilloin and his child, per se. "[T]he result of an adoption [by the child's step-father] in this case," wrote the Court, "is to give full recognition to a family unit already in existence, a result desired by all concerned, except appellant." [15] The Court's language about fathers who shoulder "significant responsibility" regarding the socialization of their children seemed to distinguish Quilloin from separated or divorced fathers who had once had a relationship with their children's mothers in the context of having been joined in a "family unit" with that mother and their children. This language also served to stress the absence of a relationship between Quilloin and the child. "[E]ven a father whose marriage has broken apart," wrote the Court, "will have borne full responsibility for the rearing of his children during the period of the marriage." [16] That statement may be true as an assumption allowed to law, but, as the Court clearly knew, does not necessarily describe the behavior of any particular father. Thus, the opinion suggests, even in the midst of a statement about the importance of unwed fathers' paternal behavior that that behavior itself is conditioned by the father's relationship with the children's mother.

The Court was certainly concerned, as commentators have stressed, that Quilloin had no substantial parental relationship with his child. But, of at least equal concern was the absence of a "family unit" involving Quilloin, and the presence of a "family unit" including Ardell Walcott, Randall Walcott, and the child. The Court declared that "[w]hatever might be required in other situations, we cannot say that the State was required in this situation to find anything more than that the adoption, and denial of legitimation [of the child by Quilloin], were in the 'best interests of the child.' "[17]

Thus, under the holding in *Quilloin*, biology alone is of minimal importance in securing legal recognition for the paternal relationship of unwed fathers to their biological children. Behavioral ties between such fathers and their children are significant, but not conclusive. The Court did not even try to delineate *how much* social responsibility an unwed father had to accept for his child in order to be guaranteed parental rights. Of greatest importance in determining a biological father's rights to a legal relationship with his child appears to be the father's inclusion in a "family unit" with the children and their mother. Although the "family unit" recognized in *Quilloin* was marital, the Court did not express an explicit preference for marital as compared to nonmarital family units. Once again, as was true under the common law, *Quilloin* implies that for most fathers at least, paternal rights are mediated by the father's relation to his child's mother, although *Quilloin*, unlike the common law, does not suggest that that relationship must be effected in the context of a marriage. In sum, the *Quilloin* Court considered each of the three factors that might provide an unwed father grounds for claiming parental rights: a biological tie to the child; a social connection to the child; and creation of a "family unit" with the child and his or her mother. Of these three factors, the first alone was given little significance; the second and third were recognized as important, but only the third factor emerged as determinative. *Quilloin* suggests, without ever stating explicitly, that the relationship which makes an unwed father most *like* a married father—a relationship founded on the establishment and maintenance of a household with the mother and child—would carry greatest weight in determining unwed fathers' paternal rights.

Thus, between *Stanley* and *Quilloin* the Court seemed to move from an equivocal willingness to recognize paternity on the basis of a biological father's commitment to his child toward a more certain reluctance to recognize paternity unless the biological father made a commitment to a "family unit" that included, at least at some point, the children's mother as well as the man and his children. In either case, paternity is distinguished from maternity as a matter of choice, and biology is not presumed to determine a father's relationship to his children. The *Quilloin* Court did not consider the disparate treatment of unmarried fathers and unmarried mothers.[18] However, the Court did separate out the mother-child relationship as the core around which "family units" form. By implication, the Court understood female, but not male, biology to encompass, and therefore to guarantee, a parent-child relationship.

In *Caban v. Mohammed*, decided one year after *Quilloin*, an unwed father, who was anxious to preserve his parental rights, presented an equal protection argument based on disparate treatment accorded unwed fathers and unwed mothers. When the case was heard, Caban was married to another woman. This fact—making Caban part of a "family"—may have played some unstated role in the Court's view of Caban. The case involved the constitutionality of a New York statute which gave unwed mothers, but not unwed fathers, the right to withhold consent for the adoption of children.[19] The parents in *Caban* never married but established and maintained a household together for five years. During that time Maria Mohammed gave birth to two children. When the children were two and four, Maria left Abdiel Caban and shortly thereafter married Kazim Mohammed. Two years after the marriage, Maria and Kazim filed a petition to have Kazim adopt the two children. A New York surrogate granted the adoption.

Eventually, the United States Supreme Court, reversing the decisions below, held New York's statute unconstitutional under an intermediate standard of review. The Court found that the statutory distinction "between unmarried mothers and unmarried fathers, as illustrated by this case, does not bear a substantial relation to the State's interest in providing adoptive homes for its illegitimate children."[20]

The Court rejected as justification for the statutory distinction the Mohammeds' argument that "a natural mother, absent special circumstances, bears a closer relationship with her child ... than a father does."[21] The Court admitted the statistical validity of this claim but expressed concern that some unwed fathers may play an important role in the lives of their children and decided that the rights of such fathers deserve protection. "The present case," wrote the Court, "demonstrates that an unwed father may have a relationship with his children fully comparable to that of the mother."[22]

Caban suggests that a biological father's paternal behavior will determine the degree of protection the Constitution provides in safeguarding his relationship with his biological child. However, the language of the opinion focuses on Caban's having "lived together as a *natural* family" with Maria Mohammed and their children rather than on the character of the relationship that Caban affected with his children.[23] It was, argued the Court, *as a member of a natural family*, that Caban cared for and supported his children. Once again, in *Caban* the Court in large part predicated the unwed father's relation to his children and his claims to legal paternity on his relation to his children's mother—on the creation of a "natural family"—as much as on his relationship with his children, per se.

Commentators analyzing *Caban*[24] have noted the Court's acknowledgment that an unwed father may have a "relationship with his children fully comparable to that of the mother,"[25] but have frequently failed to recognize the extent to which the *Caban* Court, in fact, premised recognition of the father-child relationship on the unwed father's having set up a "natural family" with the children and their mother.

Technically, the term "natural family" was used in *Caban* to refer to a social unit of *unmarried* biological parents and their children. However, the term carried additional implications. The term "family" refers, of course, to a comparable unit involving two *married* adults. "Natural family" is the marked term.[26] The traditional, ideal family can be described without use of the adjective "natural." That adjective is used to delineate a special, marginal family group. In this regard, therefore, *Caban* differed from the traditional position that to achieve legal recognition a family must include two adults *married* to each other. But the decision did not eliminate altogether the presence of "family" as a basic precondition for the protection of a biological father's legal paternity.

For the Court, the social constellation in *Caban* could be described as a family not only, not even primarily, because there were biological ties between Caban and his children, but because the adults had cohabited on the model of a married couple, together with their children. Thus, the important "natural" relationship giving Caban legal rights to his children was not his biological link to the children, nor even his unmediated social tie to them, but his continuing link to their mother after their births. *That* link made Caban part of a "natural" family and gave him *legal rights* to his biological children. Caban was able to effect the right to claim paternity by declaring his connection to his children's mother, the parent whose biological tie to her children so much more irrefutably constituted a parental tie. Thus, again in *Caban*, the choice that gives an unwed father paternal rights is the choice to relate to his children's mother as much as the choice to relate to the children, themselves.

Justice Stewart's dissenting opinion shared a set of assumptions with the Court's majority about the comparative significance of female and male biology and delineated more expressly than the majority the implications of the assumed differences between biological maternity and biological paternity. This dissent is important because it reintroduces the underlying assumptions about biology that allowed the majority and the dissent alike so facilely to distinguish mothers from fathers.

Justice Stewart wrote: "Parental rights do not spring full-blown from the biological connection between parent and child. They require relationships more enduring. The mother carries and bears the child, and in this sense, her parental relationship is clear."[27] Justice Stewart posited the mother's relationship with her child to begin with the gestation and delivery of the child. Thus, "the biological connection between parent and child" that in Justice Stewart's view does not give rise automatically to parental rights must be a genetic connection, the only biological connection available to a father. On this reading, female biology encompasses maternity, but not because the mother provides the egg from which her child develops. The gestational, not the genetic, role makes a biological mother a "mother" in a case such as *Caban*.[28] In contrast, biological paternity, understood to involve only a genetic tie carries no certain implications for the social relationship between a man and his biological child. "The validity of the father's parental claims must be gauged by other measures," wrote Justice Stewart.[29] Traditionally, continued Justice Stewart, that measure has been legitimation of the paternal relationship through the father's marriage to the mother. So far, Justice Stewart's position resembles that of the majority. The difference, and the determinative difference for Abdiel Caban, is that the majority was willing to read the creation of a "natural family" as comparable to the creation of a marital family for purposes of establishing paternal rights. That difference, although determinative for Caban, is in a more analytic context a minor difference, holding few implications for the essential character of paternity.

Like Justice Stewart's dissent in *Caban*, Justice Stevens's dissent stressed the relevance of biological maternity to the establishment of a mother-child tie and was of particular significance in foreshadowing Justice Stevens's majority decision in the next unwed father case to reach the Supreme Court. Referring to the biological ties between mother and child that develop and grow during pregnancy and birth, Justice Stevens's *Caban* dissent invoked a "symbiotic relationship" between mother and child that provided a "physical and psychological bond" between the two, "not present between the infant and the father or any other person."[30] Thus, for Justice Stevens the "natural" roots of maternity and paternity differ, and mothers differ accordingly from fathers. But it was not until *Lehr v. Robertson*, that Justice Stevens explained in detail his view of the differences between biological maternity and biological paternity.

In *Lehr*, Justice Stevens, for the Court, denied the petition of the putative father, Jonathan Lehr, to prevent the adoption of his daughter, Jessica, by the husband of the child's mother. Lehr argued that New York's failure to provide him notice of the adoption proceeding denied him due process and that the different treatment of unwed mothers and unwed fathers in the statute denied him equal protection.

Addressing the due process claim, Justice Stevens conceded that the "intangible fibers that connect parent and child" deserve "constitutional protection in appropriate cases."[31] Lehr's case was not seen to be such a case, however, because "a mere biological relationship"[32] cannot alone establish legal paternity. The majority proceeded to quote Justice Stewart's dissent in *Caban*: "Parental rights do not spring full-blown from the biological connection between parent and child. They require relationships more enduring."[33] Justice Stevens declared:

> The significance of the biological connection is that it offers the natural father an opportunity that no other male possesses to develop a relationship with his offspring. If he grasps that opportunity and accepts some measure of responsibility for the child's future, he may enjoy the blessings of the parent-child relationship and make uniquely valuable contributions to the child's development.[34]

Biology, in short, gives men options. An unwed biological father may establish his relationship with his biological child and with that child's mother through appropriate behavior and become a legal father. Alternatively, he may treat the biological relationship as irrelevant and not become a father at all.

Mothers, wed or unwed, do not have the same choices.[35] The Supreme Court implied that for mothers parental rights *do* spring from a biological, though not from a genetic, connection between parent and child.[36] The gestational bond conditions (and in most cases compels) biological mothers to be social mothers. Biology gives men the *chance* to become fathers. However, it inexorably makes women mothers—at least when they are being compared to fathers.

In responding to Lehr's equal protection argument, the Court did not openly rely on, or even expressly refer to, its own assumption that biological paternity and biological maternity are different enough to situate unwed mothers differently from unwed fathers for purposes of constitutional analysis. Rather, the Court decided that Lehr's equal protection claim failed because *he* had not "established a substantial relationship with his daughter" while the child's mother had such a relationship with the children.[37] On this basis, the Court distinguished *Lehr* from *Caban*.

Thus, the Court in *Lehr* implied that had Lehr only been a more committed father, had he "come forward to participate in the rearing of his child,"[38] his paternal rights would have received constitutional protection. This explanation is unconvincing, however, in light of the facts revealed in Justice White's dissenting opinion which indicated that the child's mother had hidden baby Jessica from Lehr who "never ceased his efforts to locate" the mother and the child.[39] When he did locate them, the mother threatened Lehr with arrest if he attempted to see the child.

The facts presented in Justice White's dissent indicate that the decision in *Lehr* rests less on Lehr's specific failure to effect a paternal role than on two broader, implicit assumptions that the Court made. First, the Court assumed that biological paternity, unlike biological maternity, carries no imperatives for fathers—implying, of course, that Lehr's equal protection argument must fail *because* men and women are *not* similarly situated with regard to their status as parents. Second, the Court assumed that the recognition of paternity depends in most cases on a connection (either "lawful" or "natural") between the father and the child's mother. Neither assumption was express.

Tacit, fundamental assumptions of the sort found in *Lehr* can direct the course of constitutional decision-making and, because tacit, can be masked by other, more express justifications. So, for example, the assumption that men and women differ as parents on the basis of innate gender differences provides at least implicit justification for differential treatment of the two groups. Often that treatment will be justified on other grounds.

But, in such cases, careful examination will generally reveal that the express grounds on which such decisions are premised prove inadequate to explain the decisions, or are even patently self-contradictory.

Thus, when the facts in *Stanley, Quilloin, Caban,* and *Lehr* are examined, the Court's decisions in *Stanley* and *Caban* are not adequately distinguished from *Quilloin* and *Lehr* on the ground that the first two fathers effected relations with their children and the second two did not. The *Lehr* Court did not expressly refer to Lehr's failure to establish a household with the mother and the child, but that fact, more than Lehr's not having "come forward,"[40] distinguished Lehr's situation, in the Court's view, from that of the fathers in *Stanley* and *Caban* and made him more like the father in *Quilloin*. For the Court, the determinative difference between the two sets of cases was that the fathers in *Stanley* and *Caban* effected relations that adequately resembled families with the children's mothers and the fathers in *Quilloin* and *Lehr* did not. The Court never focused clearly on the importance this difference played in its unwed father decisions. The Court simply assumed, quite implicitly, that through the mediation of the mother in the context of a "family," biological fathers became social fathers *and* that in the absence of such mediation, they did not.

The assumption in these cases that biology does not compel social paternity, as it compels social maternity, undergirds the demand that fathers seek other paths for securing legal rights to their biological children. By forming "families" with the mothers of their children, fathers share in the natural bonds that connect mothers and children. A man's ties to his biological child are thereby socialized.

Another set of cases regarding paternity, however, does seem to posit legal paternity on the sole ground of biological paternity and therefore calls for further explanation. These are cases in which unwed biological fathers have been held responsible for supporting their biological offspring despite the absence of any social relationship between the father and his biological child as well as the absence of a continuing relationship between the father and the mother of that child.[41] Although such cases do make declarations of legal paternity on the basis of biological paternity alone, they are essentially decisions that the biological father bears a certain contractual, financial obligation—not that he is or need be a social father (a "real" father). No relationship *with the child* is assumed to flow from the man's biological paternity in these support cases. His responsibility for the child's support is in essence, even if not literally, a matter between the man (as autonomous, individual—not as family member) and the state.

The unwed father cases decided by the Supreme Court did not involve children deprived of financial support. Thus, in these cases, the Court tacitly assumed, and relied on the assumption, that for men biology does not compel social paternity. Fatherhood, unlike motherhood, is understood to be constructed socially.[42] Through the mediation of woman ("mother"), the father chooses to proclaim (and thus to claim) his "natural" relationship to his biological child, gaining the status, and therefore the constitutional protection, that for women is viewed to stem directly from the biological connection and that has not generally been viewed as a matter of choice.

Michael H.: The Limits of Choice

This reading of *Lehr* and the other three unwed father cases that preceded *Lehr* becomes even more compelling in light of the Court's 1989 decision in *Michael H. v. Gerald D.*[43] *Michael H.* tested the principle apparently enunciated in *Lehr*—that an unwed biological father creates a liberty interest in his relationship to his child if he "demonstrates a full commitment to the responsibilities of fatherhood"[44]—and found that principle's limit easily reached in a case in which the father demonstrated a commitment to his biological child, but did not establish a marital or marriage-like familial relationship with that child's mother.

The biological father in *Michael H.* did not establish a familial relationship with the child's mother because he legally could not. The mother was married to another man. He did develop a *relationship* with his child's mother, but, in the Court's view, that relationship was neither marital nor the kind of nonmarital relationship that resembles that between spouses. The Court described a family (called a "unitary family") to include the marital family and a "household of unmarried parents and their children." "Perhaps," wrote Justice Scalia, "the concept can be expanded even beyond this, but it will bear no resemblance to traditionally respected relationships—and will thus cease to have any constitutional significance—if it is stretched so far as to include the relationship established between a married woman, her lover and their child."[45]

Justice Scalia's plurality opinion in *Michael H.* seems inconsistent with the implications of the *Stanley* line of cases if those cases are read to say that a biological father's relationship with his child will deserve constitutional protection if he effects a social relationship with that child. In particular, *Michael H.* seems inconsistent with the broad implications of *Quilloin* and *Lehr* that a putative father at least deserves the right to *develop* a social relationship with his biological child adequate to ensure constitutional protection for that relationship. If, however, *Quilloin* and *Lehr* are read to posit a putative father's relationship to his biological child to rest heavily on, and to be mediated by, his relationship with that child's mother, then *Michael H.* and the earlier cases can be harmonized.

Michael H. differed from the earlier cases involving the paternal rights of unwed fathers because in *Michael H.* the child's mother was married to another man. *Michael H.* also differed from the earlier unwed father cases in that Michael was more directly opposed in his claims to his daughter Victoria's paternity by another father than by a mother. It may be that a man's biological tie to a child carries even less weight when that tie is compared to the tie of another *man* than when it is compared to the tie of a woman. A reading of *Michael H.* and the other unwed father cases does not provide enough evidence for a clear conclusion on this point.

Carole, the mother, was married to Gerald when she conceived and bore a daughter, Victoria. During the period of Victoria's conception, Carole had a relationship with Michael. Gerald was listed as Victoria's father on the birth certificate, but blood tests later showed a 98.07% probability that Michael was the child's biological father. Michael and Carole lived together for eleven months during the child's infancy. Eventually, Carole, with the child, left Michael in California and resettled with Gerald in New York. Between those two periods, Carole moved back and forth between Gerald and Michael numerous times. In addition, she moved in with a third man, Scott, for ten months in 1982–83. During Victoria's first three and a half years, Carole and Victoria moved a dozen times among different "family" constellations (consisting variously of Victoria, Carole, and Gerald; Victoria and Carole; Victoria, Carole, Michael and Carole's mother; and Victoria, Carole, and Scott).[46]

Michael, however, appeared to have effected the kind of commitment to Victoria referred to in *Lehr* as the basis for an unwed father's right to a relationship with his biological child. Within eighteen months of Victoria's birth he filed a petition for a declaration of paternity; he provided financial support to the child; and he established a parental relationship with Victoria. The child called him "Daddy."

In 1984 Michael, and Victoria through a guardian ad litem, sought visitation rights for Michael. However, Section 621 of the California Evidence Code provided that "the issue of a wife cohabiting with her husband, who is not impotent or sterile, is conclusively presumed to be a child of the marriage."[47] For a putative father the presumption was irrebuttable. The California Superior Court granted Gerald's motion for summary judgment on the basis of affidavits submitted by Carole and Gerald that indicated that the two had lived together during the period surrounding Victoria's conception and birth and that Gerald was neither impotent nor sterile. The state court of appeals affirmed, noting that despite Michael's interest in maintaining a relationship with Victoria, "the state's interest in preserving the integrity of the matrimonial family is so significant that it outweighs most other interests."[48] Michael and Victoria then appealed directly to the United States Supreme Court.[49]

The Court, in a five-to-four opinion, affirmed the California court's summary judgment for Gerald. Justice Scalia, who authored the Court's plurality opinion, decided that Michael did not have a constitutionally protected liberty interest in his relationship with Victoria and concluded that the right of putative fathers to develop a relationship with their biological children did not include the right to rebut the marital presumption contained in Section 621. Justice Scalia analyzed Michael's due process claim as a substantive, not a procedural, claim. The Court read section 621 as a substantive rule of law, phrased as a presumption. The plurality asserted: "California declares it to be, except in limited circumstances, *irrelevant* for paternity purposes whether a child conceived during, and born into, an existing marriage was begotten by someone other than the husband and had a prior relationship with him."[50]

The plurality rejected Michael's reliance on *Stanley, Quilloin, Caban,* and *Lehr* as well as his reading of those cases. In the plurality's view, those cases did not establish a liberty interest on the basis of "biological fatherhood plus an established parental relationship—factors that exist in the present case as well."[51] Rather, as the plurality viewed them, the unwed father cases rested "upon the historic respect—indeed, sanctity would not be too strong a term—traditionally accorded to the relationships that develop within the unitary family."[52] Commentators, as well as Justice Brennan's dissent in *Michael H.*, took umbrage with Justice Scalia's interpretation of the earlier unwed father cases.[53] And, indeed, the express language in those cases conflicts with the Court's review in *Michael H.*, as Justice Brennan pointed out. However, Justice Scalia's interpretation of the earlier cases merely articulates the implicit message that runs beneath, and explains, the opinions in those cases. The way the fathers in those earlier cases were treated depended, as Justice Scalia noted, on their role in a "unitary family" (a family including the child and his or her mother). The explicit language of the earlier cases failed to explain the assumption behind the law. As Justice White recalled in *Michael H.*, the Court *had* said in *Lehr* that an unwed father receives due process protection when he "demonstrates a full commitment to the responsibilities of parenthood by 'com[ing] forward to participate in the rearing of his child.' "[54] However, the explanation offered, and quoted by Justice Brennan, is a second-level explanation. The basic explanation—the one that explains when the Court, in fact, identified a father in the unwed father cases as effecting the requisite commitment—depended on the father's relation to the mother or, as Justice Scalia put it, on the father's relationships within a "unitary family."[55]

Thus, the plurality in *Michael H.* distinguished the earlier cases by interpreting those cases to protect the rights of a father within a "unitary family." In the plurality's view, Michael and Victoria did not belong to such a family unit, and thus Michael's particular relation to Victoria became irrelevant. Justice Scalia's opinion declared a biological father's constitutional right to a relationship with his child to rest firmly on his involvement in a *family* unit. The plurality rejected the possibility, almost without exploration, that an unwed father and his biological child could form a family unit in the absence of an appropriate relationship between the unwed father and the child's mother; the opinion refused to include within "traditional," and thus protected, family units the "relationship established between a married woman, her lover and their child."

A crucial aspect of the *Michael H.* decision was the Court's delimitation of what relationships will be considered the building blocks of a "unitary family" (also called "traditional families") and will thus deserve constitutional protection. The plurality wrote:

The family unit accorded traditional respect in our society, which we have referred to as the "unitary family," is typified, of course, by the marital family, but also includes the household of unmarried parents and their children. Perhaps the concept can be expanded beyond this, but it will bear no resemblance to traditionally respected relationships.[56]

Justice Brennan referred to the plurality's depiction of a "unitary family" as a "pinched conception" and said it was "jarring in light of our many cases preventing the States from denying important interests or statuses to those whose situations do not fit the government's narrow view of the family."[57]

In any event, on the basis of its understanding of "family," the plurality denied protection to Michael's relationship with Victoria, however dear that relationship. The state was not required to consider the intensity or duration of that relationship in this case, one in which the biological mother's marriage to another man definitively precluded the biological father from establishing the sort of relationship *with the mother* that would provide constitutional protection for his relationship with his biological daughter.[58]

The implications of the assumptions behind this decision are of great moment for understanding the law's view of paternity. The opinion asserted that fathers in certain families, but not others, deserve constitutional protection. The implications of Justice Scalia's opinion are especially suggestive because he stated explicitly that fathers become fathers by forming proper "traditional" families, that the decision that a particular father is part of such a family is unrelated to notions of "biological" truth, and finally, that a man's biological relation to a child (as in the case of an "adulterous natural father," as the Court labelled Michael H.) may actually imperil the man's reliance on constitutional protection in asserting legal paternity.

The implications of Justice Scalia's opinion in *Michael H.* are dramatically illustrated by the two distinct, even opposing, meanings that underlie his use of the term "nature" (or "natural") in the opinion. Invocations of nature are often suggestive. The divergent meanings of "nature" represent a general paradox in Western culture.[59] On the one hand, that which is natural is good, moral, and inevitable. Nature, as in the phrase "mother nature," directs and protects an inexorable reality with which people toy only at their peril. On the other hand, nature is inferior to culture. Nature represents brute emotion and untrammeled instinct which must be channeled and contained for people to live together in society.

The first use of "nature" is found in Justice Scalia's claim that "California law, *like nature itself,* makes no provision for dual fatherhood."[60] In referring to "nature itself" Justice Scalia asserted that nature dictates that children have one father, not two, and that Michael, by claiming to be Victoria's father, defied that natural, and thus, proper pattern. In fact, of course, Michael's claim was that *he* was Victoria's natural father. He argued that as a result of *that* truth, his paternity deserved social and legal recognition. Moreover, the very statute that Justice Scalia's opinion fervently upheld defined a child's father to be the husband of that child's mother's *even* in cases in which the mother's husband was not the biological (genetic) father. Thus, in effect, Justice Scalia, at least by implication, argued that a child's stepfather is a more "natural" father than the child's genitor.

Later, Justice Scalia invoked "nature's" role, again suggestively, when he referred to Michael as the "adulterous natural father."[61] Now, the very "naturalness" of Michael's fatherhood seems to justify the state's decision to ignore his biological paternity. Here, the description "natural" justifies the deprivation, rather than the extension, of rights because the term now implies disorder and contrasts with social control, morality, and justice. The opinion almost suggests that Michael's claim, based on biological paternity, withered before the need to punish him for interfering with what should have been another man's paternity, for his role as "an adulterous, natural father." Justice Scalia wrote further:

> We have found nothing in the older sources, nor in the older cases, addressing specifically the power of the natural father to assert parental rights over a child born into a woman's existing marriage with another man. . . . [T]he evidence shows that even in modern times—when, as we have noted, the rigid protection of the marital family has in other respects been relaxed—the ability of a person in Michael's position to claim paternity has not been generally acknowledged.[62]

In this sense of the term "natural," people are cultured. Animals are natural. For fathers, for whom parenthood appears to be, at least in large part, a matter of choice, the "natural" facts get no legal recognition until garbed with social form.

In short, Justice Scalia applauded the preservation of "natural" patterns, as evidenced by "California law." Yet he sustained the law's obliteration of Michael's paternity, the paternity of the man he called Victoria's "natural father" and justified that act *because* the father's paternity was merely "natural."

And herein lies the moral of the tale. A "natural" father's paternity can be ignored precisely because fathers (men) are not encompassed by their biological selves. On the whole fathers represent culture and history, as opposed to women (and mothers), who stand for nature. For men, the predominant aspect of parenthood must, therefore, stem from, and be predicated upon, culture, not nature. Thus, only when the two meanings of "natural" come together, is the "natural father" the father. This occurs, of course, when the biological father effects his fatherhood in the context of a moral and proper (read, "natural," in its other sense) family.

The central difference between *Michael H.* and the earlier unwed father cases is not, as commentators have suggested,[63] that in the earlier cases biological fathers achieved the right to legal paternity by effecting social relationships with their children while *Michael H.* required something more. Rather, *Michael H.* and the earlier cases alike extended constitutional protection to a biological father's legal paternity if the man established a "family," a home, with the child and that child's mother. This assertion is based on a reading of the four cases as a whole. Within any one opinion in any one of the cases, it *is* possible to find support for popular interpretations of the cases. For instance, Justice White, dissenting in *Lehr v. Robertson* and joined by Justices Blackmun and Marshall, was more ready to protect Lehr's paternity on the basis of an independent relationship between Lehr and his biological child that did not include the child's mother. Of course, in *Lehr* it was possible to assume, on the basis of the given facts, that Lehr *would have* established a relationship with his child and even perhaps with that child's mother, had the mother been willing. However, it is important to recognize that Justice White expressly predicated his readiness to protect Lehr's paternity on the fact of a biological relationship between Lehr and the child. Justice White wrote: "The 'biological connection' is itself a relationship that creates a protected interest. Thus the 'nature' of the interest is the parent-child relationship; how well developed that relationship has become goes to its 'weight,' not its 'nature.' "[64]

The position that biological paternity deserves protection in cases in which the father establishes a home with the child and that child's mother was explicit in *Michael H.* and was implicit in the earlier cases. The difference between *Michael H.* and the other cases lies elsewhere. The difference stems from the narrowness with which the concept "family" was defined in *Michael H.* as compared with the earlier unwed father cases. If, as Justice Brennan pleaded in his dissent in *Michael H.*, Michael, Carole, and Victoria composed a family, *then* Michael was a social father, whose fatherhood deserved protection. If, however, as Justice Scalia argued, the family is to be defined more narrowly, in, as he framed it, "traditional" terms, then Michael was not part of a family involving himself, his child, and the child's mother. For *that* reason, and for no other, Michael failed to adequately effect his social fatherhood. By definition, that option—the option of forming a "unitary family" with his biological child and that child's mother—was not available to Michael H.

In fact, the fathers whose paternal rights received constitutional protection in the first four unwed father cases did fit into Justice Scalia's definition in *Michael H.* of a "unitary family." However, *Michael H.*, unlike the earlier cases, made it abundantly clear that the limits of what could constitute a "family" from a constitutional perspective would be strictly defined and uncompromisingly applied.

In sum, the unwed father cases, from *Stanley* through *Michael H.*, delineate three factors that make an unwed man a father. These are the man's biological relation to the child; his social relation to the child; and his relation to the child's mother. *Stanley* through *Lehr* seem to suggest, and have certainly been read to say, that a man can effect a legal relation to his biological child by establishing a relationship with that child. However, the facts of those cases belie the claim that that is a full interpretation. *Michael H.*, which has been read to conflict with the earlier decisions, in fact suggests an elaboration of the message implicit in *Stanley* through *Lehr*, taken as a group. In this regard, *Michael H.* clarifies the earlier cases. A biological father does protect his paternity by developing a social relationship with his child, *but* this step demands the creation of a family, a step itself depending upon an appropriate relationship between the man and his child's mother.[65]

The ambiguity of the Court's response to the unwed father cases is predicated on real ambivalence. The cases acknowledged and approved a change that carries important implications for the scope and form of the family and then quickly (though quietly) retreated. The Court proclaimed that unwed fathers may become legal fathers by establishing relationships with their biological children and then hedged that proclamation, though neither directly nor certainly, by tacitly restricting the context in which a father could demonstrate the existence of the requisite relationship with his biological children to one including the children's mother—to one defined traditionally as "family." Men are still viewed as less restricted in their commitment to parenthood by biological processes than women, and for men, as for women, family relationships are presumed to be significantly different from market relationships. A man may, indeed must, *choose* his paternity in order to guarantee its legality, but he must embed that choice in certain (familial) forms and processes. The relationship between a father and a child cannot be effected like any relationship between two autonomous individuals, free to come and go as they agree. A man becomes a father by relating to his child *in the context of family*. That context is prototypically[66] created by the development of a spousal or spouse-like relationship between a father and his child's mother.

Thus, in the end, the father *is* required to effect his relationship with his biological children through acts in the world in order to protect his paternal relationship under the law. However, not any acts will do. The acts that make a biological father a social, and thus a legal, father are *familial* acts, acts that socialize the "natural" facts by inserting themselves in, and thus defining themselves through, a certain ordering of the relationship between the father and his child's mother. In that way, the preservation of traditional family forms is supported.

II. What Makes a Mother a "Mother"?

At least since the nineteenth century, claims to maternity, unlike claims to paternity, have been recognized as predicated on biology. That belief supported the "cult of motherhood" as it developed during the nineteenth century and as it was elaborated further in the middle decades of the next century. In the words of the English anthropologist Marilyn Strathern: "Between mother and father, the mother is recognized; the father, by contrast, is constructed." Strathern means that in traditional

European-American thinking a mother's identity is understood as a natural fact while a father's identity, itself a product of his relationship to the mother, is understood as a social fact.[67]

In part, this difference in understandings of maternity and paternity can be attributed to the comparative certainty with which biological maternity, unlike biological paternity, could be presumed. However, that is an aspect, more than an explanation, of presumed differences between maternity and paternity. The inexorability of the connection that linked mothers to their children gave women fewer choices than men. Mothers, unlike fathers, were understood, in the *nature* of their maternity, as bonded to their children and their homes.

In this sense, recognition of the biological tie between a woman and her child as the essence of maternity furthered the preservation of traditional family forms. Fathers chose fatherhood. Women *were* mothers, a fact presumed to have been at once demonstrated and effected by the simultaneity of biological and social motherhood. This notion of mothers and motherhood has been absolutely essential to society's understanding of family for almost two centuries.

Now, society faces a number of challenges to deeply embedded understandings of "mother." Central among these challenges is the generalization of an ideology of autonomous individuality into the home, an ideology which grants new options to women, increasingly understood at least sometimes and at least in theory as equal to men. The contractualization of maternity represented by surrogacy arrangements provides an especially stark, and therefore especially troubling, instance of the erosion of romantic images of woman and mother first constructed at the start of the Industrial Revolution. That women may negotiate the conditions of their biological maternity before becoming pregnant, and that they may further *choose* to undertake biological maternity without desiring or presuming that social maternity will follow, completely disrupts traditional understandings of motherhood. In particular, the possibility that women can negotiate the social consequences of biological maternity and that social motherhood can follow from bargained arrangements and financial exchanges as well as from the inevitability of biological reproduction suggests a new kind of mother. However, in responding to cases occasioned by surrogacy, courts, even while recognizing the contractualization of motherhood, have largely tried to preserve traditional understandings of mother and of family. That becomes increasingly difficult, and so, in cases such as *Baby M.*, as well as in cases of gestational surrogacy, involving the separation of gestational and genetic maternity, courts, often implicitly and sometimes unwittingly, are redefining the meaning of mother.

This process of reconstructing motherhood has been accelerated by the advent of reproductive technology which, more and more, enables people to control the processes of human reproduction. However, the challenge now presented to traditional understandings of motherhood cannot be attributed completely, or even primarily, to technological advances. That becomes clear in light of the major disruption that traditional surrogacy presents to established understandings of motherhood and of family. Certainly, as the discussion in chapter 5 indicates, the possibility of separating biological maternity into discrete aspects that can be distributed among different women, as well as other alterations in the process of human reproduction becoming possible through technology assistance, compel society and the law to reconsider the meaning of motherhood. However, the changes are broader and more fundamental than those occasioned by the use of new technologies. The reexamination of motherhood in cases such as *Baby M.* and in others involving gestational surrogacy, is being directed by, and against, an emerging understanding of family that supersedes that forged during the nineteenth century and elaborated in subsequent years.

In these cases, mothers are being compared with other kinds of mothers, and they are being compared with fathers. Thus, the cases occasioned by surrogacy arrangements, comment, though generally obliquely, on the understanding of fatherhood suggested by the cases about the paternal rights of unwed fathers.

From the unwed father cases, one would expect that a biological mother who entered, and then regretted entering, into a surrogacy agreement would bring more powerful arguments to an adversarial proceeding at which the baby's parentage was in dispute than would the contracting and genetic father. This would seem to be the case for both surrogates such as Mary Beth Whitehead and for surrogates lacking a genetic connection with the child. Moreover, one would conclude, at least on the basis of Justice Stewart's dissenting language in *Caban*, quoted favorably in Justice Steven's majority opinion in *Lehr*, [68] that, everything else being equal, gestational mothers would be preferred to genetic mothers. Discounting the importance of biological paternity per se, Justice Stewart recognized the gestational link between a woman and a child to constitute the foundation for an "enduring" relationship (for a mothering relationship). "The mother," wrote Justice Stewart, "carries and bears the child, and in this sense her parental relationship is clear."[69] Thus, the unwed father opinions assert clearly that genetics (biological paternity) plays a limited role in making a man a father; they suggest, by implication, that genetics plays a similarly limited role in making a woman a mother. But these cases say that for women there is a biological basis for the construction of motherhood—the relationship formed between a woman and the baby she gestates and bears.

Thus, the unwed father cases would seem to support the claims of a surrogate seeking recognition of her maternity in opposition to the biological father, as well as the claims of a gestational surrogate, seeking recognition of her maternity in opposition to the claims of the biological father and/or the genetic mother. Yet, the surrogacy cases do not reflect this pattern. Rather, courts in both traditional and gestational surrogacy cases have been ready to negate absolutely, or to minimize seriously, the significance of the biological bases of a surrogate's claims to legal maternity. *Baby M.*, along with a gestational surrogacy case decided in California in the early 1990s, *Johnson v. Calvert*, illustrate the law's response.

In *Baby M.*, as described in chapter 3, both New Jersey courts that heard the case initially recognized William Stern as the baby's father and Mary Beth Whitehead as her mother. Even the trial court, which concluded by terminating Whitehead's maternal rights, appeared at the start to presume that on biological grounds the claims of Whitehead and of Stern argued for each one's parentage of Baby M. The court began by stating:

> Justice, our desired objective, *to the child and the mother, to the child and the father*, cannot be obtained for both parents. The court will seek to achieve justice for the child. This court's fact finding and application of relevant law must mitigate against the heartfelt desires of one or the other of the *natural* parents.[70]

Accordingly, the court examined the child's best interests. However, in that examination, the court returned again and again to the "natural" bases of Whitehead's maternity with the apparent, though unstated, purpose of reducing its significance.

Although the court could not, and did not, find that Whitehead was an unfit mother, it did question her fitness to be a mother *to this child*. In a clever, though possibly uncalculated, move, the trial court predicated its concerns about Whitehead's fitness to be a mother to Baby M. on the very motherliness of her maternity. The court wrote:

> Mrs. Whitehead has been found too enmeshed with this infant child and unable to separate her own needs from those of the child. She tends to smother the child with her presence even to the exclusion of access by her other two children. She does not have the ability to subordinate herself to the needs of this child. The court is satisfied that . . . Mrs. Whitehead is manipulative, impulsive and exploitive [sic].[71]

The court also wrote: "[Whitehead] exhibits an emotional overinvestment. It was argued by defendant's counsel that Mrs. Whitehead had loved her children too much. This is not necessarily a strength. Too much love can smother a child's independence. Even an infant needs her own space."[72]

Whitehead, as the court viewed her, had become too much a mother. To the extent that her claim to legal motherhood rested on the invocation of her "natural" maternity, the court viewed that maternity, in her case, to have run amok. She smothered the child and failed to separate herself reasonably from it. She had come to love the child too much. Her natural mothering instincts, perhaps due to her effort to reclaim the child she had earlier chosen to give to others, developed uncontrolled. Her exaggerated maternity had become a parody of motherhood. As depicted by the court, Whitehead, selfish from the start, had obstructed her own maternity by agreeing to bargain it away. Whitehead had presumed to choose what no "real" mother would dare select. She chose to abdicate maternity. The court wrote: "Mrs. Whitehead was anxious to contract. . . . She knew just what she was bargaining for. This court finds that she has changed her mind, reneged on her promise and now seeks to avoid her obligations."[73] When later she "changed her mind," she was unable to resume a normal mothering role. Her maternal instincts had become exaggerated and deformed.

In this way, the social force of Whitehead's biological maternity and in particular, of her gestational role, was dispelled. Never denying the importance of gestation as a symbol and as a guarantor of social maternity, the court defined Whitehead as an exception. More specifically, by entering into a contractual arrangement aimed at determining her child's parentage, Whitehead was understood as an antagonist of tradition, and in particular of traditional conceptions of family which depend on the separation of home and work—of love and money.

Against Whitehead's uncontrolled, strangulating motherhood, the court balanced Stern's proper home, proper job, and proper wife. In this context, the court stressed the importance of Stern's biological role. Unlike Whitehead, Stern behaved as a father should, and thereby strengthened the social impact of his biological paternity. Here, a component of biological paternity not stressed in the unwed father cases emerges. That component consists of the ownership rights of a biological father to his child in cases in which the father *is* deemed part of a traditional family. The court, concluding that Stern had not paid Whitehead *for the baby*, justified that conclusion by asserting that in such cases "the father does not purchase the child. It is his own biological genetically related child. *He cannot purchase what is already his.*"[74]

The genetic link made the baby Mr. Stern's. It did not automatically make him a social father. Had Stern been only a biological, and not a social, father, the ownership component of Stern's paternity could have created obligations, but not rights. But Stern's social fatherhood was confirmed for the court by his relationship with Elizabeth Stern and by their joint appearance, in the court's view, as an old-fashioned couple anxious to be parents. For the trial court, the two factors—Stern's genetic connection to the child and the character of his familial role—together made the decision irresistible: William Stern and his wife were to be the child's only parents. Elizabeth Stern, who became a mother *through* her husband, was to replace the mother whose social maternity had been thwarted even before her biological maternity commenced.

Stern, like Whitehead, had entered into a contract that involved the purchase of his biological child, but unlike Whitehead he did not thereby hinder his own parenthood. Within traditional understandings of family, mothers, representing nature, home, and family, cannot negotiate the terms of their maternity through the use of market forms. Fathers apparently can.

Thus, as the trial court arranged the pieces, the assumptions behind *Baby M.* harmonized in large part with those behind the unwed father cases. Stern's biological paternity assumed importance—even importance superior to that of the biological mother—*because* he had effected a proper relationship with the woman who would be the baby's mother.

That woman's maternity could substitute for the maternity of the biological mother whose untoward, exaggerated maternity deserved only evisceration. As a result, the Stern family would survive as an instance of what a family ought to be. The only stumbling block, Whitehead's biological maternity, was bypassed by recognizing that she herself dissolved that maternity through her initial choice to enter into a contract. By that choice, the surrogacy contract, unlike other sorts of contracts, became, in effect, unbreachable. By entering into the contract, Whitehead so completely opposed nature's design that she destroyed the usual social consequences of biological maternity.

An obvious contradiction endures, however, between the court's treatment of William, and by implication of Elizabeth, Stern as contract partners and its treatment of Whitehead. The trial court's decision rests on its recognition that families can be successfully created through market interactions. Thus, the decision though ostensibly siding fully with tradition, disrupts tradition thoroughly.

The state supreme court's decision, which restored Whitehead's maternity but left custody with William Stern, contains assumptions similar to those of the trial court with regard to the effects on Whitehead's maternity of her having entered into the surrogacy contract. Rather than viewing the "natural" parents as analogous to those in the unwed father cases— in which event, Whitehead's claim to maternity might have predominated over Stern's claim to paternity—the court viewed the two as it would a divorcing couple battling for the custody of their child.

For the New Jersey Supreme Court as (more strongly) for the trial court, Whitehead's "natural" ties to her child were marred and weakened by her willingness, as the courts saw it, to redefine them as commodities. By entering into a contract for "the sale of a child, or, at the very least, the sale of [her] right to her child," she forfeited the protection normally afforded a biological mother. She agreed to interrupt her "natural" maternity, and that interruption persuaded the state supreme court to deprive Whitehead of her child's custody. This decision was less radical than that of the trial court, largely because the supreme court refused to recognize the surrogacy contract entered into among the parties and thereby determined custody, but not parentage. Even so, the supreme court read the "facts" to downgrade the significance of Whitehead's biological maternity.

Each New Jersey court began its inquiry with the assumption that

Whitehead was the baby's mother. Each deprived her of her maternity, in full or in part. In doing that, neither court renounced the model presented in the unwed father cases whereby motherhood, though not fatherhood, is an aspect and a continuation of biological processes. Instead, each court defined Whitehead as an exception. By presuming to define her child in the terms of the market, rather than of the family, Whitehead obstructed her own maternity. In the eyes of the trial court that act was total. Whitehead's maternity was eradicated absolutely by her willingness to define her child as a commodity and by her later, hysterical attempt to compensate for the original agreement. In the eyes of the state supreme court, Whitehead's maternity, though intact, had been deformed by the consequences of her agreement to sell her child. Neither opinion denied the presumption underlying the unwed father cases, that biological maternity, especially in its gestational aspect, symbolizes and constitutes motherhood. Rather, both courts, though in somewhat different ways, characterized Whitehead as an example of nature gone askew. Thus each opinion defended tradition and at the same time each opinion rewarded an attachment to modernity that permitted the Sterns to enter into a contract for a child.

Johnson v. Calvert, a case similar to *Baby M.* except that the surrogate had no genetic link to the child, brought a new consideration into play and required an elaboration, and ultimately a transformation, of the assumptions underlying traditional understandings of mother. Now, for the first time in a litigated case, there were two women whose claims to motherhood could be grounded on biological links to the child.

In this case all three parties predicated their parenthood on a biological connection to one baby. Crispina and Mark Calvert, married for several years, wanted to have a baby. Although a hysterectomy had made it impossible for Crispina to gestate a fetus, the surgery had not interfered with her body's production of ova. Anna Johnson, a vocational nurse at the hospital where Crispina worked as a registered nurse, volunteered to serve as a gestational surrogate for the Calverts. At the time, Johnson was the single parent of a young daughter.[75] The Calverts and Johnson agreed that Anna Johnson would gestate and bear a baby produced from Crispina Calvert's ovum and fertilized in vitro with Mark Calvert's sperm. Johnson agreed that at the baby's birth she would relinquish "all parental rights" to Mark and Crispina. In return, the Calverts agreed to pay

Johnson $10,000 in a series of installments and to pay for a $100,000 life insurance policy on Johnson's life.

In January 1990, an embryo produced from the Calverts' gametes was implanted in Johnson's uterus. Johnson's pregnancy was soon confirmed. In July, during the seventh month of her pregnancy, Johnson sought the balance of the payments due her from the Calverts, even though under the contract, the payments were not all due. In fact, the last payment was not due until six weeks after the birth of the child. Johnson threatened to keep the baby if the money was not forthcoming. In response, the Calverts sued, seeking a declaration of their parental rights.

The legal decisions in this case, far more dramatically than those in *Baby M.*, reveal a basic disruption in understandings of familial relationships, and of motherhood, in particular, as the society attempts to make sense of new forms of biological reproduction made possible by technology. Three California courts reached decisions in *Johnson*. All held for the Calverts, but the three decisions represent remarkably different responses to, and interpretations of, gestational surrogacy. The trial court, characterizing Anna Johnson as a "gestational carrier," but a "genetic hereditary stranger" to the child, identified the "family unit" by reference to the "shared genes" among the baby, Crispina, and Mark. The appellate court affirmed, relying on state statutes that regulated the law's recognition of the parent-child relationship. Thus, the appellate court recognized Crispina Calvert as the baby's natural mother because blood tests identified genetic similarities between her and the baby but not between the baby and Johnson. However, unlike the trial court, the appellate court explicitly acknowledged the existence of other rational schemes for identifying a baby's mother in such cases.

Finally, the state supreme court expressly recognized the disruption to familiar biological assumptions about human reproduction and human kinship presented by gestational surrogacy. That disruption not only made it impossible to continue relying on such truths in determining the parentage of children born to gestational surrogates but made statutory schemes, promulgated in light of such assumptions, largely irrelevant to the resolution of such cases. In consequence, the supreme court side-stepped around familiar biological truths and established statutory definitions in determining the parentage of Christopher, the baby involved in the case. The supreme court construction of the case, unlike the decisions of the two lower courts in *Johnson*, acknowledges that the old rules do not apply and embodies a new—though almost certainly transitory—approach to the understanding of parentage. That decision, and its implications, are analyzed in chapter 6 along with other decisions in other cases occasioned by the new reproductive technologies.

The trial court, faced with a set of reproductive facts that would have been almost unimaginable only a few years earlier, proved unwilling to abandon a traditional approach to the creation of family relationships. That court, in trying to model its response on familiar understandings of mother—understandings in which maternity is the inevitable consequence of biological facts—altered familiar understandings, though not as obviously and certainly not as self-consciously as did the state supreme court.

In *Johnson* any court presuming to rely on biological facts in settling Christopher's parentage was practically compelled to compare the significance of the genetic and gestational aspects of biological maternity. The trial court made this comparison and concluded, in marked contrast to the message about the importance of gestation underlying the unwed father cases, that gestation was of little moment in determining maternity. Judge Parslow, presiding in the trial court, paid heed to the part Anna played in the creation of the child, but clearly and unhesitatingly described her role in social, environmental—but not biological—terms. The court compared her to a foster parent who surrenders her parental role as soon as the child's "real" parent is able to resume a parenting role. For the trial court, genetics emerged as the primary factor linking a biological parent to his or her child. Judge Parslow, who gave his opinion orally, declared:

> Who we are and what we are and identity problems particularly with young children and teenagers are extremely important. We know that there is a combination of genetic factors. We know more and more about traits now, how you walk, talk and everything else, all sorts of things that develop out of your genes, how long you're going to live, all things being equal, when your immune system is going to break down, what diseases you may be susceptible to. They have upped the intelligence ratio of genetics to 70 percent now.[76]

Accordingly, the trial court identified the Calverts as Christopher's parents on the basis of their genetic connection to the child. "You have," the judge concluded, "Mark Calvert, Crispina Calvert and their child they call Christopher; three people in a family unit."[77]

Thus, the court unequivocally defined kinship through relationships based on a natural substance (genes). The family, as a legal entity, was delineated as a unit anchored in shared substance. The claims of the woman who carried and bore the baby, characterized by Justice Stewart in *Caban* as the party whose "parental relationship is clear," were no longer paramount. The great importance paid the gestational role in the earlier cases is replaced in *Johnson* by a clear statement that families are a matter of shared substance, a matter of genes. The trial court judge recognized this apparent shift and offered an explanation. He said: "One of the reasons we had a presumption that the person from whom the child emerged was the mother is it made that side of the transaction clear at birth. Paternity was always a matter of opinion, but you could always establish who delivered the child."[78] This explanation suggests that gestating and bearing a child were never important per se.

However, that questions the significance given to gestation as evidence not just of *who* the mother was but of *what* the mother was in the unwed father cases. For instance, in Justice Stewart's description in *Caban*, quoted by the Court's majority in *Lehr v. Robertson*,[79] carrying and bearing a child constituted a parental relationship. Until reproductive technology made other options available, gestation was not just the easiest way of identifying the mother, but was viewed as an inevitable correlate of being a genetic mother. The gestational role both signaled, and followed from, the substantial (genetic) link between a mother and her child.

In order for Judge Parslow to premise the legitimacy of Crispina Calvert's claims to motherhood on her "natural" maternity, he had to rend Anna's gestational role asunder from the biological links that make a mother a "mother." He accomplished this in two ways. First, he located the gestational role in a social, rather than a natural, domain. He defined gestation as a social role, akin to that of a temporary caretaker or foster parent. Then, and more forcefully, he redefined gestation as a matter almost entirely unrelated to familial affairs. He characterized Anna's gestation of the baby as primarily a business deal and thereby separated it decisively from any claim that gestation signals or symbolizes "real" maternity. Anna, concluded Judge Parslow, was to be paid $10,000 under the contract for her "pain and suffering." "I haven't carried a child myself," declared the judge, "but from what I've seen, it's a tough program. And I think altruism aside, there is nothing wrong with getting paid for nine months of what I understand to be a lot of misery and a lot of bad days."[80] Thus, Anna's gestational role was essentially a contractual, and not a biological, matter and could, as a result, be defined to exclude maternity.

In contrast, the Calverts' genetic connection to the child had to be defined to constitute parenthood *and* to harmonize with the notion that the gestation of the baby was a business deal. Accordingly, the judge characterized the Calverts' genetic contribution in multidimensional terms, as a link that constituted parenthood and as evidence of the privileges of ownership. The Calverts, said the court, were "desperate and longing for their *own genetic product.*"[81]

The court, unlike the New Jersey courts in *Baby M.*, did not base its decision on an express consideration of the baby's best interests. Rather, the trial court in *Johnson* presumed to identify the child's real parents on the basis of biological facts. However, as in *Baby M.*, the court found parental rights to lie in the couple that more fully reflected a traditional, middle-class family. Anna, who was part-black, part-Native American, and part-Irish, had from time to time been a welfare recipient.[82] Mark Calvert was white and Crispina, a Filipina. During the trial, Crispina's heritage, unlike that of Anna, was rarely mentioned by the media. Nicole Healy has suggested that it was almost as if Crispina, married to a white man, became white, and thus ethnically unmarked in contrast with Anna.[83] Whatever the precise effect of race in this case—and it was widely debated at the time of trial—the judge portrayed the biological "facts" to accord with and support a declaration of legal parentage in the married, middle-class couple rather than in the single, black, poorer woman who gestated the baby.

The state appellate court, relying on California statutes to affirm Judge Parslow's opinion, also stressed the significance of a genetic tie as the basis of a claim to parenthood. The court described genetics as "a powerful factor in human relationships. The fact that another person is, literally, developed from a part of oneself can furnish the basis for a profound psychological bond. Heredity can provide a basis of connection between two individuals for the duration of their lives."[84]

However, Justice Sills, writing for the appellate court, suggested, obliquely and almost in passing, that other "rational" bases for claims to maternity or paternity might exist. In the end, the appellate court, in declaring Crispina Calvert the "natural" mother, relied on statutory law that allowed a man or woman to be presumed a "natural" parent on the basis of blood tests which identified genetic similarities between the man or woman and the child. The court, expressly describing the rule as "rational and not arbitrary," allowed by implication for the possibility that other equally rational schemes might exist.

In fact, the viability of such alternative schemes was suggested by the Uniform Parentage Act itself, the key statute on which the appellate court relied in the case. The act provided that "between a child and the natural mother [the parent and child relationship] may be established by proof of her having given birth to the child." The court dismissed Anna's reliance on this section as a basis for her claims to "natural" maternity by asserting that the statute only gave a woman otherwise identified as a "natural mother" the right to refer to the birth process as proof of maternity. That reading is not, of course, inevitable. The legislative body that promulgated the statutory provision at issue simply assumed that the genetic and gestational mother were one; it is therefore not possible to presume anything about the legislative definition of "natural mother" in this case from a reading of the statute at hand. In fact, legislative bodies, both in the United States (where there is still relatively little legislation) and abroad, have tended to define motherhood as flowing more directly from the gestational, than the genetic, aspects of biological maternity.[85]

Johnson, unlike *Baby M.*, and unlike the unwed father cases, forced a selection between two women whose claims to motherhood could both be premised on biological facts. In *Johnson*, it was possible to demarcate genetics as the predominating biological fact without equating biological maternity and biological paternity. None of the opinions in the case spoke about the comparative significance of sperm and ovum donors vis-à-vis each other. The case required a choice between mothers, or more accurately between one mother and another mother plus her husband, the father, and did not call for selecting between claims to maternity and claims to paternity. For this reason, it seemed possible to minimize the significance of gestation in effecting maternity, to define gestation as social and contractual, but not biological, and to avoid threatening the presumption that men stand in relation to culture as women stand in relation to nature.

However, these conclusions were only fragiley grounded. As the state supreme court in *Johnson* recognized, neither the biological frame on which the trial court relied nor the statutory frame on which the appellate court relied, provided real guidance in resolving the questions the case presented. In fact, both common assumptions about biological parentage and the California parentage statute—itself based on the same essential assumptions about biological reproduction—could have been used to justify judicial recognition of Anna Johnson or of Crispina Calvert as the child's mother. Further, assumptions about the connections between biology and kinship and the statutory scheme that reflected those assumptions *could* have justified a decision to recognize both women—or neither woman—as mother to the child.

The state supreme court opinion in *Johnson* (presented and discussed in the next two chapters) recognized expressly the profound disruption presented by the new reproductive technologies to familiar assumptions about biological reproduction and accordingly to assumptions about the connection between biological reproduction and relations of kinship. As a result, that court rejected both biology and state law as guideposts for resolving the dispute.

The disruption to established expectations and understandings caused by the development of the new reproductive technologies seriously complicates the society's ongoing, and related, efforts to make sense of the transformation of the family away from the model developed during the nineteenth century—a transformation that was occurring obviously for several decades before the advent of the new reproductive technologies. In that transformation the family, once understand as the domain of life in which enduring, hierarchically organized relationships were more important than the individuals composing them, has come increasingly to be understood as a collectivity of autonomous individuals, more or less free to choose how, for how long, and in what ways to associate together as family members.

In deciding the unwed father cases and traditional surrogacy cases such as *Baby M.*, courts can preserve and have preserved the illusion that change to the family, although undeniably occurring, can be assimilated into traditional patterns and can thereby be contained. Thus, in the unwed father cases, certain fathers were given apparently new rights to their biological children but only in cases in which those fathers established relations with the mothers of their children that, even though nonmarital, resembled old-fashioned spousal relationships. And, similarly in *Baby M.*, the trial court, in particular, was able to recognize a surrogacy contract but only because the family produced by that contract reflected the court's own image of an old-fashioned nuclear family including a mother, a father, and their mutual child. These cases did not involve, and did not challenge, long-standing assumptions about the social implications of biological reproduction.

The effort to accept change, while apparently assimilating it to tradition, continued in *Johnson* but with less success—as the state supreme court, on appeal, explained. In *Johnson* and other, similar cases, the threat to traditional understandings of family is especially intense because the social and biological correlates of familial relationships are being challenged simultaneously. With gestational surrogacy—as well as a number of other reproductive possibilities such as embryo cryopreservation—the effort to preserve the illusion that nothing essential has changed collapses. Too much has changed too obviously. Moreover, the possibilities presented by the new reproductive technologies challenge central assumptions about the connections between biological reproduction and kinship. The change can genuinely be labeled revolutionary.

The remainder of this book examines the efforts of society and law to preserve order in the face of the breathtaking acceleration in rates of change to family life (already undergoing major transformation) and to understandings of the family introduced by the new reproductive technologies.

FIVE

Social Implications
of Biological Transformations

Disruptions to traditional understandings of family presented by surrogacy cases such as *Baby M.* and by cases questioning the state's response to unwed fathers are magnified many times in cases occasioned by the new reproductive technologies. Judicial responses to *Johnson v. Calvert,* reviewed in the previous chapter, suggest the enormity of the disruption.

Now, the society and the law must determine not only who is the mother, the father, or the baby, but what is a "mother," a "father," or a "baby." The simultaneous challenge to the social facts of family and to the biological facts of family precludes certainty of almost any sort. It becomes increasingly difficult to argue convincingly that biology is fate. Consequently, the actual fates that await children, or families, produced through assisted reproduction become potentially more variable and uncertain.

By threatening central assumptions about the biological correlates of family—assumptions that until recently were rarely examined at all— the new reproductive technologies endanger the ideological framework within which family has long been understood. In consequence, reproductive technology and the families it produces herald a more complete transformation of the American family than that which has already occurred. This chapter examines the complicated interaction between changing facts about human reproduction and the social transformation of the family.

I. The Biological "Facts"

Only within the past two decades has it become possible for humans to orchestrate the processes of human reproduction in a wide variety of ways. Previously, whatever people might have imagined the "miracle of birth" to imply, they viewed the process of reproduction as the essentially unchanging product of natural or supernatural forces. Even in recent centuries, Western society, reflecting the views of Western science and the perceived limits of scientific technology, understood human reproduction as a continuous process beginning with sexual intercourse between a man and a woman, including the fertilization of an egg (provided by the woman's body) by sperm (provided by the man's body), the subsequent development of the embryo within the woman's body, and then the birth of a baby from the body of the woman in whom conception occurred. Until the last few decades, only artificial insemination provided a means for humans to alter this process, and that procedure, although subject to harsh criticisms in the first half of the twentieth century, appeared to be an isolated and not particularly disrupting possibility. Then, within less than two decades, in vitro fertilization (IVF), cryopreserved embryos, and the transfer of embryos between women became routine medical procedures. In 1993, less than twenty years after the birth of the first baby conceived in vitro, over 30,000 IVF procedures were performed in the United States.[1]

IVF, originally known as "extracorporeal mammalian fertilization," was the first, and is still probably the most well-known, of the new reproductive technologies. The procedure, which separates reproduction from sexuality, involves fertilization outside a woman's body. IVF usually begins with a woman's undergoing a series of hormonal treatments to stimulate the production of multiple ova within a particular monthly cycle. Then, mature ova are retrieved from the woman's ovaries with minor surgery through the abdomen or the cervix. These ova are placed in a culture dish where they are combined with sperm. Fertilization, if successful, occurs here.

In 1981 two Englishmen, Robert Edwards and Patrick Steptoe, first announced that human embryos could be successfully frozen and stored.[2] Thus ova not implanted following retrieval and fertilization can be stored rather than discarded.[3] These fertilized ova (variously called zygotes, preembryos, or embryos) can be preserved in cryoprotectants for years and can, later, be thawed for implantation in the body of the woman in whom the ova was produced or in the body of some other woman. In the United States the first live birth following implantation of a thawed embryo occurred in 1985.[4] Also in the early 1980s, a pregnancy was first produced using donated ova. Thus, gestational surrogacy became a possibility.

Embryo transfer, used in gestational surrogacy, and the cryopreservation of human embryonic and gametic matter clearly disrupt temporal and spatial expectations about the processes of human reproduction. In addition to these possibilities others, which seem similarly to disrupt expectations about reproduction, have already been used to produce a pregnancy or seem likely to be used to produce a pregnancy in humans within the next few years. It is already possible to obtain viable sperm from recently dead men. In theory, eggs could be similarly removed from the body of dead women. Eggs removed from livestock immediately after slaughter have been fertilized and have been used to produce successful pregnancies. As a result of posthumous insemination or the posthumous fertilization of eggs, children can be conceived after the deaths of both genetic parents. The possibility of retrieving and maturing ova from aborted fetuses and then using those ova in donation programs could soon become a technological reality. That would lead to the gestation of children whose "mothers" had never been born.

These possibilities occasioned by assisted reproduction present such novel scenarios as children with multiple biological mothers (or arguably with no "real" biological mother), as seen in *Johnson v. Calvert*, or embryos stored in test tubes for extended periods so that a woman would be able, for example, to gestate her own mother's or grandmother's sibling (her own "aunt," "uncle," "great-aunt," or "great-uncle"). For instance, a woman, call her Sue, could become the mother of her own sibling if the gamete donors (Sue's parents) had an embryo cryopreserved and then, years later, that embryo was thawed and implanted in Sue's uterus. Sue could then gestate and give birth to the resulting baby. Had the embryo in question developed in vivo, without the interruption that cryopreservation allows, the embryo would have been born a generation earlier as its mother Sue's "sister" or "brother." Similarly, a woman could become mother to her aunt or uncle in a case in which the cryopreserved embryo was donated by her grandparents rather than by her parents. Obviously the use of the words "sister," "brother," and "aunt," as well as "mother," could be vigorously debated.

The challenge to definitions of family is far-reaching and social responses are still sparse and generally inadequate. That notwithstanding, the new reproductive technologies have developed in concert with existing scientific paradigms that explain human reproduction. The development of reproductive technology has not depended upon the development of a new vision of human reproduction. Reproductive technology multiplies the ways through which human reproduction can occur but has not widely challenged existing scientific paradigms that explain the biological facts of human reproduction. In fact, reproductive technology uses existing paradigms and even serves to demonstrate their accuracy and power by multiplying the possibilities for controlling the processes of reproduction. The technology is not revolutionary because it challenges a contemporary scientific vision. Rather, it is revolutionary because it actualizes that vision through the control and manipulation of biological processes previously understood as "natural" and as impervious to human manipulation.

In short, reproductive technology has not unsettled a familiar and important scientific theory, and, therefore, changes occasioned by reproductive technology do not challenge the theories that explain how reproduction occurs. Rather, these changes disrupt the very notion that the science of human reproduction reflects a natural, unyielding process, and question the fundamental assumption that human reproduction is the result of natural processes which inevitably define social relationships. Already this technology challenges traditional understandings of mother, father, and child.

Other, far more dramatic possibilities seem decades, rather than centuries, away. Once babies can be manufactured in laboratories, a possibility that has not (yet) been realized but that is no longer imaginable only as science fiction, then the biological correlates of human reproduction will no longer—or at least will no longer easily and automatically— ground securely the values and beliefs that Americans have traditionally attached to family. The loss of the biological anchor has not yet, and may never, completely negate those values and beliefs, but it does remove the certainty with which traditional values and beliefs about family were assumed and invoked.

As a result, disputes occasioned by the new reproductive technologies provide remarkably fruitful contexts for furthering the more fundamental debate about the form and future of the family itself. Since family disputes resulting from gestational surrogacy or cryopreserved embryos occur in a context in which both the social and biological aspects of family are questioned, traditional understandings of the social order can be invoked to justify, to condemn, or to mask the significance of the transformations. However, as options for defining and regulating the family multiply, expectations about the family and about the contours of familial relationships are less and less widely agreed upon and actualized. The biological facts, especially as they become increasingly subject to change, can be invoked and analyzed to justify decisions about the scope and design of the social order or to condemn changes that seem to defy the dictates of what could once be taken unequivocally as natural truth. Litigants and courts, like the society of which they form a part, can no longer continue to assume that the biological facts of human reproduction ground the family and familial relationships in an unyielding reality. Increasingly, the traditional anchors—the biological and social correlates of family—are being simultaneously dislocated. And so the terms through which such disputes are aired and resolved are being constructed. The terms chosen, and the meanings attached to those terms, broadly suggest emerging understandings of family and of personhood.

The new reproductive technologies are being taken to signal the end of order or alternatively the achievement of unprecedented possibilities of choice and happiness. For some, reproductive technology and the social arrangements that may accompany it, violate the natural order, and thus augur social chaos. The anthropologist Robin Fox, for instance, argues as a matter of scientific fact that a woman bonds with a child that she carries in her body. He therefore concludes that "if we try to force bonded mothers to give up their children in the name of contract . . . we will fail—or at least deserve to fail."[5] For others, reproductive technology simply affords more joy by providing more routes, and thus more opportunities, to create families and familial relationships. Those families can be imagined on the model of traditional families or on other, less traditional models. One British journalist, arguing that reproductive technology does not alter the character of families, proclaimed: "This is what science is for, the extension of human happiness through choice."[6] Thus, reproductive technology can be viewed as disturbing the social incidents of family as it alters the biological dimensions through which families are created or it can be viewed as leaving the social incidents of family essentially untouched. Other, intermediate positions are possible and are being voiced.

In the face of the myriad confusions and uncertainties posed by reproductive technology, disputing parties in cases involving this technology rely with remarkable consistency on biological facts to present their arguments in court. Since the moral and existential implications of the facts of human reproduction, but not the facts per se, are usually in dispute, opposing litigants rely on essentially the same biological facts. Those facts are then presented to the court, by the disputing litigants taken as a group, as conclusive evidence of contradictory social truths.

Consequently, the biological facts dim in significance. For example, if the biological facts can demonstrate equally that a genetic mother and a gestational mother are "real" mothers (or that neither is fully a mother), then a dispute such as that in *Johnson* between competing mothers must ultimately be resolved without appeal to biology. In the end, defining the family as a social reality that follows clearly and inevitably from the biological facts of family becomes increasingly difficult. That is of tremendous significance to a society that has assumed for hundred of years that kinship follows from biological relationships.

II. What Is a Biological Mother?

Many of the interpretive conundrums to which gestational surrogacy gives rise emerged in the context of *Johnson* and *McDonald v. McDonald* (a 1994 New York case), taken together. While *Johnson* involved a couple each of whom provided a gamete to be joined and then gestated in another woman's uterus, *McDonald* involved a wife who gestated an embryo formed from the fertilization of a donated ovum with her husband's sperm.

Johnson v. Calvert

As described in chapter 4, the two lower courts that rendered decisions in *Johnson* relied respectively on biology and on statutory law to give the baby Christopher to Mark and Crispina Calvert, the genetic parents, rather than to Anna Johnson, the gestational parent. The California Supreme Court affirmed that holding but on very different grounds. The state supreme court, concluding that neither biology nor the state's statutory definition of mother provided adequate criteria for selecting between Crispina and Anna, relied on neither. Moreover, the court refused to accept the plea of amicus curiae that both women be denominated "mother." In reaching its holding in *Johnson*, the state supreme court (affirming the holdings of the lower courts which named the Calverts as the child's only parents) relied on the notion of parental intent. That notion, as well as its implications and potential usefulness in cases such as *Johnson*, is examined in chapter 6.

Even though the highest California court largely ignored the biological correlates of Crispina's and Anna's respective claims to maternity, the litigants did not. The Calverts and Johnson based their appeals to the court on alternative interpretations of the reproductive process that led to the birth of baby Christopher.

In premising her parenthood on biological truth, Anna Johnson, for instance, argued that nature inevitably creates a bond between a woman and a baby that she gestates and bears, and that the preservation and development of that bond establishes the mother-child connection. She further argued that the link between a woman and the baby she gestates is more significant from a biological perspective "than [that] of the genetic donors."[7] The Calverts stressed their biological link to the child as conclusive of their parentage and of Anna's essentially incidental role in the creation of their child. They argued that the embryo, produced from their gametes and fertilized in vitro, was "already defined [as] a new human individual"[8] before it was implanted in Johnson's uterus. Thus, in the Calverts' presentation, Johnson could not premise her maternity on biology since, as a biological matter, the embryo—and thus the complete being that was their child—existed before uterine implantation.

The briefs as a whole demonstrate the remarkable flexibility with which society and the law can invoke and interpret biological definitions of reproduction. Once assumed to present the essence of natural parentage, genes can be defined variously and may, among other things, represent an almost incidental donation to the woman who maintains a "blood relationship" with a baby she has gestated and to which she has given birth.[9] Similarly, gestation takes on new meanings as judicial responses to *Johnson* suggest. Gestation was long understood, and was described specifically by the U.S. Supreme Court in the cases involving the paternal rights of unwed fathers, as the symbol and essential instance of biological maternity—as the inviolable biological fact that distinguished maternity from paternity and that made biological maternity synonymous with social and legal maternity. Now gestation can be interpreted, as it was by the trial court in *Johnson*, as creative of a social and incidental, rather than a biological and thus permanent, connection between a woman and the baby she gestates and bears. Thus, Judge Parslow could describe Anna's role as "analogous to that of a foster parent." [10]

The facts of *Johnson* challenge—and affirm—a wide array of meanings that society presently attaches to the terms that define human reproduction—terms such as fertilization, embryo, fetus, blood relationship, and gene. Despite growing indications as the case moved through the California courts that biological truths would prove conclusive for neither side, each side continued vehemently to argue that its biological connection to the child should be determinative.

Each prospective mother argued that her connection to the child was more substantial than the connection of the "other mother" in the sense that her connection was more real. Crispina Calvert and Anna Johnson each tried to distinguish the real, enduring relationship (her own) from the more ephemeral one. Each defined her relationship to the child in terms of an inexorable biological connection. Each woman argued that her own biological connection was more significant, either qualitatively (e.g., more natural) or quantitatively (e.g., involving a greater investment of pain, time, or energy). Yet, for both sides, the shadow of the other's biological connection to baby Christopher, however fleeting, made it impossible to rely upon traditional assumptions about the substantial connection that links mothers to their children.

The power of the claim that biological mothers could once make in asserting their maternity depended on the exclusivity of the claim. In cases occasioned by reproductive technology, assertions of biological maternity no longer necessarily determine social maternity. Once the traditional assumptions about maternity—and "blood" relations more generally—are challenged by novel reproductive possibilities, the entire scheme within which those relations once made sense collapses.

In the wake of that collapse, the old terms continue to seem important—even momentarily conclusive. In fact, the frame within which their conclusiveness was once assured has eroded. Consequently, the parties in *Johnson*, and in other similar cases, continue to argue back and forth, each asserting her special claim to maternity in light of traditional understandings of motherhood. But as the arguments proceed, each side's claims are confused with, and ultimately become substitutable for, those of the other. Thus, the claims of both sides flounder and, in their attempt to undermine each other, ultimately undermine themselves. Moreover, the respect once accorded biological truth as an arbiter in defining familial relationships necessarily diminishes.

In *Johnson*, the differences between, and comparative significance of, genetic and gestational contributions to the production of a child define the terms of the debate. In other cases, the terms of the debate are differently defined. In cases occasioned by reproductive technology, the debate about the significance and implications of particular biological facts becomes a debate about something even larger. Ironically, *Johnson*, and other cases like it, question the fundamental relevance of biological facts to the definition of family relationships. Consequently, such cases almost inevitably enter the contemporary debate about the changing meaning and implications of "family" in American society.

Thus it becomes important to examine in detail the shifting meanings of the symbols of maternity in *Johnson*. Several sorts of contentions, more or less expressly articulated by the parties, constituted the principal themes presented to the courts in *Johnson*. Among these were conflicting contentions about the meanings of mother and parent, the particular meaning of the term "blood mother," and conflicting contentions about the role that choice can or should play for the society and the law in determining parentage. The parties considered each of these contentions through reference to the comparative significance of genetic and gesta-tional contributions to the creation and development of a baby.

Significantly, none of the parties in *Johnson* argued that familial, including maternal, relationships should be determined without refer-ence to biological connection. In fact, either side could have argued that culture, not nature, should determine parentage. Johnson, for instance, might have emphasized that based on her social and psychological bonds with the baby, forged in fact during the long months of gestation, she, and she alone, had already psychologically become a parent—the only "parent" figure in the newborn child's life. The Calverts, in turn, might have presented (as the California Supreme Court did) the surrogacy contract and the parties' preconception plans as conclusive of the child's parentage. Although the Calverts obviously argued for the legality and enforceability of the surrogacy contract entered into between themselves and Anna Johnson, even that argument was embedded in the discussion of the parties' comparative biological claims.[11]

Instead, each side premised its claim to parenthood on the unique significance of its biological connection to the baby. The Calverts argued that a person is the consequence of his or her parents' combined gametic material, and that, accordingly, at the fertilization stage of development, the identity of a new human individual has already been defined.[12] The Calverts defined Anna Johnson's role as essentially indistinguishable from that of the laboratory in which the egg was fertilized and developed before implantation in Johnson's uterus:

> From the moment that sperm successfully penetrates the ovum and im-pregnation is achieved a new generation of human exists. It is within the care and custody of medical experts that in the laboratory provide the environment in which the embryo grows and matures until it is ready for implantation into the uterus. These laboratories and experts sustained the embryo during a time when it could not survive in utero, at a time when Anna Johnson could not provide the environment and care needed.
>
> Likewise, Crispina Calvert could not provide the uterus with which to care for the embryo, Anna Johnson could. She was entrusted with the embryo's care until it developed and matured and Crispina and Mark Calvert were able to provide the proper environment and care.
>
> It cannot rationally be said that there is a distinction between paying for the care of the ovum by the doctors and clinic and paying for the care of the ovum by the gestational mother.[13]

Thus, the Calverts suggested that while Anna Johnson's role may have been biological, it was not the role of a biological mother.

Johnson, in response, took issue with the Calverts' (and the trial court's) understanding of biological reproduction. "There is no founda-tion in science," she declared in presenting her case to the appellate court, "to define Biology . . . to contribute to the conclusion [sic] that an actual birth mother is not a natural Biological parent."[14] Johnson defined her psychological relationship to the child as a natural consequence of her having gestated and given birth to the baby. She further argued that because her biological maternity (unlike that of Crispina Calvert) en-tailed a relationship to the baby, her gestational role, unlike the Calvert's genetic role, reliably predicted that she would not just be a mother but that she would be a good mother—a better mother—to the baby.

In presenting her case to the appellate court, Johnson quoted exten-sively in her brief from the testimony of Dr. Michelle Harrison, a psychia-trist who had served as an expert for Johnson at trial. "The baby in Anna Johnson's womb," Dr. Harrison asserted, "is not the same baby that would have been in the womb of Mrs. Calvert. Therein lies the total misconception." That misconception, Dr. Harrison explained, was that "a baby is made from DNA."[15] Harrison agreed without qualification when asked at trial whether it could be said that "the biological contribution of the birth mother to the creation of the baby is greater than the biological contribution of the commissioning parents who donate egg and sperm."[16]

Harrison further characterized Johnson's gestational bond to the baby as the bond of "love":[17]

> In my interview with Ms. Johnson, she talked tearfully about the experience of nursing the baby . . . of her belief that he recognizes her by odor, and when she has him he roots to nurse since she has continued to nurse even during the visitations. She believes that he feels safe and falls asleep easily in her arms.[18]

When Harrison was later asked to explain the assertion that the baby recognized Johnson "by odor," she responded:

> There are actually some scientific studies demonstrating newborn's [sic] familiarity with the odor of the mother whey [sic] they have been nursed. And Anna in this case . . . described how it felt to her when he began to root. In other words, when she would pick him up after many days of not seeing him and he would begin to root for her breast.[19]

Finally, Johnson's lawyer asked Harrison what "make[s] a woman a mother." She answered:

> What makes her a mother is her emotional and physical work in the nurturing of the fetus, and the way in which . . . her body builds the baby. Her body brings it oxygen, her body takes away waste, her body protects it . . . from bacteria [and] from external assault.[20]

Harrison further declared that the mother's body "treats [the embryo] as though it were the same tissue as the tissue of her hands or her heart or anything else. And as that process goes on, she also incorporates the baby into her psychological development."[21]

Harrison's testimony answered the Calvert's claim to genetic exclusivity and allowed Johnson to argue that her biological connection to the baby, unlike that of the Calverts, encompassed, and thus guaranteed, the fact and the success of her psychological and social maternity. Johnson proclaimed that she was the baby's social mother *because* she was the gestational mother. In short, she argued that her social relationship to the child was an inevitable result of a natural process and therefore, superior to any relationship the Calverts might effect with the child.

As each woman relied on biological facts to prove herself the only natural mother, both parties engaged in several subsidiary controversies. Anna Johnson and Crispina Calvert each presented herself to the court as the baby's blood mother. Traditionally, the term "blood mother" has been synonymous with "real mother"; for centuries "blood" has been understood, at least metaphorically, as the essential substantial connection between a mother and her child. In the post-Mendelian era, at least until recently, the terms "blood mother" and "genetic mother" have generally been understood as synonyms. Now, with the availability of gestational surrogacy, it has become possible to argue that a child's genetic mother and blood mother are two different people. The genetic mother, according to this argument, is the ovum donor; the blood mother is the woman who gestates the fetus, sharing her blood with that of the fetus during the period of fetal development. Until the early 1980s however, it was assumed that the real relationship between a woman and her child results not from a literal contribution of maternal blood to a fetus but from a woman's genetic contribution to the embryo.

In a curious twist, the advent of gestational surrogacy, along with other technological possibilities such as DNA blood testing, once again encourages people to understand blood literally as a substance shared between a woman and baby and as an indicator of fetal-maternal identity. Thus each woman was able to present herself as the baby's blood mother. Presumably, in characterizing herself as the blood mother, each woman intended to draw on the power traditionally associated with the metaphoric attribution "blood mother." Each woman used the language of scientific and legal discourse, not the language of poetic metaphor, to show concretely that her maternity could conclusively and uniquely be premised on similarities between her blood and that of the child.

The Calverts invoked several provisions in California law that together allowed a child's genetic mother to be declared the child's legal mother. The provisions in questions, repealed in 1992, the year after the birth of Christopher, were found in the Uniform Parentage Act, enacted in California in 1975 as part of the California Civil Code. Focusing on the blood testing which can be used to establish genetic relationships, the Calverts hypothesized:

> Assuming this, or for that matter, any child were confused with a number of other children in the hospital nursery. Assuming further that no other identifying data is available. Could then Anna Johnson prove her maternity? Indeed, only Crispina Calvert could, by blood tests, prove her maternal connection to the child.[22]

The Calverts also urged that the law recognize the continued importance of preserving "human blood lines." The "social value" of human blood lines, they declared, "is incalculable, for it is through our progeny that we perpetuate culture, traditions and history."[23]

The Calverts specifically denied that there was a "blood relationship" between Johnson and the baby.[24] Presumably, the Calverts intended the term "blood relationship" to serve as a synonym for genetic relationship. Anna Johnson, in turn, presented herself as the child's blood mother. In doing so, she relied on her gestational connection to the baby, referring to the "mixing of blood between mother and baby" that occurs through the placenta and at birth.[25] Dr. David Chamberlain, who testified for Johnson at trial, described Johnson and the baby as "intimately attached and biochemically related." In the language of medical science, he described that attachment concretely:

> There is a flooding of catecholamines. The mother's blood stream carries adrenal hormones through the placenta to the baby's blood. Virtually everything that the mother has going on in her body and blood stream goes directly through to the baby. This is absolutely main stream medical thinking.[26]

Finally, in characterizing herself as the baby's blood mother, Johnson argued that she too could claim parenthood on the basis of blood tests. In response to the Calverts' claim that they alone could demonstrate parentage on the basis of blood tests, Johnson maintained:

> Respondents [the Calverts] claim that it would be impossible for Anna Johnson to prove her maternity if the hospital nursery had mixed up the babies in the hospital. Not only was this issue never litigated or proved at trial, but the premise, once again is a total falsehood.
>
> Dr. Klaus, Dr. Call, Dr. Chamberlain and Dr. Harrison all agreed that the baby was born with Anna Johnson's antibodies and hormones.[27] Test-

ing the antibodies and hormones could therefore prove maternity and clearly identify the baby.[28]

Thus, both the Calverts and Anna Johnson used expert testimony presenting the biological facts of maternity to persuade the courts that Anna or Crispina, respectively, should be exclusively identified as Christopher's blood mother—and therefore as his real mother.

In the end, the parties' claims about the identity of the baby's blood mother prove inconclusive, as do their claims about the comparative significance of Anna's gestational, and Crispina's genetic, contribution to the baby's development. Indeed, the parties' contentions almost neutralize each other, so that the identification of a single "real" mother on the basis of the biological facts and arguments presented becomes largely a matter of social choice.

The obvious challenge such controversies pose to the biological facts themselves—and, more importantly, to the relevance of biological facts altogether in defining the family and characterizing familial relationships—encourages new interpretations of human reproduction and its social implications. Two further examples from the *Johnson* case illustrate this point.

The first involves Johnson's suggestion that Crispina Calvert, more like a father than a mother, could not premise her parenthood on a biological connection to the child. The second, in direct contrast, involves the suggestion, made expressly by amicus curiae, that Christopher was the child of two mothers.

Anna Johnson, responding to the Calverts' presentation of the biological facts, reinterpreted the social implications of those facts so as to define the Calverts, or at least Crispina Calvert, as biologically—and thus socially—abnormal. Anna acknowledged Crispina's genetic contribution, but redefined that contribution to be something other than that of a mother.

Dr. Harrison, testifying as an expert for Johnson at trial, declared:

[I]t's really I think more like Anna is the mother and the Calverts are the other half, the other interest. Like as I say, again, much more like a father, and again, that's not—I mean, our language is gender related so it has implications which I don't mean in this sense, but they are the genetic part of the child.[29]

Accordingly, Johnson argued: "Both appellees stood in the shoes of an expectant father, as each provided genetic material which impregnated Appellant." [30]

The argument illustrates the remarkable flexibility with which the symbols of human reproduction are being interpreted and the far-reaching social consequences of such interpretations. By elaborating the implications of a traditional association between gestation and maternity and between a seminal (genetic) donation and paternity, Johnson defined a genetic mother as more like a father than a mother. Johnson thus asserted that she should be recognized as the baby's real mother—the parent for whom biology both encompasses and assures an ongoing social connection with the child—and that the Calverts together be recognized as the baby's "father." Thus Johnson's interpretation of the biological facts associates Johnson and her claims to maternity with familiar, old-fashioned understandings of motherhood, and in contrast defines Crispina's role as incidental (since the child clearly has a father already) or as perverse, with the lurking suggestion that a woman so distorted should not be recognized as the mother of a child who has a normal mother already on hand.

Even more, the very same biological facts on which Johnson relied, were used by other parties to suggest that Christopher had not one mother (Johnson) and two fathers (the Calverts) but two mothers (Anna Johnson and Crispina Calvert) and one father (Mark Calvert). The American Civil Liberties Union, writing as an amicus curiae, declared that Anna and Crispina should each be recognized as mother.[31] The courts, anxious to preserve a more traditional view of family, rejected the notion.

Certainly, the courts could have identified three biological parents, including two biological mothers. Had they been determined to define the biological, rather than the contractual or social, parents as the baby's legal parents, then, a conclusion that both Anna and Crispina were biological mothers would have been quite plausible—even perhaps inevitable. While none of the courts accepted this conclusion, each court's reasoning allowed for such a possibility.

The state supreme court directly addressed the possibility of two biological mothers, declaring that both women "have adduced evidence of a mother and child relationship as contemplated by [California law]. Yet for the child California law recognizes only one natural mother,

despite advances in reproductive technology rendering a different outcome biologically possible."[32] The assertion is reminiscent of one found
in Justice Scalia's plurality opinion in *Michael H.* There, denying paternal rights to an unwed biological father given the mother's marriage with
another man, the Court declared that "California law, like nature itself,
makes no provision for dual fatherhood."[33] The facts in *Michael H.*
support the invocation of nature as arbiter of social truth. Those in
Johnson do not.

Even the Calverts, who had argued consistently for their exclusive
biological parentage, responded to the ACLU's recommendations by
asserting that a judicial finding of two mothers (or three parents) would
ill serve the child's best interests.[34] That contention averts, but does not
gainsay, Anna Johnson's claim to biological maternity.

In fact, the unanimity with which the courts rejected the possibility of
a three-parent family is partly explained by the threat that such a possibility poses to traditional understandings of family, apart from *any* account-
ing or interpretation of the biological facts. In divorcing families, steppar-
ents may be understood clearly as social parents, related to the children
through marriage to one of the biological parents. The increasing inci-
dence of divorce and stepparent families in the last several decades has
itself threatened the traditional family; but that threat is understood as
one of social change rather than of changes in the very nature of things,
and therein differs from the threat to traditional notions of the family
posed by gestational surrogacy cases. The latter threat at once directly
challenges traditional assumptions about the biological correlates of parentage and traditional assumptions about the parameters of family.

The social contours of family have been consistently defined through
reference to the biological correlates of familial relationships. As a result,
shifts in the meaning or use of the biological facts of family more
seriously threaten traditional understandings of the family than do shifts
in what appear to be social patterns. Social patterns can be altered, and
later rejected; but biological facts, Western society has long held, reflect
the very nature of things and thus pose seemingly secure limits to the
definition of family.

Gestational surrogacy simultaneously suggests both a new form of
family and a new understanding of the biological facts through which
shifts in social patterns might be understood and assimilated. As a result
of this simultaneous shift in society's understanding of the social and

biological facts of family, the possibilities for new forms of family multiply accordingly.

In the world of gestational surrogacy—a world in which parties can press their claims by arguing that a child has two fathers and one mother or, with apparently equal sanity, that the same child has two biological mothers and one father, the traditional anchors, that made family relationships inexorable, have vanished. Various interpretations of family, and of the connections between the biological and social components of family, may continue to align themselves with tradition. However, understandings of family can no longer be grounded in absolute and inexorable truth.

McDonald v. McDonald

McDonald, a divorce action filed in New York in 1990, resembles *Johnson*, in that it too involved a dispute over the parentage of children born to a gestational mother. In *McDonald*, however, the woman who intended from the start to be the social mother provided the gestational, but not the genetic, component of biological maternity. The case further differs from *Johnson* in that the dispute in *McDonald* was between a man (a father) and a woman (a mother) rather than between two women (or rather, one woman and another woman together with her husband).

The McDonalds, he a podiatrist, she an M.D., married in 1988. Unsuccessful at conceiving a child, the couple sought medical assistance from an infertility clinic. Eventually, embryos were created through the use of donor eggs, fertilized by Robert McDonald's sperm. The embryos were implanted in Olga McDonald's uterus, and in February 1991 twin girls were born.

Before the birth of the children, Robert filed for divorce. He sought sole custody of both children. As described by a New York appellate court,[35] Robert argued that he, as the "only genetic and natural parent available,"[36] brought the superior claim to parentage. Accordingly, he contended that Olga, as a gestational, but not a genetic, parent, should play no custodial role as long as a genetic parent was available to do so. The appellate division disagreed and affirmed the trial court's grant of custody to Olga.

From a biological perspective, the facts in *McDonald* are a mirror image of those in *Johnson*. The two cases differ in that in *McDonald*, the "intending" mother was the gestational, but not the genetic, mother. In contrast, Crispina Calvert was Christopher's genetic, but not his gestational, mother. Almost reflexively, courts and others, including the media, have characterized the role of the gestational mother entirely differently in the two sorts of cases. Anna Johnson is called a gestational surrogate and the case is referred to as a gestational surrogacy case. In contrast, Olga McDonald is described as a gestational mother or as a mother who used donor eggs to conceive her child. In either case, she is described as a mother, and *McDonald* is characterized as an "ovum donor" case. The California Supreme Court in *Johnson* justified those differences by concluding that, in such cases, the intentional mother is the natural (and thus legal) mother. Some commentators have posited that class differences that often exist between intentional mothers and gestational surrogates have affected the assumptions that society and the law bring to such cases. On the other hand, class differences do not generally distinguish intentional/gestational mothers from ovum donors. Many anonymously donated ova are provided by women who are themselves undergoing infertility treatments. In fact, such women are sometimes encouraged to donate ova in exchange for reduced IVF fees. As a group such women are at least moderately well-off. Moreover, the very issue of class differences between gestational/intentional mothers and ovum donors is usually masked for the parties because the identity of ovum donors, unlike that of gestational surrogates, is usually not revealed to the intending parents. Similarly, ovum donors generally will not know the identity of the intending parents.

In fact, the appellate court in *McDonald*, like the state supreme court in *Johnson*, found the intending mother to be the "natural" mother. *McDonald* is significant in this regard because the conclusion that Olga McDonald was the twins' "natural" mother was not compelled by statutory law. In contrast, the conclusion of the California Supreme Court in *Johnson*, that the intentional mother was the "natural" mother, arguably followed from parts of California's statutory provisions that regulated the identification of a child's "natural" mother.

Relying expressly on the decision of the California Supreme Court in *Johnson*, the *McDonald* court determined Olga to be the natural mother because she was the intentional mother. *McDonald* relied on a footnote in *Johnson* in which the court elaborated the implications of its decision that in cases of split biological maternity, the woman whose "acted-on intention" caused the child to be conceived and born should be named the child's "natural," and thus only, mother. The *Johnson* court explained: "Thus, under our analysis, in a true 'egg donation' situation, where a woman gestates and gives birth to a child formed from the egg of another woman with the intent to raise the child as her own, the birth mother is the natural mother under California law."[37] Relying on that characterization, the *McDonald* court concluded:

> In the case at bar, we have a true "egg donation" situation, and we find the reasoning of the Supreme Court of California on this issue to be persuasive. Accordingly, the Supreme Court, Queens County, correctly held that in the instant "donation" case, the wife, who is the gestational mother, is the natural mother of the children, and is, under the circumstances, entitled to temporary custody of the children with visitation to the husband.[38]

In *McDonald*, as in *Johnson*, the parties supported their claims to parenthood through references to the biological facts. And as in *Johnson* the parties interpreted those facts to support contradictory conclusions about the parentage of the twin daughters born to Olga.

Robert, in claiming parentage and asking for sole custody of the children, relied largely on his genetic connection to the babies and the absence of a comparable connection between Olga and the twins. He described himself as "the sole genetic parent among the parties" and Olga as a "genetic stranger" to his children.[39] In large part, his arguments parallel arguments asserted by the Calverts. However, unlike the Calverts, who presented themselves as a traditional, married couple, Robert asked for custody as a divorcing man and single parent.

Olga's arguments to the court contrast with those of Robert and with the arguments presented by all the parties in *Johnson* in that Olga focused on the social correlates of her maternity. Certainly, she described her biological contribution to the babies' creation, but for the most part she presented that contribution as evidence of her motherliness (a social matter) rather than as evidence of an inexorable claim to "natural" maternity. For a number of reasons, Olga, unlike Anna Johnson, was able to stress the maternal behavior she had exhibited, and continued to exhibit, toward the children. In contrast, Anna Johnson's ability to present herself as a good mother was curtailed by the very fact of her having entered into the agreement to gestate, and then to forego, maternal claims to a baby. Moreover, Olga, although in the midst of divorce proceedings, was married to the father of the babies she had gestated and borne and thus had the advantage of having started her relationship to the babies in a traditional mother-father-children triad. In addition, Olga, unlike Anna, had retained custody after the children's births and had continued to serve as their custodial parent. Finally, Olga's claims to maternity, unlike those of Anna, opposed the claims of a father and not those of another mother. For all these reasons, Olga was able to construct her case by relying on a set of arguments that had not been available to Anna Johnson.

Olga explicitly distinguished *Johnson* from her own case. She submitted her brief prior to the California Supreme Court's ruling in *Johnson*, which, to Olga's benefit, relied on maternal intent to establish "natural" maternity. Refuting the relevance of the lower court rulings in *Johnson*, Olga declared that she could not be described as a "surrogate."[40] She further asserted:

> In the instant case, there is no contest between the egg donor and the respondent [Olga] for custody, and therefore it is still a one (1) mother/one (1) father scenario. There is no need for this Court to be concerned about the psychological impact it might have on a child to be brought up with two (2) mothers.
>
> Conversely, it is the appellant who would like to deprive the children [of] the only mother that they have ever known. It is respectfully submitted that such deprivation would in fact have a devastating effect upon the children.
>
> This Court is not bound by the *Calvert* ruling and may find that there is much more significance to the individual who actually gives the children life. In the analysis of the instant case, it is important to note that the child was born during a legal marriage and therefore is presumed to be the legitimate issue of *both* parents.[41]

Certainly, Olga referred to her gestational role as a significant aspect of her maternity. However, in describing that role, she stressed the pain and suffering that the embryo implantation and the subsequent pregnancy had brought her, rather than the physiological processes of maternal bonding on which Anna Johnson had focused. Olga portrayed the history of her pregnancy in detail. In doing so, she focused on her own endurance, and asserted that Robert had continually attempted to undermine the pregnancy's success. For instance, Olga claimed she responded to an early period of spotting in the pregnancy with devastation and grief. In contrast, she proclaimed that Robert had expressed delight that " 'the experiment had failed.' "[42] She further described Robert as having thought of the developing fetuses as " 'freaks, monsters and anomalies' "[43] and to have urged termination of the pregnancy. Olga said that later stages of the pregnancy brought her continuing anxiety and illness. Each diagnostic sonogram, she reported, "was a veritable nightmare" for her.[44] Later, beset with serious symptoms caused by the ongoing pregnancy, Olga chose to continue the pregnancy rather than risk a seriously premature birth:

> The respondent decided to sacrifice her own life and try to endure the complicated pregnancy a little longer so that the children could be born healthy and normal. The toxemia got so much worse that the respondent experienced swelling all over her body, had extensive nose bleeds and was totally unable to walk, and required a wheelchair to get around.[45]

At the birth Olga, treated with local rather than general, anesthesia, was "aware of every incision, cut, contraction and the incredible pain, yet was only concerned about the welfare of the children. Out of that near death experience came two very healthy and beautiful girls."[46]

Olga's biological maternity, as she described it, involved almost unrelenting emotional and physical agony, from conception through birth. For Olga, her constant sacrifice and courage during that period indicate the quality of her maternity. Thus, she claimed that her experiences and reactions during pregnancy, especially when compared with Robert's disdain, proved her the better parent.

Alongside this characterization of her pregnancy and maternity, Olga presented another type of argument about the biology of reproduction. She suggested that the new options for human reproduction made available by technological advances such as in vitro fertilization call for a far-reaching reevaluation of the social implications of biological maternity and paternity. "This court must recognize," Olga declared, "that such onerous terms, like 'genetic stranger,' [sic] have no place in a world which has embraced new reproductive technology as a necessary means to assist individuals in their desires to procreate."[47] The argument rests on the presumption that reproductive technology is good. Olga supported that presumption by arguing that reproductive technology provides a new set of solutions to an old and troubling problem—the problem of infertility. Using herself as an example, Olga asserted that she, "[l]ike many individuals . . . so desperately desired to either bear a child or have one borne for her, that she turned to the advances of medical technology to assist her in that important goal."[48]

Thus, Olga argued that reproductive technology should rightly be viewed as a means for relieving human suffering—suffering created in the absence of family—and that, in consequence, the requisite reinterpretation of human reproduction could be justified by reference to the significance of family. Analyzing the sort of strategy Olga took (though writing about a different context), the English anthropologist Marilyn Strathern, explains: "Arguments in favour of embracing the new reproductive technologies can point to them as techniques that will alleviate suffering and provide remedies for disability, and thus enable the family to take its proper and traditional form."[49] For Olga, a societal decision to adopt reproductive technology preserves traditional families by helping to create them. The likelihood that this decision may challenge society's most fundamental assumptions about the biological correlates of family is presented as essentially inconsequential. Thus, Olga suggests that parentage should not be exclusively premised on a genetic connection between parent and child.

In place of that familiar assumption, she offers a view of family epitomized by her own sacrificial role as the gestator of her twin daughters. Olga pled that the social implications of biological reproduction be reexamined asserting that the essence of the traditional family—which she identified as love—be preserved. Thus, Olga described gestation as one stage in the "nourishment and care" that a good mother gives her children.[50] Genetics does not produce that concern. In a remarkable twist on traditional definitions of family, Olga characterized Robert's concern with his genetic connection to the twins as evidence that he would be a *bad* father:

> It was not until the appellant learned of his paternity did [sic] he begin to illustrate a desire to be a parent to the twins. In effect, his love for the children was conditioned upon his genetic link to the children. Now he is asking this Court to award his [sic] custody based upon his genetics alone.[51]

For Olga, the invocation of family—even of traditional families—in this new context, a context that expands the universe of traditional families, requires a shift in old assumptions. Those old assumptions grounded traditional views of family in the inevitability of natural truth. Without such assumptions, the notion of enduring, committed relationships that traditionally describes and constitutes the family lacks a sustaining force.

Thus, in *McDonald*, as in *Johnson*, parties associate their opposing cases with tradition. Robert McDonald relied on his exclusive genetic connection to the children and suggested that, in comparison, Olga was a "stranger" seeking custody of his children.[52] He ignored Olga's gestational role in order to assert that he and his children could constitute a traditional family, one in which the parent-child bond was grounded in natural truth.

Olga also premised her claim to maternity on tradition. She defined herself in terms of traditional portraits of a good mother—self-sacrificing, loving, unendingly committed to her children. She connected that self-portrait to her biological (gestational) role, but she also proposed that the advent of reproductive technology necessitated new understandings of parent and child. In effect, she suggested that the social and biological dimensions of parenthood be disassociated so that the social dimension might be preserved in its most traditional form. In this vision, for instance, "good mothers," even if infertile, might be enabled to create families and to raise children who would benefit, as children always have benefited, from their mothers' loving care.

III. What Is an Embryo?—Or Is It an Embryo?

Disputes involving the disposition of frozen embryos resemble those involving children produced as a result of gestational surrogacy arrangements or ovum donation, in that the invocation of biological facts furthers a larger debate about the nature and future of family. Here too, arguments apparently about the biological facts of human reproduction serve as a pretext for voicing and resolving controversies about the meaning and limits of personhood. And, here too, the disruption to long-standing assumptions about the scope and contours of family is profound.

A New Time and Space for Human Reproduction: In Vitro Fertilization and Cryopreserved Embryos

In 1978, Louise Brown, the first baby conceived in vitro, was born in England. Six years later in Australia, another child conceived in vitro was born. In the Australian case, however, the embryo, fertilized outside the body, was cryopreserved and only later thawed and implanted in the uterus of the woman from whose body the ovum had been extracted. Thus, within an extraordinarily short period of time, both the spatial and temporal dimensions of human reproduction became subject to technological manipulation. For the first time in history, human reproduction could begin outside a woman's body and could be suspended for long periods of time after conception and before further development of the embryo. Thus, in vitro fertilization, and the cryopreservation of early embryos, make it impossible to continue assuming that human reproduction is spatially contiguous and temporally continuous. The consequent disruption to traditional views of the family can be acute.

The advent of in vitro fertilization and cryopreservation necessitates that the law settle controversies about the rights to, and the rights of, frozen embryos. Several types of disputes have arisen in the wake of these new reproductive technologies. One line of cases has involved disputes between gamete donors and the infertility clinics that helped to create, and then store, their embryos. In *York v. Jones*, Steven York and Risa Adler-York went to court to force the Howard and Georgeanna Jones Institute for Reproductive Medicine in Norfolk, Virginia, to transfer their frozen embryo to a fertility clinic in Los Angeles. The couple had been treated for infertility at the institute. During the course of the treatment, they had one embryo cryopreserved for possible later implantation. However, before that implantation was attempted, the couple moved to Los Angeles. The Jones Institute refused to transfer the embryo. A federal district court in Virginia, relying on the terms of the Cryopreservation Agreement between the couple and the institute, concluded that the agreement had created a bailor-bailee relationship between the couple and the clinic. The court found that the Jones Institute had "fully recognize[d] plaintiffs' property rights in the pre-zygote and . . . limited [its own] rights as bailee to exercise dominion and control over the pre-zygote."[53]

In addition to disputes such as that in *York*, there have been disputes between two gamete donors who, having had embryos frozen for future implantation, later decided not to become parents together as a result of their deteriorating relationship. *Davis v. Davis* represents the latter sort of case.

Unlike gestational surrogacy cases, frozen embryo cases have a rela-

tively long, impassioned, and self-conscious history because of the controversy about the legality of, and limits upon, abortion. The abortion
debate has been marked by unending and generally inconclusive appeals
to the biological correlates of embryonic development.

Those appeals were given legal significance by the framework within
which the Supreme Court analyzed the abortion issue in *Roe v. Wade.*
In *Roe*, the states of Texas and Georgia, whose abortion statutes were
under constitutional attack, argued that the protection of fetal life constituted a "compelling state interest" that justified infringing on the privacy
interests of pregnant women wanting to terminate their pregnancies. The
Supreme Court, in response, expressly refused to "resolve the difficult
question of when life begins,"[54] but agreed that the privacy interests of a
pregnant woman are not absolute. The Court concluded that the state's
"interest in protecting the potentiality of human life" counterbalances
the rights of a woman seeking an abortion at the point of "viability." The
Court placed the point of viability at about twenty eight weeks, noting
that in some cases viability could occur as early as twenty four weeks.[55]
Since *Roe*, the point of fetal viability has been located a few weeks earlier
than was the case at the time of the decision. In 1982, dissenting in *Akron
v. Akron Center for Reproductive Health*, Justice O'Connor asserted that
the trimester framework on the basis of which the Court decided *Roe*
was being called into question as a result of advances in medical technology.[56]

At the time of *Roe*, the court explained its conclusions about "the
point of viability":

> With respect to the State's important and legitimate interest in potential
> life, the "compelling" point is at viability. This is because the fetus then
> presumably has the capability of meaningful life outside the mother's
> womb. State regulation protective of fetal life after viability thus has both
> logical and biological justifications.[57]

Thus, in the law regulating abortion after *Roe*, conclusions about the
point at which life begins were displaced by more concrete, though
changing, conclusions about the point of fetal viability. *Roe* promised to
displace theological debate, at least within the universe of legal discourse,
with empirical observation. *Roe* thus appeared, at least momentarily, to
justify its trimester approach to the regulation of abortion. However,
after *Roe*, the biological "facts" of embryonic development remained as

significant as ever to the law's regulation of abortion. Within the society, *Roe* has intensified, rather than stilled, the controversy about when life begins.

Since *Roe*, a woman's right to abortion before viability has been premised on her privacy right to control her body. At both the beginning and the end of pregnancy, that scheme is threatened by technological advances which permit fetal development outside a woman's body. *Roe*, common sense, and most of Western theology and philosophy state clearly that, once born, a baby (even if still exhibiting what would previously have been fetal development) is a person and therefore cannot be killed. However, no comparable agreement exists about the existential or moral status of the embryo during the earliest stages of development. This disagreement is problematic because, through in vitro fertilization, embryos can be conceived outside a woman's body and can develop there for at least several days. Of course, those embryos are not viable (as the term was used in *Roe*) because they cannot develop into babies unless implanted in a woman's uterus for gestation beyond the first few days of development. However, embryos produced through in vitro fertilization can survive outside the body and, if frozen, may be available years after their creation for implantation and gestation in a woman's uterus. Thus they may lead eventually to the birth of a child.

This possibility has required the legal system once again to consider when life begins. Thousands of embryos are now being stored at fertility clinics in the United States. Some will be implanted in the woman from whose ovaries the ova were extracted; some will be implanted in other women, some of whom will not expect to become mothers to the babies they gestate ("gestational surrogates") and others of whom will expect to become mothers ("intentional mothers"); some will be used for research; and others will eventually be discarded.

If, however, as some argue,[58] early embryos are human life, the entire enterprise and, in particular, any decision to discard a frozen embryo, becomes problematic. As a result of this controversy, in a number of recent cases involving the fate of frozen embryos, courts have been asked to decide the status and fate of cryopreserved embryos. The first publicized case of this sort occurred in Australia. Heralded in the media and elsewhere as the tale of "frozen embryo orphans," the case involved a wealthy California couple, Mario and Elsa Rios, who went to Australia to receive IVF treatments. Several embryos resulted from the treatment; two were frozen for later use. The Rioses were then killed in a plane crash. The case led to questions about the fate of the frozen embryos and their potential right to inherit an intestate share of the Rioses' large estate.[59]

Other cases, such as *Davis* and *Kass v. Kass*, decided in New York several years after *Davis*, arose as divorce proceedings between parties who had earlier, while more happily married, undertaken infertility treatments together.

Davis v. Davis: Were the Embryos Children, Property, or Something in Between?

Mary Sue and Junior Lewis Davis married in 1980. In the early years of the marriage, Mary Sue suffered a series of ectopic pregnancies that resulted in the loss of her fallopian tubes. Then, in 1985, the couple entered an in vitro fertilization program at a Knoxville fertility clinic. Mary Sue tried the in vitro procedure without success several times during the next few years. In 1988, on the advice of their infertility doctor, the couple decided to cryopreserve embryos for future use should Mary Sue not become pregnant during the next cycle in which ova were extracted. In December 1988, nine ova were retrieved. Two were fertilized and implanted, but did not result in a pregnancy. Seven were cryopreserved and stored in the Knoxville clinic. Two months later, in February 1989, the Davises' marriage failed.

The couple agreed about all the terms of their divorce except the disposition of the seven frozen embryos. At first, Mary Sue hoped to use the embryos to become pregnant herself. She later remarried (becoming Mary Sue Stowe) and requested that the embryos be donated to an infertile couple. Junior Davis opposed both uses, proposing instead that the embryos be stored indefinitely. At the time, indefinite storage was understood as "tantamount to destruction" since it was believed that frozen embryos would likely not be viable after a couple of years.[60] Later, Junior asked that the embryos be discarded.

In the course of litigation, three Tennessee courts heard the case. Each based its opinion on a view of the embryos' existential condition radically different from that of the other two courts. To Judge Young of the trial court, the embryos were children. "The Court finds and concludes," he asserted, "that the seven cryopreserved embryos are human."[61] For Judge Young, that conclusion delineated what he then described as the essential question in the case: "What then is the legal status to be accorded a human being existing as an embryo, *in vitro*, in a divorce case in the state of Tennessee?"[62] He answered, expressly asserting the court's parens patriae power:

> [I]t is to the manifest best interest of the children, *in vitro*, that they be made available for implantation to assure their opportunity for live birth; implantation is their sole and only hope for survival. The Court respectfully finds and concludes that it further serves the best interest of these children for Mrs. Davis to be permitted the opportunity to bring these children to term through implantation.[63]

The court further vested "temporary custody of the parties' seven cryogenically preserved human embryos" with Mary Sue.

The Court of Appeals of Tennessee reversed. In the appellate court's decision, the trial court's focus on the moral and existential status of the embryos disappears, and was replaced by a focus on outcome. "The sole issue on appeal," declared the appellate court, "is essentially who is entitled to *control* seven of Mary Sue's ova fertilized by Junior's sperm."[64] The court concluded in effect that, whatever the status of the fertilized ova, they would be afforded a status somewhere between property and body organs available for transplant. Citing the Uniform Anatomical Gift Act, as passed in Tennessee, the court concluded that Mary Sue and Junior shared "an interest" in the cryopreserved embryos and, accordingly, vested "joint control" in both of them.[65] The decisions went further toward defining the embryos' status than toward determining their practical fate.

The state supreme court affirmed the holding of the appellate court, but separated itself from any implication in the lower court's opinion that the parties' interest in the embryos was "in the nature of a property interest."[66] The court explained:

> [P]reembryos are not, strictly speaking, either "persons" or "property," but occupy an interim category that entitles them to special respect because of their potential for human life. It follows that any interest that Mary Sue Davis and Junior Davis have in the preembryos in this case is not a true property interest. However, they do have an interest in the nature of ownership, to the extent that they have decision-making authority concerning disposition of the preembryos, within the scope of policy set by law.[67]

In its conclusions and holding, however, the state supreme court evaded the question of how to respect cryopreserved embryos and turned instead to the interests and rights of the gamete donors. The court finally decided that, given the lack of either a current or prior agreement between the parties about the embryos, it became necessary to weigh the "relative interests of the parties in using or not using the preembryos."[68] The court wrote:

> Ordinarily, the party wishing to avoid procreation should prevail, assuming that the other party has a reasonable possibility of achieving parenthood by means other than the use of the preembryos in question. If no other reasonable alternatives exist, then the argument in favor of using the preembryos to achieve pregnancy should be considered. However, if the party seeking control of the preembryos intends merely to donate them to another couple, the objecting party obviously has the greater interest and should prevail.[69]

In the aftermath of that conclusion, the embryos were transmitted to Junior Davis by the Knoxville infertility clinic where they had been stored for over four years. In June 1993, Davis announced that he had had the embryos destroyed.[70]

Each of the three state courts that rendered opinions in *Davis*, as well as the parties and amici curiae who presented arguments to the courts, reviewed the biological facts of embryonic creation and development in order to justify the decision reached or desired. Thus, while the parties (along with amici curiae) disagreed about the description, the definition, and the "personhood" of the embryos, they used the same medical facts surrounding in vitro fertilization to support their respective claims.

This case differed from *Johnson v. Calvert* in that the opposing parties in *Davis* had each donated a gamete to produce the embryos in question. Thus neither party could use the biological facts as they are now generally understood to demonstrate a greater or more "natural" relation to the embryos. Other understandings do exist, but were not stressed by the parties in *Davis*. In fact, for instance, folkculture often ignores the scientific understanding of gametic donation—which characterizes the male and female gametes as similar apart from the X and Y chromosomes—in order to view the donation of the male as superior to that of the female. Helena Ragoné notes the use of this folk-theory among surrogate mothers who hope to minimize their own biological connection to the child.[71] In fact, Dr. Jerome Lejeune, a French geneticist who testified for Mary Sue Davis at trial, did assert that in his view, the gamete provided by the male is not genetically comparable to that provided by the female. He argued that certain sorts of genetic information are carried by sperm and other sorts of information are carried by ova.[72] Mary Sue did not stress this understanding in her own arguments before the courts. The parties in *Davis* did, however, invoke biological facts to define the moral and existential status of the embryos, and thus hopefully the controversy, so that the fate of the embryos would be decided as each, respectively, desired.

The briefs and the arguments presented to the courts in *Davis* suggest three broad views of the embryos' status. Each of the three views was adopted by one of the three courts that rendered decisions in the case. The trial court viewed the embryos as children and therefore understood the case as a custody battle between two parents. The intermediate appellate court viewed the embryos as animate commodities, much as other courts have viewed genetically engineered matter.[73] The court therefore framed the case to resemble a property dispute between divorcing spouses. Finally, the state supreme court sought a middle course, one that avoided expressly viewing the embryos as either people or property. The court determined that the embryos, although not persons, were entitled to "special respect because of their potential for human life." This view allowed the court to distinguish its treatment of the embryos from the treatment it would afford inanimate commodities in another case, while also allowing the court to bypass the interests of the embryos (which would be determinative if they were "children").

In fact, the Tennessee Supreme Court, after emphasizing the respect owed the embryos, turned to a world of contractual negotiations, and a world concerned with the preservation of people's (in this case, the gamete donors') constitutional rights in the context of intimate familial relationships. The court encouraged the use of prefertilization contracts between gamete donors interested in together becoming the parents of a child, and suggested that the terms of such contracts be conclusive in future disputes. If such a contractual agreement did not exist, the court suggested focusing, as it did in *Davis* itself, on the interests of the gamete donors. Thus, in the end, the state supreme court in *Davis* did not exactly treat the embryos as having a status intermediate between that of people and that of property. Rather, the court held that treatment of disputes over embryos should vary depending upon the existence of agreement. Where an agreement exists, the court will treat the dispute more like one involving property. On the other hand, when there is no agreement between the gamete donors, the court will treat the dispute more like one involving family members. Thus, as will be considered in detail in chapter 7, although the court premised its conclusions on the "special respect" owed embryos "because of their potential for human life," the decision in fact reflected concern for the gamete donors instead.[74] More specifically, the decision did not respect the embryos, except to the extent that the embryos' interests were encompassed by the interests of the donors. Moreover, the donors were respected only insofar as the court—*unable* to rely on a contractual, or other, agreement between them—focused on their procreational autonomy as protected by the Constitution.

In fact, none of the three courts' respective conclusions about the existential status of the embryos necessitated the holding that each court reached about the fate of the embryos. Their conclusions about the embryos' status did, however, establish the terms of the debate. For instance, a conclusion that the embryos are, or resemble, children establishes that the case should be handled as a custody dispute. Within that dispute, the court could theoretically have decided that the best interests of the embryonic children lay with perpetual storage, with donation to an infertile couple, or with some other use or disposition. Similarly, a conclusion that the embryos are, or resemble, property establishes that the case should be handled by reference to the parties' comparative claims to "control" the property at stake. That perspective does not, however, clearly dictate the proper use or disposition of the *Davis* embryos.

While the rhetoric in *Davis* does not necessitate a particular outcome, it serves a very important role in structuring the current debate about family. Clearly, *Davis* was about far more than the fate of seven embryos. Encompassing the controversy about the fate of the seven *Davis* embryos is a much broader debate about the meaning and parameters, indeed the very nature, of the family, and of the persons who compose families. The case provided a concrete forum in which the larger debate could be conducted.

In carrying on that larger debate, the parties consistently invoked the biological facts of embryonic development. As in *Johnson*, each side claimed that the weight of scientific truth demonstrated the unique value of its perspective and its proposed use for the disputed embryos. And, as in *Johnson*, the invocation of biological facts proved generally inconclusive. No conclusions about the status of the embryos could fairly be derived from the total testimony of the medical experts. Yet each court relied on some of that testimony to justify its view of the embryos and its conclusions about their fate.

Of the three courts that heard the case, the trial court most emphatically embraced biological facts to support its conclusions about the embryos' existential and moral status. That court relied heavily on the interpretations of Dr. Jerome Lejeune, the French geneticist who testified for Mary Sue Davis at trial. Dr. Lejeune was known in the scientific world for his discovery of the chromosome responsible for Down's syndrome. He had been appointed in 1974 by the Pope as a member of the Pontifical Academy of Sciences and had worked actively to have abortion declared illegal.[75] Dr. Lejeune premised his arguments for Mary Sue on the position that in vitro fertilization does not differ fundamentally from fertilization within a woman's body. After describing the process of fertilization within a woman's body, Dr. Lejeune asserted:

It is not at all the inseminator who makes fertilization, he just puts on the right medium, a ripe ovum, active sperm, and it is the sperm who make the fertilization. Man would be unable to make a fertilization. It has to be done directly by the cells. And it's because they were normally floating in the fluid that this extracorporeal technique is at all possible.

Now, the reproduction process is a very impressive phenomenon in the sense that what is reproduced is never the matter, but it is information.[76]

In this statement, Dr. Lejeune attempted to support two arguments. First, he wanted to establish that embryos produced through in vitro fertilization are no different from embryos produced through sexual intercourse. Second, he set the scientific stage for concluding that the embryos, cryopreserved at the four-to-eight cell stage, represent unique human beings, just as they would had they been conceived and allowed to develop in a woman's body. Dr. Lejeune argued that, because each embryo contains all the information necessary to produce a unique human being even before the eight-cell stage, each is a human being. "[S]cience," he asserted "has a very simple conception of man; as soon as he has been conceived, a man is a man."[77] When Charles Clifford,

Junior Davis's attorney, asked whether a zygote deserves "the same respect as an adult human being,"[78] Dr. Lejeune responded:

> I'm not telling you that because I'm not in [the] position of knowing that. I'm telling you, he is a human being, and then it is a Justice who will tell whether this human being has the same rights as the others. . . . But as a geneticist you ask me whether this human being is a human, and I would tell you that because he is a being and being human, he is a human being.[79]

After discussing the implications of cryopreserving cells, Dr. Lejeune suggested that alternatives to in vitro fertilization, and the cryopreservation of any resulting embryos, were on the horizon. He further suggested that these alternatives offered biologically and socially superior results to those produced through the present methods. "[L]ove," he declared, "is the contrary [sic] of chilly. Love is warmth. . . . [T]he best we can do for early human beings is to have them in their normal shelter, not in the fridge."[80]

Dr. Lejeune was one of five experts who testified at trial. He alone testified that, as a scientific matter, human life begins at conception; yet, the trial court relied on Dr. Lejeune's testimony for just that conclusion, which it proclaimed in a list of twelve "findings of fact and conclusions of law resulting in judgment."[81] Reviewing Dr. Lejeune's scientific testimony, and comparing it with that of other expert witnesses,[82] the court concluded that nothing in the testimony of the other experts effectively disputed Dr. Lejeune's assertion that the cells of an early embryo are differentiated. In describing the early embryo's cells as "differentiated," Dr. Lejeune hoped to show that the early embryo is unique, autonomous, and human—thus, "an early human being."

Whatever the validity of Dr. Lejeune's controversial conclusions about the biology of early embryos, they hardly compel the conclusion that four-cell embryos are human beings. However, Dr. Lejeune's testimony, and the court's characterization of that testimony, dramatically illustrate how the facts of nature are used to justify social and moral conclusions. The court justified its holding by referring to Dr. Lejeune's explanation of the biological facts of embryonic development, even though it acknowledged that Dr. Lejeune's conclusions about the differentiation of cells in early embryos were "highly technical, incapable of observation by the Court and require[d] the Court to either accept or reject the scientist's conclusion."[83]

At least two broadly dissimilar strategies can be employed in responding to Dr. Lejeune's testimony and to the trial court's conclusions based on that testimony. First, an alternative description and/or interpretation of the biological facts might be presented to dispute the details, or the implications, of Dr. Lejeune's testimony. Second, the biological facts might be bypassed, and the terms of discourse shifted to another domain entirely. Junior Davis and the two higher courts, each of which disagreed with the trial court's analysis, employed each of these strategies at one time or another.

Junior Davis offered an alternative description of the seven cryopreserved embryos. "As just two or eight cell tiny lumps of complex protein," he argued, "the embryos have no real value to either party."[84] Moreover, he offered competing theories for interpreting the social significance of embryonic development. Junior differentiated a fetus from an embryo, and stressed that the early embryo lacks a nervous system. Quoting the work of John Robertson, one of Junior's experts at trial, Junior declared:

> Even if one takes a very cautious position on when a nervous system begins, the earliest possible time of arguable relevance is the formation of the primitive streak, the precursor to the nervous system. Yet this first structure of the embryo proper does not develop until implantation has occurred, some ten to fourteen days after fertilization.[85]

In a similar vein, the state court of appeals, with almost no elaboration, simply replaced the trial court's interpretation of the relevant biological facts with its own:

> There are significant scientific distinctions between fertilized ova that have not been implanted and an embryo in the mother's womb. The fertilized ova at issue are between 4 and 8 cells. Genetically each cell is identical. . . . It is important to remember when these ova were fertilized through mechanical manipulation, their development was limited to the 8 cell stage.[86]

The Tennessee Supreme Court expressly dismissed Dr. Lejeune's scientific testimony. While acknowledging Lejeune as "an internationally recognized geneticist," the court noted that his "background fails to reflect any degree of expertise in obstetrics or gynecology (specifically in the field of infertility) or in medical ethics." Moreover, "his testimony revealed a profound confusion between science and religion."[87] The court described in some detail the testimonies of Dr. Ray King and other experts, all of which controverted Dr. Lejeune's testimony about the stages through which a fertilized ovum proceeds during gestation. At the heart of this alternative depiction of embryonic development is the "biologic difference between a preembryo and an embryo."[88] Dr. King's testimony, as summarized by the court, characterized the preembryonic stage as continuing until cellular differentiation begins, about fourteen days after fertilization. Whatever the scientific merit of the distinction, it can be used to arbitrate social and moral disagreements. Finally, the court concluded its description of the embryo's development with its own disclaimer about the relevance of the distinction it had just described between the preembryo and the embryo. "Admittedly, this distinction," the court acknowledged, "is not dispositive in the case before us."[89]

The biological facts can be debated and revised. As that debate proceeds, the implications that the biological facts hold for the social contours of family are reconstructed. Almost always, in cases such as *Davis* there are alternative responses to a disconcerting characterization of the biological facts for one party as presented by another party, or by a court. For instance, when faced with an unsettling presentation of the biological facts, it is possible to shift the level of discourse so that the biological facts become background to a discussion about social, cultural, psychological, or theological matters. Junior Davis did precisely this. In arguing his case to the courts, he largely bypassed the biological facts of embryonic development, in order to present his case in social, rather than biological, terms. Not surprisingly, in almost all of his arguments before the courts, Junior Davis focused upon family, and highlighted his desire to preserve a traditional view of familial relationships.

Junior referred to his genetic connection to the embryos in order to support his constitutional right not to become a father. In this manner, he defined the controversy as essentially unrelated to the facts of embryonic development. For instance, in concluding his brief to the Tennessee Supreme Court, he expressly stated that the dispute was not about embryos but about "whether or not the parties will become parents."[90] This shift in focus made relevant a variety of social and legal arguments and analogies that would have been irrelevant had the case been about the existential status of the embryos, demonstrable only through reference to the biological facts of embryonic development. If, as Junior argued, the central question in the case involved the definition and regulation of family, then Junior did not need to focus exclusively on disputing the trial court's understanding of the biological facts of embryonic development. Instead, he could turn—as he did—to a variety of laws and legal interpretations about the family that did not require any consideration of the facts of embryonic development, or any further consideration of the biological underpinnings traditionally thought to limit and define family relations. He could, for example, rely on the numerous constitutional decisions rendered in the last three decades that define a right to family privacy or autonomy. Those cases include *Griswold v. Connecticut* and *Eisenstadt v. Baird*, discussed in chapter 2, as well as *Roe v. Wade*. As a group these cases, and others like them, protect the right of individuals to establish familial, and other intimate, relationships without state interference. Junior's definition of the case similarly allowed him to invoke various statutory rules and regulations whose implications for the social and moral dimensions of family relationships favored his case.

If, after all, the essential issue in *Davis* was not whether the embryos were human, but the constitutional and statutory rights of the gamete donors (the potential parents), then evidence about the specifics of embryonic development was peripheral. Accordingly, Junior argued:

> Tennessee specifically recognizes the high importance of family or genetic relationships in conferring rights and benefits and allocating burdens among citizens. In many areas of the law, the mere fact of biological kinship alone is sufficient to confer a right or impose a duty. In such areas the State acknowledges the most ancient and fundamental rights and duties springing from human kinship and will not intrude, even if more modern concepts of fairness or equity might dictate otherwise.[91]

At this point, Junior was able to invoke a series of statutes regulating the relations between family members, such as those controlling intestate inheritance, those imposing an obligation on a biological parent to support his or her child, and those regulating the donation of a deceased person's body organs by family members.[92] In relying on these statutory rules, Junior suggested first, that whatever the existential status of the embryos, he could be obliged to support any child produced from them, and second, that such a development should not occur without his consent.

For example, Junior analogized rules regulating the donation of body organs to the regulation of the fate of the *Davis* embryo. Under Tennessee law, the organs of a deceased person, absent a statement left by the deceased, may be donated if the deceased's next of kin agree. If more than one person is next of kin to the decedent (e.g., children or siblings), agreement must be unanimous among all members of the group before donation can occur. Junior suggested that similarly in the case of frozen embryos, a decision to donate (though apparently not to discard) the embryos, should only be affected upon agreement of both gamete donors. Junior explained: "Each party's interest in the disposition of the embryos springs from the same ancient wellspring of kinship involved in the policy of organ donation set out above. No disposition should be made of their embryos unless they both agree."[93]

Somewhat more implicitly, Junior used the organ donation statute to invoke the importance of family and to connect himself, and his position, to family. Tennessee rules regulating organ donation by a dead person, he asserted, illustrated "the high degree of respect and deference due human kinship."[94] In this way, Junior transformed the debate from one about the humanity of the embryos into one about the parameters of family. As a result, he was able to associate his position with the "ancient wellspring of kinship."[95] Ironically, Junior's invocation of family, and of the "ancient wellspring of kinship," aimed to protect his right to remain free of family. He alluded to family and tradition in order to safeguard his right to autonomous choice. Junior's allusion reflected the pervasive transformation of the American family from a holistic unit structured in hierarchical terms to a collectivity of separate individuals, unconnected until and unless they choose connections.

The Tennessee Supreme Court, after considering and evaluating the extensive testimony about biological facts, and the consequent status of the embryos, similarly shifted the level of discourse. First, the court switched from the biological to the legal dimensions of the case, in order to draw conclusions about the status of the embryos. Later, the court turned away entirely from the question of the embryos' status or rights, and considered instead the competing constitutional rights of the two gamete donors.

After considering the "scientific testimony" presented to the trial court about the facts of embryonic development and concluding that that testimony failed to compel any particular judicial response, the court turned to an examination of the state's treatment of fetuses in the womb.[96] Reviewing the United States Supreme Court decision in *Roe v. Wade* which asserts that fetuses are not "persons" under the law, the court concluded that the embryos in *Davis* should certainly not be treated as legal persons. The court still had to decide, however, what to *do* with the Davis' embryos. The legal conclusion that embryos are not persons offered almost no more assistance than had the parties' and experts' interpretations of the biological facts.

In order to reach and justify a concrete decision, the court shifted the focus of its analysis even further from the existential status of the embryos. After deciding that the embryos were neither persons (on the basis of some combination of the biological facts and the law) nor property (on the apparent basis of the court's own sense of things—including perhaps the very fact that the embryos' biology could be, and had been, extensively considered), the court focused on the rights of the gamete donors rather than on the rights of (or "respect" owed) the embryos. In this regard, the court relied on Junior Davis's view that the case was not about the embryos or where to store the embryos, but was rather about "whether the parties will become parents."[97]

After reviewing federal and state assurances of a "right to privacy," the court declared:

> Obviously, the drafters of the Tennessee Constitution of 1796 could not have anticipated the need to construe the liberty clauses of that document in terms of the choices flowing from *in vitro* fertilization procedures. But there can be little doubt that they foresaw the need to protect individuals from unwarranted government intrusion into matters such as the one before us, involving intimate questions of personal and family concern.[98]

The court then addressed two equal rights deriving from the "right to procreational autonomy" that it defined as being at stake in *Davis*—the "right to procreate" and the "right to avoid procreation"[99]—and undertook to weigh "the relative interests" of Junior and Mary Sue in regard to the embryos.[100]

Thus, the court all but abandoned its concern with the existential status of the embryos. The court's holding effectively disregarded its own determination that the existential status of the embryos demanded they be given "special respect" because of their potential for life [101] and instead favored the status and rights of the gamete donors. By asserting that the case was essentially about the contours of family—even if a disintegrating family—the court apparently satisfied its condition that the law respect the embryos, and therefore felt free to focus on the interests of the gamete donors. In effect, the decision presumes that the gamete donors as family, or potential family, to the embryos would demonstrate the requisite respect for the embryos in any decision about the embryos' use or disposition.

Essentially, the court was able to rely on the possibility inherent in Western views of the family of separating biological from social fact. As Marilyn Strathern has asserted:

> Arguments in favour of embracing the new reproductive technologies can point to them as techniques that will alleviate suffering and provide remedies for disability, and thus enable the family to take its proper and *traditional* form. The domains of biological and social fact are not, in this view, to be confused. Medical intervention is strictly intervention in the biological process. And while it may alter the disposition of kin, that is, alter expectations about who becomes related, the traditional family as a social unit is not necessarily challenged. [102]

The possibility of separating the biological and social facts of family allows parties and courts to premise their arguments on the significance of preserving traditional families even in cases in which the biological facts are unknown, ambiguous—as in *Davis*—or in apparent conflict with the view, pervasive in Western cultures, that specific biological relationships anchor family relationships.

The state supreme court in *Davis*, unlike the trial court, was unable or unwilling to ground its decision on the certainty of inexorable natural fact. Instead the court shifted the level of discourse, and focused on a domain of social interaction, that of the family. That domain has long held a special, even sacred, place in Western culture, and has been understood through reference to biological facts that have more generally been assumed than delineated and described. Thus, again, the respect the court declared that the law owed the embryos on the basis of their existential status was satisfied by actualizing the respect owed the two people who might have become the embryos' parents.

In fact, the court's opinion allowed for, and even encouraged, explicit contractual regulation of cryopreserved embryos in future cases. In the absence of any agreements between the Davises, the court ultimately effected a disposition that relied, more than anything, on its own sense of the harm Junior would suffer by having children produced from the embryos, as compared to the relative benefit to Mary Sue if the embryos were to survive to become children.

In the end, the court was able to "respect" and to avoid considering fully the biological reality of embryonic development and of four-cell cryopreserved embryos. It was able to connect the extensive testimony provided by experts at trial to its characterization of the embryos as deserving of "respect." The court accomplished this without considering the concrete implications of "respecting" embryos, and without directly actualizing the presumption of respect at all. Moreover, the court was able to preserve traditional views of family by premising its decision on the parties' familial status, while simultaneously defying tradition almost entirely by suggesting that contract, rather than family, law could best deal with cryopreserved embryos.

Thus, the opinion of the supreme court can be read both to connect biological truth to the social order, and to disassociate the two almost completely. Further, the opinion can be read to herald, or at least to encourage, a radically new view of intimate (family) relationships and yet to focus chiefly on safeguarding old-fashioned rights and responsibilities connected to the family. It can be read in these various, often contradictory, ways in large part because the court appeared to ground its decision in a reasoned assessment of what Justice Daughtrey, writing for the state supreme court in *Davis*, called the "scientific testimony" (the biological facts), while acknowledging quite forthrightly that those facts failed to direct the court to a clear holding in the case. In a sense, the biological facts offered solace where they failed to offer guidance. They allowed the court to invoke tradition and the sacred order of old-fashioned families, while at the same time permitting the court to suggest that, to resolve disputes such as those in *Davis*, contract law might be better than family law.

In short, the *Davis* case, taken as a whole, shows the continuing interest of the law and the society in predicating family relationships on biological truths, as well as the general disruption and some of the specific options available when those truths are difficult to decipher or do not provide clear direction for resolving controversies occasioned by reproductive technology. Even if the assumed connections between family relationships and biological facts can be rent asunder by reproductive technology, or already have been, to whatever degree, it remains possible to invoke tradition as if it has remained intact.

IV. Transforming Assumptions

The varied responses of courts to cases occasioned by reproductive technology suggest the depth and significance of the social and legal transformation of the family now occurring. Taken as a whole, the legal system, much like the larger society, is reacting with uncertainty and confusion. In *Johnson*, for instance, each of the three courts that considered the case relied on widely discrepant understandings of maternity and of the origin of the parent-child bond in determining the parentage of baby Christopher. Similarly, each of the three Tennessee courts that rendered decisions in *Davis* depended on three completely different understandings of the moral and existential status of frozen embryos.

Reproductive technology developed within a world already witnessing widespread changes in the meaning of family. At present, however, the new reproductive technologies confront a legal system still committed in significant part to old-fashioned conceptions of family with families that often cannot be assimilated into those conceptions. In cases occasioned by reproduction technology, biological truths may be invoked to identify a child's "real" parents, but opposing parties often present the same biological facts to demonstrate contrary conclusions. In consequence, the implications for society of the biological facts of reproduction cannot be taken for granted. That precludes the law's defining and regulating families in a familiar, consistent fashion. As the assumptions that previously undergirded the law's approach to families are challenged, the law is compelled to invent new approaches.

Sometimes, the recognition that biological facts no longer securely anchor the society's understanding of family and family relations presents a new challenge to the biological facts themselves. Sometimes, the biological facts may be elided by an appeal to tradition that focuses on the social facts of family. And sometimes a new view of family clearly emerges, a view that values autonomy more than connection, and therefore suggests that family relationships are grounded in individual choice—open to change and to negotiation—rather than in shared assumptions about the essence of familial connections—connections our society once understood as grounded predominantly and securely in unalterable, and thus eternal, truths.

The "Intent" of Reproduction

Disputes occasioned by reproductive technology force courts to recon-sider—and thus often to reinvent—assumptions that undergird notions of mother, father, child, and family. In cases such as *Johnson*, *McDonald*, and *Davis*, the law is confronted with possibilities that challenge virtually every presumption the society has held about the essence of familial bonds. Moreover, the law is being asked to respond to the disruptions presented by reproductive technology, just as traditional assumptions about the social dimensions of family and the character of kin relations are being questioned and eroded more generally. For the most part the task has fallen to the judiciary. Courts are responding by settling particu-lar disputes. But they are doing much more than that. They are beginning to erect a set of frames, within which to think about and develop the family of the future. They are, in short, being asked to develop a new social—even a new moral—vision of families and familial relationships *so that* they can determine the appropriate response to the social and moral dilemmas created by the new reproductive technologies.

Courts have begun this task often unaided by statutory law, because rules promulgated to guide courts faced with disputes involving custody and parentage determinations still generally reflect traditional assump-tions about the biological parameters of the parent-child relationship and about the meanings attached to human reproduction. Most state legislatures have not yet promulgated rules aimed directly at handling dis-putes engendered by surrogacy and the new reproductive technologies.

In fact, courts, in considering and resolving concrete disputes involv-ing reproductive technology, are providing a potential laboratory, whose results legislators may review when, as must eventually occur, states respond to the conundrums presented by the new reproductive techno-logies and surrogacy with comprehensive statutory rules.

So, for instance, courts deciding cases such as *Johnson* and *McDonald* (in each of which two women claimed to be the biological mother of one child) were poorly assisted by existing law since state statutes addressing matters of custody and parentage were largely promulgated during a period in which only science fiction envisioned a separation of biological maternity into genetic and gestational aspects with different women carrying out each role.

Some courts facing such cases bypass existing statutory rules and formulate new approaches aimed expressly at resolving these unprecedented dilemmas. Others, however, adapt established statutory approaches to situations not imagined by the legislators who formulated the exiting rules. Thus, not surprisingly, courts are both designing new rules and stretching existing rules in resolving disputes occasioned by the new reproductive technologies. Both sorts of responses are altering the contours and meaning of family.

The first sort of response is represented by the decision of the California Supreme Court in *Johnson*. There the court relied on parental intent to distinguish between two women claiming to be a child's biological mother. The court, obviously struggling to mediate among conflicts presented by various images of family, ultimately sided with one vision of family. The second sort of response is illustrated by *Baby M*. There, the New Jersey trial court and the state supreme court, despite very different decisions, each relied on the familiar best-interest standard to determine the child's parentage and/or custody. Judicial reliance on the best-interest standard, which asks courts to determine a child's best interests in determining that child's custody or parentage, inevitably presumes some understanding of family. For that reason, reliance on the standard is more likely to reflect than to resolve contradictions that develop as families are defined at once through the terms of the marketplace and through those of the traditional family (including the inevitabilities associated with blood and genetic connection).

Neither sort of approach—neither that which bypasses established rules for resolving disputes involving custody and parentage nor that which attempts to adapt established rules to new contexts—has as yet proved adequate to the general task of defining and regulating familial bonds produced through reproductive technology. This chapter and the next examine instances of each approach, respectively. This chapter focuses on the implications and consequences of relying on parental intent to resolve disputes about parentage. The next chapter, in turn, examines the implications and consequences of adapting the best-interest standard to resolve parentage or custody disputes in cases occasioned by reproductive technology and surrogacy. Each approach depends on, and intensifies, existing confusions about the meaning and limits of the family.

I. The Generalization and Redefinition of Choice

Courts deciding a number of cases involving reproductive technology have fastened upon the concept of intent and charged it with the task of resolving disputes about parentage and custody as well as, more generally, of mediating between the demands of tradition and those of modernity. Reliance on the deceptively simple concept of intent inevitably involves the vastly, perhaps endlessly, complicated study of motivation. The charge of the courts to themselves has been that the study of motivation will, somehow or other, enable diverse and contradictory understandings of family to be reconciled.

The results have not been impressive. Intent is very difficult to determine. It has been asked by the courts in particular cases to shuttle between diverse conceptions of family in a dizzying and almost random fashion. Because of its nature, the concept of intent cannot in good faith act as mediator and has fulfilled its task only sometimes and tentatively, if at all. Thus courts invoking intent to mediate between very different understandings of family such as bargained interaction and love, profane business and sacred connection, have rendered decisions which have uniformly resisted any absolute identification with either understanding. In consequence, a significant confusion has been compounded by the introduction of a concept designed to resolve the initial confusion.

Intent is the practical reality that underlies the abstract concept of choice. Intent precedes choice and is "played back" to the person choosing "in the consumer idiom of *choice*."[1] Choice is essential to the world of the marketplace. The presumption of unfettered choice defines that world and the actors who operate in it. The consumer society, consistently, and almost everywhere, stresses the appeal of unending choice. Represented by television and the advertising industry, this society assures people that a better everyday life depends only on the appropriation of choices not yet tried. So, for instance, if one brand of shampoo, laundry detergent, or breakfast cereal fails to make life better, a new and better brand surely will soon appear.[2]

Reproductive technology, if appropriated and understood through the idiom of the market, asserts that choices about parentage and familial relationships are fully comparable to other choices of the market. Yet, the market's presumption of choice—that everything has been chosen and that everything could have been chosen differently—increasingly is found in connection with the family not only in cases occasioned by reproductive technology but much more generally. The very fact of infertility, for example, a fact that may result in the use and purchase of reproductive technologies, is described as unfortunate precisely because it limits or precludes choice.[3] Thus reproductive technology helps to create a certain kind of choice—the choice to have children and to create "families."

Generally speaking, reproductive technology, simply by unfolding, invites human beings to become increasingly autonomous, and to enter into a range of contracts that may prove unlimited. It thus invites, and values, choice. In this, reproductive technology inevitably challenges a traditional conception of family which in many respects regards choice as essentially destructive. This is understandable, since a world defined by unchanging truths rooted in tradition and immutable law tends, of its nature, to prefer a validated status quo to untested change. Thus choice justifies the development and use of reproductive technology and simultaneously threatens traditional understandings of family.

That being the case, it is obviously imprudent to establish choice as the mediating principle between families or aspects of families understood as traditional and families or aspects of families understood as modern. Nonetheless, it has been so established by courts anxious to reconcile contradictory understandings of family, uncertain about how to proceed, and naively hopeful that, somehow or other, a society increasingly intrigued by the contractual choices offered by reproductive technology will, of its own volition (by choice) turn away from them, and back toward traditional definitions of family.

This hope—essentially, the quixotic expectation that choice will deconstruct itself—underlies much of the heightened confusion and ambivalence evident in a number of cases occasioned by the new reproductive technologies, in which courts have relied on the notion of intent in order to resolve conflicting ideological claims.

While intent precedes choice, choice enables intent. Moreover, the "real" meaning of a particular choice can be discovered through analysis of the motivating intent. Thus intent explains choice. Clearly, therefore, a legal system prepared to deal with the challenges posed by reproductive technology through the analysis of intent has implicitly conceded the inevitability of choice in allowing people significant freedom to define the scope and meaning of family. The failure of such a system to realize that it *has* conceded the inevitability of choice merely assures that the system will adjudicate the conflicting demands of tradition and modernity in a confused, self-contradictory fashion.

And this it has done, and continues to do.

Courts relying on intent to resolve disputes engendered by reproductive technology, have failed to delineate the parameters and implications of intent. Several law review articles, suggesting that intent should become the central tool through which to settle disputes involving reproductive technology, have delineated the contours of the concept.[4] In each case, intent has been equated almost completely with the sort of choice understood as paradigmatic of contractual negotiations. Thus, the articles urge that courts recognize and enforce contractual agreements concerning the creation of children and families. Courts have generally not been willing to do that. Although they have relied on intent, courts have failed to address the obvious questions raised by that reliance. The decisions that exist have all failed to explain how a party's real intent is discerned, even though people's intentions are often obviously multidimensional, complicated, and confused. The decisions have failed, as well, to explain why any one intent is preferred over another in cases in which a party's intent changes. If intent were understood to be synonymous with contract, as has been suggested,[5] the questions raised by courts' reliance on intent could be resolved through the principles of contract. But that has not generally been the case. Courts have explicitly distinguished a party's intent from the same party's contractual agreements. In effecting a party's intent, some courts have referred to, and even relied directly on, a contract as evidence of intent. But in such cases, the courts have insisted that the need to effect a party's intent, rather than the obligation to enforce a contractual agreement, has necessitated their holdings. Thus, the courts have denied that they are simply applying rules of the marketplace to the regulation of family life.

The concept of intent has been attractive to courts in these cases, precisely because reliance on intent has seemed to allow courts to mediate between images of the marketplace and those of the traditional home. As will become clear from a review of the cases, courts have used the concept of intent so that, quite remarkably, it suggests the rational negotiations of the market and at the same time resembles "blood" (or genes) as the ground on which familial connections are rendered real.

Thus, the concept of intent suggests a world of contract, offering unlimited free choice, but courts, relying on the concept in cases occasioned by reproductive technology, have constructed the concept to invoke images of traditional family relationships as well as those of contract. For instance, courts have relied on intent so as to effect certain kinds of choices, choices that reflect the parameters associated with traditional family life. Other courts, hearing cases calling for a determination of parentage or for the right to control gametic material, have limited the choices that can be effected through judicial reliance on intent by suggesting that use of the concept be restricted to the resolution of cases involving some biological connection between the parties and the disputed gamete or child. As a result, the freedom to choose implied by judicial reliance on intent may become the freedom of only certain parties (those with a biological connection to the gamete or child) to choose, or it may become the freedom to select only certain choices (those that support traditional family values).

Judicial reliance on intent as the essential determinant of parentage in these cases has not, and probably cannot successfully mediate, and thereby comfortably combine, traditional and modern conceptions of family. In fact, this reliance has engendered a set of confusions and inconsistencies which seem inevitable if, as has been the case, the law fails to specify how relevant intentions are to be identified in any case. Indicatively, courts relying on the notion of intent have generally used the term in the singular (a usage followed in this chapter for the most part) as if to suggest that each disputant can be clearly identified with one, predominant, motivating intent. The presumption that a person will likely have acted on the basis of one intent and that that intent can be identified by others assumes too much about the complicated workings of the human mind. Human intentions are almost invariably complex and most judges, like most people, are unable to delineate and decipher the multidimensional motivations that engender human action.

Courts could define intent as a matter of law to be identifiable only by reference to a contract or other, similar documentation. One commentator has suggested, for instance, that in cases involving artificial insemination "the parties' preconception intent" should "govern paternity" and that law makers should consider "requiring that some documentation of that intent be filed with the state."[6] In general, however, courts handling disputes occasioned by reproductive technology have not directed that intent be specified through reference to preconception documentation (such as a contract) for a simple, though unfortunate reason: that the courts, in their confusion, find intent attractive precisely because it can be constructed to serve the apparent interests of tradition and of modernity (of status and of contract). A party's intent may indicate the terms of a contract into which that party has entered; or, equally, it may be taken to refer to an undeclared sense of self in connection to others (including familial others). Not surprisingly, therefore, in the process of constructing intent to serve various, often contradictory ends, the meaning of the concept shifts.

If the law were clearly to define intent in such cases to reflect principles of contract, the concept would lose its usefulness in mediating conflicting understandings of family. In fact, each court that has relied on the concept of intent in confronting the challenges of reproductive technology has constructed the meaning of the notion intent independently. In each case, the meaning constructed suggests a parallel reconstruction of the relations understood to differentiate and connect home and work, including related images of tradition and modernity. Moreover, construction of the notion of intent in these cases reflects, and then affects, the differences and similarities between the person as an autonomous individual and the person as an essential part of an enduring constellation of familial relationships.

The relevant cases illustrate the pressures on the judiciary, and on the legal system more generally, to decide what constitutes a family and what the implications of *that* decision are for competing claims to gametes, embryos, or children. Moreover, those cases illustrate the deep confusions and inconsistencies in the law's response at present to the possibilities that reproductive technology occasions.

II. The Judicial Response: Intent as an Option

In *Davis v. Davis*, the Tennessee divorce case in which Junior and Mary Sue Davis fought for control of their seven frozen embryos, the conflict between a vision of the embryos as children and a vision of the embryos as property was both transparent and acute. As a result, the case frames dramatically the attraction that a procedure promising to permit contract and choice but to preserve tradition holds for courts. The state supreme court forged an approach which apparently promises to do just that—to preserve tradition and to recognize modernity. In fact, the promise is illusory.

The court bowed to traditional understandings of family by demanding that "special respect" be paid to the embryos, defined as valuable because of their "potential to become ... children."[7] However, in reaching a specific holding, the court bypassed the interests of the embryos and focused on those of the progenitors. The court explained that ideally such disputes should be resolved by effecting "the preferences of the progenitors,"[8] but that, if the progenitors disagreed, courts should look to any "prior agreement concerning disposition" of the embryos. The court further explained that in cases such as *Davis* in which the parties did not agree, and had never expressly agreed, about alternative dispositions of the embryos, "the relative interests of the parties in using or not using the preembryos must be weighed."

In theory, this third approach followed from the right to privacy protected by the federal and state constitutions. However, the right to privacy offers no guidance in selecting among disputants' conflicting rights to procreational privacy. The constitutional frame within which the court balanced the parties' preferences posed the right to procreate against the right to avoid procreation. The court described these as "rights of equal significance."[9] That frame did not compel any particular decision. And so, the state supreme court considered such factors as the "emotional stress and physical discomfort" that IVF causes women, the "joys of parenthood," the "anguish of a lifetime of unwanted parenthood," the "emotional burden" of knowing that IVF had been undertaken for naught, and the burden of "wondering" about one's "parental status."[10] Thus, the court examined, characterized, and compared the parties' preferences and the emotional underpinnings of those preferences. Presuming to balance the parties' constitutional interests, the court in fact examined their preferences, and then effected one party's preference.

The court's asserted respect for the embryos, on the one hand, and its attention to the wishes and interests of the parties, on the other hand, appear to recognize, and thus to provide for, alternative visions of family. In fact, however, the language of the decision reflects, but the holding fails completely to reconcile or even acknowledge, the contradictions presented by the case. By invoking the embryos and defining them as it did, the *Davis* court appeared to acknowledge and favor traditional families, defined in contrast with the dictates of the marketplace. But in recognizing as definitive the preferences and contractual agreements entered into by the progenitors, the court defined the Davises as associates in the business of human reproduction. Even the approach actually followed, whereby the court presumed to balance the Davis's respective constitutional interests, reflects a view of family members as essentially unconnected, autonomous individuals. The United States Supreme Court clearly delineated that view in *Eisenstadt* (in proscribing a statutory prohibition against the distribution of birth control to unmarried individuals) as well as in latter privacy cases. However, it is a view almost completely at odds with traditional understandings of the family as a connected, enduring whole.

In *Davis* the contradictions between alternative visions of family as well as the court's failure to mediate those contradictions are transparent. That is so because the *Davis* court failed even to attempt to reconcile its conclusions about the embryos' ontological status with its focus on the progenitors' preferences and interests in actually resolving disputes such as that in *Davis*.

The same set of contradictions appears in a number of other cases in which courts, asked to settle disputes occasioned by reproductive technology, defined parentage through reference to parental intent. In these cases, however, the contractions between traditional and modern understandings of family are far less transparent than in *Davis*, largely because the courts attempted to construct the concept of intent itself to reflect both the parameters of the marketplace and those of the traditional home.

Maternal Intent

In both *Johnson v. Calvert* and *McDonald v. McDonald*, courts relied expressly on the notion of intent to establish the parentage of a baby with two biological mothers (one genetic, one gestational). Each case involved IVF and the gestation of the resulting embryo in the uterus of a women unconnected genetically to that embryo. In *Johnson* the gestational mother (called the surrogate) was paid to gestate an embryo produced from the gametes of Crispina and Mark Calvert, the intending parents. In *McDonald*, in contrast, the gestational mother was the intending, though not genetic, mother. Both the California Supreme Court in *Johnson* and the New York appellate court in *McDonald*, expressly following the model erected in *Johnson*, identified the intending mother as the baby's "natural" and legal mother.

As seen from the discussion of *Johnson* in the previous chapter, the California Supreme Court in that case looked to the notion of intent only after concluding that neither of the traditional methods for establishing parentage in California—through reference to biology or to existing statutory rules—could be applied satisfactorily to the case. Thus, the court sought an alternative method for establishing maternity. However, in relying on the notion of intent to establish Crispina Calvert's maternity, the court reconstructed the meaning of the term. This chapter is concerned primarily with the implications of that sort of reconstruction.

As reconstructed in *Johnson*, the term "intent" denotes alternative, even contradictory, views of person, parent, and family. In this sense, the decision in *Johnson* resembles that in *Davis*. However, the *Davis* court delineated two essentially unconnected approaches to the case, and then, without explanation, relied on only one of them. In contrast, the state supreme court in *Johnson* relied on the single concept of intent to recognize favorably the creation of families through choice and to acknowledge the value of traditional families.

As used by the court in *Johnson*, the concept of intent represents a contractual, *and* a traditional, view of family. The decision certainly acknowledges that through agreement, familial connections can be imagined, produced, and then, with the law's assistance, enforced and solidified. Also, however, the term is used as a symbol of familial connection, as a new alternative to terms such as blood and genes, which constitute the connection between generations. In this sense, the term "intent" suggests the essence of familial loyalty and love associated with traditional understandings of family.

Again and again, the court in *Johnson* elaborated upon the notion of intent by invoking simultaneously the assumptions central to the world of the marketplace and those central to the world of traditional families. The assumptions of the marketplace seem obviously associated with the concept of intent. Intent suggests will and reason; it depends on choice and negotiation, and it provides for changing perspectives and shifting interactions. In almost complete contrast, biology, as a ground on which familial relations have long been rendered sensible, makes those relations inevitable and their termination unlikely.

The supreme court in *Johnson* recognized expressly that its reliance on the notion of intent implies a contractual view of family. The court explicitly approved, although it did not directly enforce, the contract into which the parties had entered and on which the court relied in discerning the parties' intentions. Such contracts, explained the court, are not inconsistent with public policy.

But, the notion of intent was fashioned by, and was useful to, the court in *Johnson* because that court *did not* abandon a view of family based on a traditional conception of inexorable connection and replace it with one based firmly and exclusively on autonomous individuality—traditionally perceived as appropriate to the marketplace but not to the home. Rather, the court relied on the notion of intent, and defined that notion variously, if confusedly, as associated with both traditional family bonds and with contract and autonomous individuality.

Thus, the court asserted unhesitatingly that its reliance on intent was not merely a pretext for identifying the genetic parents as the legal parents and declared accordingly that parental intent is determinative not only of legal maternity, but of "natural" maternity. Although the egg donor emerges as the natural mother in *Johnson*, in other cases, the gestator, if also the intending mother, would be the natural mother. Exactly that identification was made in *McDonald*. There, the court identified the gestational mother, Olga McDonald, as the children's natural mother because Olga, not the egg donor, had intended to become their social mother. These decisions expressly separate the designation "natural mother" from biological considerations; that notwithstanding, the designation "natural mother" in cases such as *Johnson* and

McDonald performs the same service—that of identifying a child's "real" mother—usually performed through reference to biology.

Neither the court in *Johnson* nor that in *McDonald* used the term "natural mother" as a synonym for "better mother." The *Johnson* court was explicit. It sought to identify the *real* mother. That becomes clear from the court's response to the dissent. Justice Kennard's dissent suggested that the case should be decided by identification of the parent or parents who would best serve the child's interests:

> This "best interests" standard serves to assure that in the judicial resolution of disputes affecting a child's well-being, protection of the minor child is the foremost consideration. Consequently, I would apply "the best interests of the child" standard to determine who can best assume the social and legal responsibilities of motherhood for a child born of a gestational surrogacy arrangement.[11]

The majority described the dissent's position as "confus[ing] concepts of parentage and custody." "Logically," the court continued, "the determination of parentage must precede, and should not be dictated by, eventual custody decisions."[12] The court explained that decisions about parentage—about who the parents *are*—must be made before decisions about custody.

That is so, however, only in a world in which inexorable, incontestable truths (such as those traditionally represented by claims based on blood, or genetic connections) dictate the facts of family. The dissent presumed that it could establish parentage as well as custody through a best-interest determination. That presumption suggests that parents can be linked to their children without reliance on inexorable truths about the everlasting essence of the parent-child connection and that the identification of parentage is a social choice. The majority, however, in sharp contrast, self-consciously and unequivocally sought the real and natural mother, not the best mother.

Apart from the replacement of blood or genes with intent, the court's understanding of the connection on which it predicated the existence of family is remarkably traditional. For instance, following a model of old-fashioned, traditional families, the court depicted relations in the family and at home ideally to be relations of enduring and solidary commitment, exactly the type of relations that have long been taken to make the family different from the world of work—a world in which relations are transient and oriented toward specific goals. In large part, therefore, the court responded to the challenge that the facts in *Johnson* presented to traditional views of family by preserving a traditional view but, within that, substituting new assumptions (for example, intent is productive of familial connections) for old assumptions (for example, blood connections produce familial relations). In this sense, the court replaced blood and genes with intent as the inexorable foundation of familial commitment. To this extent, therefore, intent becomes a substitute for blood as the basic connection between parents and their "natural" children.

Thus, the court used the notion of intent as a justification for, and as an elaboration of, its central determination—"that Crispina is the child's natural mother."[13] This use of the notion of intent may initially appear effective, and thus perhaps even determinative, because it seems to bring the correlates of traditional family life into harmony with the correlates of the marketplace, with each pointing to Crispina Calvert as the baby's mother.

However, that harmony can be easily shattered. In fact, the court's approach to determining parentage in such cases is self-contradictory and inherently unstable. The court presented the parties' intentions as revealing the baby's real and only mother; but at the same time, the court itself connected the parties' intentions to the contractual agreement among them. More particularly, the court embedded a contractual understanding of family in the rhetoric of family as a realm of status, a hierarchical realm defined through love, loyalty, and enduring commitment. Complications and contradictions are evident. For instance, the court recognized the strength of biological connections in order to transcend the implications that such connections carry. Thus, the court explained that in what it called a "true 'egg donation' situation," a situation in which the gestational, rather than the genetic, mother was the intending mother, then the "birth mother" would be "the natural mother."[14] *McDonald* represented exactly that case, and there, the New York court, relying on *Johnson* for a model, denominated the gestational and intending, but not genetic, mother, the "natural mother."

The courts in *Johnson* and *McDonald* unhesitatingly claimed to have identified a real and natural mother. In one case that mother was genetically related to her child but did not gestate nor give birth to the child; in the other she gestated and gave birth to her child but was not linked to that child through genetics. The courts' conclusions in each case depended on reconstructing the concept of intent. If intent is ultimately allied with the world of contract, with the world of the marketplace, then, as the dissent assumed, courts may select the best parent in such cases, but they cannot identify and distinguish the real parent. If, on the other hand, parentage flows inevitably from the facts of nature or from the facts of family, then, at least in theory, courts can identify the real parent (as well perhaps as the best parent) in such cases only by reconstructing the concept of intent so that intentions, or at least intentions that have been articulated and announced, become nonnegotiable. Such intentions must be separated from the world of the marketplace and allied with the sort of inexorable truths long thought to underlie familial connections.

Clearly, *Johnson*, and *McDonald* in its wake, are self-contradictory. The contradictions underlying these cases reflect a set of contradictions found pervasively within present-day family life and family law. They are thus worth exploring further. That exploration can continue by examining in greater detail the responses of Justice Kennard, who dissented in *Johnson*, to the arguments through which the majority elaborated upon the notion of intent as the central determinant of parentage and the court's responses to Justice Kennard's dissent.

Justice Kennard asserted that the court in *Johnson* looked to "tort, property [and] contract law" and should instead have relied on "family law, as the governing paradigm and source of a rule of decision." [15] That observation is not inaccurate. However, on deeper examination, the majority did not simply rely on the laws of the market; rather, it appropriated those laws and refashioned them to reflect the correlates of an ideology of status as well as of contract. For instance, the court justified its reliance on intent by claiming that "the child would not have been born but for the efforts of the intended parents." [16] Certainly, "but-for" arguments, familiar to the law of torts, have not generally been invoked in the resolution of disputes concerning parentage. However, the court framed its discussion to suggest that Crispina Calvert's causative intention effected a fundamental and enduring connection between her and the baby—a connection as strong and certain as any predicated on the biological correlates of maternity. So understood, intent becomes connective, joining people more strongly and more securely than any contract can.

The court explained:

[T]he mental concept of the child is a controlling factor of its creation, and the originators of that concept merit full credit as conceivers. The mental concept must be recognized as independently valuable; it creates expectations in the initiating parents of a child, and it creates expectations in society for adequate performance on the part of the initiators as parents of the child.[17]

The dissent, describing this language as reminiscent of the laws that protect intellectual property, wrote,

[I]t may be argued, just as a song or invention is protected as the property of the "originator of the concept," so too a child should be regarded as belonging to the originator of the concept of the child, the genetic mother.

The problem with this argument, of course, is that children are not property. Unlike songs or inventions, rights in children cannot be sold for consideration, or made freely available to the general public. Our most fundamental notions of personhood tell us it is inappropriate to treat children as property.[18]

The court did not, however, simply equate children with songs and inventions. Rather, the court interpreted Crispina's intent to *constitute* her maternity and therefore, to provide evidence of her ability to parent well. In the court's view, Crispina's intent, similar to another mother's blood or genes, connected Crispina to the child and made that child hers.

The *Johnson* court further justified its reliance on intent by declaring that " 'intentions that are voluntarily chosen, deliberate, express and bargained-for ought presumptively to determine legal parenthood.' "[19] The dissent responded:

The unsuitability of applying the notion that, because contract intentions are "voluntarily chosen, deliberate, express and bargained-for," their performance ought to be compelled by the courts is even more clear when the concept of specific performance is used to determine the course of the life of a child. Just as children are not the intellectual property of their parents, neither are they the personal property of anyone, and their delivery cannot be ordered as a contract remedy on the same terms that a court would, for example, order a breaching party to deliver a truckload of nuts and bolts.[20]

Again, however, the court did not simply appropriate rules promulgated for resolving disputes in the marketplace and apply those rules to determine a child's parentage. Instead, the court reconstructed the meaning of the rules, and thus the rules themselves, so that, in the context of decisions about parentage, those rules assume connection as well as autonomy, and unalterable truth as well as negotiated, changing arrangements. The court did not enforce the parties' "bargained for" intentions as it would enforce any contract. It effect those intentions as the embodiment of a set of truths about familial relationships compelled the conclusion that Crispina was the baby's "natural" mother. The court enforced the contractual arrangement entered into by the parties only incidentally in actualizing the intent that the contract revealed.

In declaring Crispina the "natural" mother because she had *intended* to be the mother, the court presumed her the better mother as well because the court understood maternal intent to indicate, even more completely than the biological components of motherhood in other cases, that the intending mother would be the better mother. The court explained that "the interests of children, particularly at the start of their lives, are '[un]likely to run contrary to those of adults who choose to bring them into being.' "[21]

In response, the dissent argued that the court's approach would always prefer the genetic mother in cases such as *Johnson* and that in certain cases, that preference would not serve the best interests of the child or children involved. In fact, the court had expressly asserted that the gestational mother, if the intending mother, should be denominated the natural mother under state law. However, on its reading of the majority's decision (perhaps referring only to that subset of cases in which the gestational mother did not initially intend to become the social mother), the dissent explained:

> It requires little imagination to foresee cases in which the genetic mothers are, for example, unstable or substance abusers, or in which the genetic mothers' life circumstances change dramatically during the gestational mothers' pregnancies, while the gestational mothers, though of a less advantaged socioeconomic class, are stable, mature, capable and willing to provide a loving family environment in which the child will flourish. Under those circumstances, the majority's rigid reliance on the intent of the genetic mother will not serve the best interests of the child.[22]

Yet, courts generally prefer a biological parent to anyone else in disputes involving a child's parentage or custody, without assuming that that parent will necessarily be the wisest or most impressive parent or custodian among those seeking the role. A biological parent may be declared unfit, thereby obviating the strength of the biological connection in disputes over parentage or custody. That, however, is understood as the extreme and unusual case. Generally, courts stress the importance of the biological connection per se and presume that preference for a biological parent in cases involving disputes over parentage will best serve a child's interests even if other contenders for the role of parent seem psychologically, sociologically, or economically superior to the biological parent. The position of the majority in *Johnson* that an intending parent should be preferred to anyone else is analogous.

In fact, the presumption in *Johnson* that an intending parent will be a good parent is arguably stronger than the comparable presumption about biological parents in other cases. The claim presuming that biological parents are better parents relies on the correlates of an ideology of status only—on the notion, for instance, that that which is "natural" is good, or at least better than alternatives. The comparable claim for an intending parent relies on the correlates of status along with those of contract. In addition to being the "natural" mother, the intending mother is a rational parent. She chose to be a parent and actualized that choice as an autonomous actor negotiating an agreement to produce her child. Thus, Crispina, in the court's view, became Christopher's mother even before the child's birth as a matter of nature (signified by her gamete donation along with her intent) and as a matter of culture (signified by her contractual agreement that demonstrated her intent). The court did not expressly separate Crispina's maternity into a natural and a cultural aspect. Rather, the court described each aspect so that it strengthened the reality and legitimacy of the other.

Thus, the court attempted, perhaps not self-consciously, but quite obviously, to combine the correlates of an ideology that prizes autonomous individuality and bargained negotiations with the correlates of an ideology that prizes enduring, inexorable connection among family members. Ultimately, however, the contradictions inherent in that effort prove it unworkable. The state supreme court in *Johnson* never directly addressed those contradictions nor the implications that flow from them.

For instance, the *Johnson* court never addressed, and appears not to have recognized, the difficult but inevitable problems presented by shifting or confused intent. Yet, if the law is to predicate parentage on intent in cases involving disputes occasioned by reproductive technology, courts that rely on intent to determine parentage must be able to identify the parties' real intentions. In fact, however, people's intentions are rarely unidimensional or everlasting, and it is rarely possible to identify a person's one, true intent.

The court in *Johnson* did not consider the difficulties posed by changing intent and uncertain intent. Perhaps, the court avoided that task because consideration of these difficulties would likely have entailed an analysis more clearly embedded in the world of the marketplace than that which the court produced. Instead of delineating expressly a procedure available to future courts involved in identifying a party's intent in such cases, the *Johnson* court imagined implicitly an almost primordial moment during which the parties' intentions were rendered unalterable at least for purposes of judicial analyses and conclusions. By locating that moment at the baby's creation, the court presumed a moment of clear, eternal intention and thereby avoided the reality of changing intent:

> But for [the Calverts'] acted-on intention, the child would not exist. Anna agreed to facilitate the procreation of Mark's and Crispina's child. . . . [I]t is safe to say that Anna would not have been given the opportunity to gestate or deliver the child had she, prior to implantation of the zygote, manifested her own intent to be the child's mother. No reason appears why Anna's later change of heart should vitiate the determination that Crispina is the child's natural mother.[23]

The court thereby posited an initial, inviolable intent that would determine all future interactions and connections. Changes of heart may occur and be unfortunate for the parties, but they cannot challenge the force of the original intent or the law's readiness to ensure the actualization of that intent. The court justified its preference for that initial, almost mystical, intent through reference to the contractual arrangement among the parties, but the court did not enforce that contract.

Courts or legislatures could decide to enforce such contracts. That is not what the *Johnson* court did, however. Had the court simply enforced the contract into which the parties had entered, the court would have avoided the need to presume intent. But the court would, as well, have definitively defined the family in market terms, as a collection of free, essentially unconnected, uncommitted individuals. Had the case been decided on the basis of ordinary contract principles, it would not have been necessary, or even possible, to infer Crispina's "natural," and thus exclusive, maternity from the agreement. In fact, the court neither enforced nor dismissed the gestational surrogacy contract. It acknowledged that contract, and then used it to safeguard a world understood through the prism of relations founded on status rather than contract.

As a result, maternity as defined in *Johnson* is fragile. The court's efforts to ground its identification of the mother in natural fact notwithstanding, the identification and definition of mother do become matters of negotiable choice once the definition of mother is separated from connections (such as those based in blood or genes) understood by the larger society as inevitable. The notion of intent cannot reflect and preserve autonomous individuality and at the same time substitute convincingly for blood or genes as the enduring essence of familial love and loyalty. Judicial reliance on intent in such cases will prove impractical or will be expressly transformed into a more straightforward reliance on ordinary contract principles.

A Dead Sperm Donor's Intent

For a few decades before *Johnson*, courts faced with conundrums posed by the use of AID (artificial—or alternative—insemination, donor) invoked consent—though not intent—in identifying a child's father. In none of those decisions, however, was a consenting father thereby designated a "natural" father.

Donor Sperm and the "Consenting" Father

Long before the appearance of the new reproductive technologies, courts faced disputes occasioned by the use of artificial insemination (sometimes now referred to as alternative insemination). In the first half of the twentieth century, this form of reproductive assistance was problematic for the society and the law. Most controversial were cases of artificial insemination that involved use of sperm from a man other than the husband of the woman being inseminated. This form of insemination, referred to as AID has generally been used by women whose husbands were sterile, had low sperm counts, or were deemed likely to produce children with genetic diseases, or by women choosing to become mothers without the active involvement of a male partner. Artificial insemination cases involving use of sperm from the mother's husband (AIH) have been much less controversial.

Slowly, during the course of the twentieth century, the law recognized the mother's husband as the father of children produced through use of donor sperm in cases in which the mother's husband consented to the insemination. In several AID cases, courts determined a mother's husband to be her child's legal father, or at least to be responsible for child support, despite the absence of a biological connection between the man and the child. In those cases, the husband's paternity was premised on his consent to the artificial insemination of his wife with donor sperm.

For instance, in *People v. Sorensen,* the California Supreme Court decided in 1968 that a man who had agreed to the artificial insemination of his wife with donor sperm remained responsible for the child thereby produced after his divorce from the child's mother. *Sorensen* involved a criminal prosecution for failure to support the child. Sorensen argued he had no duty of support. The court disagreed with him and asserted that Sorensen, having "consent[ed] to the production of a child," and having thereby made it "safe to assume that without [his] active participation and consent the child would not have been procreated," became the child's father and as a result became responsible for supporting the child.[24] The court in *Sorensen* expressly and carefully differentiated such a father from a "natural" father:

> The determinative factor is whether the legal relationship of father and child exists. A child conceived through heterologous artificial insemination [insemination using donor sperm] does not have a "natural father," as that terms [sic] is commonly used. . . . Since there is no "natural father," we can only look for a lawful father.[25]

In *Sorensen,* a consenting father was a clear alternative to, rather than a variant of, a natural parent. "In California," the court concluded, "legitimacy is a legal status that may exist despite the fact that the husband is not the natural father of the child."[26]

Other courts similarly predicated paternity on the consent of the mother's husband in cases involving AID. In *In re Adoption of Anonymous,* a New York court allowed a father who had consented to the conception and pregnancy from donor artificial insemination of his wife to veto the adoption of the child by the mother's new husband. In *Gursky v. Gursky,* a father was held responsible for support of a child conceived by his wife through AID. In that case, a New York court held the father responsible, despite the annulment of the marriage on grounds that it was unconsummated, because he had consented to the insemination.

Thus, courts have been considering issues engendered by cases involving artificial insemination for many decades. For that reason, these cases invite contrast with more recent ones involving the use of the new reproductive technologies. The earliest cases and commentaries involving the use of donor insemination, decided before mid-century, focused on dangers and advantages of artificial insemination using donor sperm for the character of the family and, more particularly, for the stability of marriage.

In *Orford v. Orford,* one of the earliest legal cases involving AID, the Ontario Supreme Court declared in 1921 by way of dicta that, under Ontario divorce law, a married woman allegedly artificially inseminated with sperm from a donor, without the knowledge of her husband, was guilty of adultery. The court defined adultery to include the voluntary surrender by the guilty person of the reproductive powers to someone other than the spouse. Thus, the court clearly understood marriage as a status relationship, not as a negotiated association between two essentially separate people. The court declared: "[I]n the case of the woman [adultery] involves the possibility of introducing into the family of the husband a false strain of blood. Any act on the part of the wife which does that would, therefore, be adulterous."[27] The *Orford* court presumed that family relations, including the relations between spouses were (or at least should be) anchored decisively and exclusively in a natural order. Anything perceived to deviate from that order deserved condemnation.

Only by the middle of the twentieth century did courts in the United States begin to recognize the legitimacy of children produced from donor insemination in cases such as *Sorensen* in which the mother's husband had given his consent. At about the same time, states began to provide by statute for the recognition of families created through artificial insemination using donor sperm. In 1964, the first statute regulating artificial insemination was promulgated in Georgia,[28] and at present about three-fifths of the states have statutes that permit and regulate artificial insemination.

With the first cases approving artificial insemination and legitimizing the children involved, the husband's consent became pivotal. However, that consent was not equated or confused with intent. Thus, a husband who consented to the donor insemination of his wife could not deny paternity by arguing that he had never in fact intended to effect the terms of his apparent consent.[29] Neither could a wife deny the paternity of her divorcing husband to children born during the marriage by donor insemination if the husband consented to the procedure.[30]

To a significant extent, the developing rules governing the use and implications of artificial insemination have continued to reflect old-fashioned family values. Courts and legislatures have worked to ensure that artificial insemination would occur within a social context associated with traditional families; the law accomplished this by allowing paternal consent to be substituted for biological paternity in determining the implications of artificial insemination using donor sperm. That substitution reflected the traditional notion that a mother's husband was the father of her children. Relevant, contemporary statutes routinely treat a mother's husband who consents to donor insemination as they treat a "natural" father, but do not label him as such. More specifically, statutes regulating artificial insemination treat a consenting mother's husband as the child's father, giving him the rights and holding him to the responsibilities of any father, without requiring that he adopt the child involved. The husband's consent—not his intent—is central to the existing rules. The aim has been to ensure that the husband's rights and responsibilities would be preserved with regard to any child resulting from donor insemination of his wife, and concomitantly that families produced through donor insemination would resemble traditional families as closely as possible.

The law has been slower to provide expressly for the rights of women seeking nonmarital motherhood by choice. In the mid-1980s, Carol Donovan reviewed this area of the law and found a continuing absence of protection for unmarried women anxious to establish families without legal fathers.[31] Since then, a number of cases have involved sperm donors claiming paternity of children born to unmarried mothers. Largely, in these cases courts have relied on existing statutes to determine the respective rights of the parties. For instance, in *Jhordan C. v. Mary K.*, the court found the sperm donor to be the father of the child because a statute provided that the "donor of semen *provided to a licensed physician* for use in artificial insemination of a woman other than the donor's wife is treated in law as if he were not the natural father of a child thereby conceived."[32] In the case, however, the insemination had occurred without physician involvement.

Can Dead Men Have Children?

The response the law has developed over the last few decades in regulating artificial insemination is today being tested anew. With the availability by the 1950s of cryopreservation to store sperm indefinitely in a frozen state, new possibilities have begun to emerge. One such possibility, the use of a man's sperm after his death, challenges the law's assumptions about the meaning of paternity and cannot be regulated through reliance on existing rules since the law has not yet responded to the possibility of posthumous insemination, conception, and birth. Legislators have not yet defined the familial relation between a dead sperm donor and a child conceived through use of his sperm. In general, the law in the United States does not yet regulate control over frozen sperm or clarify such matters as the inheritance rights of children conceived after the deaths of their genetic parents.

Therefore, courts are confused in cases occasioned by posthumous insemination. In such cases, the meaning of father must be reexamined and clarified, just as the meaning of mother demands reexamination and clarification in cases occasioned by gestational surrogacy. Posthumous use of sperm stretches existing statutory schemes for regulating family relationships beyond their limits. In particular, it becomes difficult to sustain the broad approach to artificial insemination, widely institutionalized in the 1960s, as an exception that can be comfortably harmonized with traditional views of family.

Torn between the security of old understandings of family and the pull of novel understandings engendered at least in part by the new reproductive technologies, courts are attempting to bypass, or sometimes to incorporate, both, and to construct new categories through which to think about, and govern, the creation of families. And, as with cases involving gestational surrogacy, courts faced with disputes about the control of a dead man's sperm have declared the intent of the parties to be determinative.

Two cases, one decided in France in 1984 (*Parpalaix c. CECOS*) and the other in California in the 1990s *(Hecht v. Superior Court)*, have presented courts with just such a dispute. In France at the time, no laws directly addressed the questions presented. In several regards the California court was able to, and did, refer to existing state statutory provisions, but the central question in *Hecht* could not be answered by the state's existing law. Thus, both courts chose not to infer a response to the disputes before them from related, existing rules. Each court fashioned its own responses to the dilemmas presented by posthumous insemination.

In *Hecht v. Superior Court* the California courts were asked to determine the fate of William Kane's frozen sperm. Kane was already dead. In October 1991, Kane deposited fifteen vials of his sperm with California Cryobank, Inc., a Los Angeles sperm bank, and signed an agreement authorizing the bank to release his sperm to Deborah Hecht, the woman with whom he had lived for five years.

Specifically, Kane signed a "Specimen Storage Agreement" which provided that in the event of his death, the sperm bank should "[c]ontinue to store [the specimens] upon request of the executor of the estate [or] [r]elease the specimens to the executor of the estate."[33] In fact, a few weeks before Kane deposited sperm with California Cryobank, he executed a will that named Hecht as executor of his estate and that provided that "any specimens of my sperm stored with any sperm bank or similar facility for storage" be bequeathed to Hecht. Hecht was not in fact serving as executor of Kane's estate when the California appellate court heard the case, and the record before that court was apparently unclear as to whether reference to Kane's executor was a reference to Hecht or to anyone serving in the role of executor.[34] In another provision of the agreement into which Kane entered with the sperm bank (labeled "Authorization to Release Specimens") Kane authorized the bank to "release my semen specimens to Deborah Ellen Hecht. I am also authorizing specimens to be released to recipient's physician Dr. Kathryn Moyer."[35]

Then, at the end of the month (October 1991), Kane committed suicide. After his death, Hecht asked that the sperm be released to her. Kane's two adult children from a former marriage, Katharine Kane and William Everett Kane, Jr., contested Kane's will and asked that Kane's sperm be destroyed. Kane's children invoked traditional family values in urging the court to order destruction of their father's sperm.

Kane's will, executed on September 27, 1991, a month before his suicide, explicitly provided: "I bequeath all right, title, and interest that I may have in any specimens of my sperm stored with any sperm bank or similar facility for storage to Deborah Ellen Hecht."[36] Kane's children asserted that even were his will declared valid, public policy argued against both the artificial insemination of Hecht as an unmarried woman and the use of a dead man's sperm. In the view of Kane's children, destruction of the sperm would "help guard the family unit" by precluding the creation of an untraditional family (one composed of Hecht, the child, and the memory of Kane) and would, equally, protect an existing family unit (their own) from invasion by a posthumous sibling and the "emotional, psychological and financial stress" that such a child's birth would create. They described their father's interest in producing a posthumous child as "egotistic and irresponsible"; such a description may harmonize with social views of expected, and even permissible, action in the marketplace, but is strongly at odds with almost any account of a good father. Thus Kane's children suggested that in their father's decision to supply and freeze sperm for posthumous reproduction, Kane showed virtually no real fatherly interest in the potential welfare of the children who might result from the posthumous use of his sperm.

The trial court agreed with Kane's children and ordered the sperm destroyed. When asked by Hecht's counsel to explain the legal bases of this order, the trial court judge replied:

> It really does not matter does it? If I am right, I am right and if I am wrong, I am wrong. As you know, I am persuaded by the arguments in the moving papers. This is something that is going to have to be decided by the appellate courts. Let's get a decision.[37]

The California Court of Appeal vacated the order of the trial court and remanded the case for determinations as to the validity of the will, the validity of the sperm bank contract, and the enforceability of settlement agreements regarding probate of Kane's estate that had been entered into by Hecht and Kane's two children.

The appellate court did determine that Kane had an "ownership" interest in his sperm sufficient to permit inclusion of those sperm within Kane's probate estate. Curiously, the court concluded that the character of Kane's ownership interest in his sperm made those sperm part of his probate estate (assuming a valid will), but precluded the sperm's being the object of a gift (either *inter vivos* or *causa mortis*). The court's opinion left the distinction unexplained:

> We conclude that at the time of his death, decedent had an interest, in the nature of ownership, to the extent that he had decision-making authority as to the use of his sperm for reproduction. Such interest is sufficient to constitute "property" within the meaning of [state law]. Accordingly, the probate court had jurisdiction with respect to the vials of sperm.
>
> In concluding that the sperm is properly part of decedent's estate, we do not address the issue of the validity or enforceability of any contract or will purporting to express decedent's intent with respect to the stored sperm. In view of the nature of sperm as reproductive material which is a unique type of "property," we also decline petitioner's invitation to apply to this case the general law relating to gifts of personal property or the statutory provisions for gifts in view of impending death.[38]

The court concluded that decedent's interest in his sperm "falls within the broad definition of property [provided for in the California Probate Code], as 'anything that may be the subject of ownership and includes both real and personal property and any interest therein.' "

The court's decision that cryopreserved sperm is among the types of property that can be bequeathed at death did not ensure that Hecht would inherit those sperm. That assurance depended, among other possibilities, on the validity of Kane's will. In fact, Kane's children questioned the validity of their father's will, claiming that Kane was "of unsound mind, subject to the undue influence of. . . . Hecht and/or suffering from insane delusions" when he designed and executed the will.[39] That claim, if supported by the facts, would erode Hecht's right to receive the sperm under the will and would preclude her referring to the will as evidence of Kane's intent regarding disposition of the sperm that he had deposited with California Cryobank, Inc.

Thus, in theory, a finding that Kane was in fact competent when he executed the will, and in particular that he had not been unduly influenced by Hecht, would allow probate of the will and transmission of the sperm to Hecht. In addition, such a finding would establish Kane's intent that his sperm be used posthumously to inseminate Hecht, thereby providing alternative grounds (not dependent on the ultimate fate of the will) for granting Kane's sperm to Hecht. The court explained that the will "evidences the decedent's intent that Hecht, should she so desire, is to receive his sperm stored in the sperm bank to bear his child posthumously."[40] Were Kane incompetent, subject to undue influence, or the victim of fraud when he executed his will, then that will would not provide evidence of his intent.

In fact, on remand, the trial court made no finding about Kane's competence as a testator. Rather, the court relied on a settlement agreement into which the parties had entered in December 1991. Eventually, under the settlement agreement, the trial court entered an order in March 1995 directing the administrator of Kane's estate to distribute three vials of sperm to Hecht. Kane's children appealed, but in August 1995, the court of appeal ruled that the trial court order had to be carried out immediately because it was issued on the ground that Hecht, then past forty years of age, was "at imminent risk of loss if she had to wait out the appellate process before attempting to be impregnated with Kane's sperm."[41]

In its initial decision, however, the appeals court *assumed*, for purposes of its decision, that Kane had intended that his sperm be used to inseminate Hecht. The court explained:

[W]e are not adjudicating the validity or invalidity of the will or any contract or settlement agreement at issue in this case; we also do not purport to adjudicate any claims of decedent's competence or Hecht's undue influence. For the purpose of addressing this rationale for the trial court's order, we *assume*, arguendo, particular intention on the part of the decedent.

The court proceeded to consider the public policy concerns raised by Kane's children. In doing that, the court framed its recognition that families can be created and regulated in contract terms, with an extended discussion of families understood as units of status.

Katharine and William Everett, Jr., argued that single women, such as Hecht, should not be encouraged to have children and create families. They further described the posthumous use of their father's sperm as "in truth, the creation of orphaned children by artificial means with state authorization."[42] The court rejected both policy concerns raised by the Kane children, but did so without strongly denying or accepting the children's claim for status—the claim that the law should encourage traditional marriage and traditional families.

Instead of focusing on families in general, the court focused on *this* family. So, in denying that public policy would limit the use of artificial insemination to married women, the court concluded that the dispute over Kane's sperm carried no far-reaching implications for the "institutions of family and marriage" since the case involved "no existing marriage relationship involving decedent at the time of his death and obviously there can be none after his death."[43]

In addressing the children's argument that public policy precluded the use of a dead man's sperm to produce a posthumous child, the court turned to the one directly relevant precedent of which it was aware— *Parpalaix c. CECOS*, decided in 1984 by a French trial court in the suburbs of Paris.

When the California Court of Appeal first decided *Hecht* in 1993, only a few cases involving the posthumous use of sperm had been decided anywhere. All but *Parpalaix* differed from *Hecht* in important regards. Among these other cases was that of a French widow, Claire Gallon, who desired to become pregnant through the use of her dead husband's sperm, frozen in a state-run sperm bank. The sperm bank in which Michel Gallon had deposited semen in 1985 refused. The case differed from *Hecht* and *Parpalaix* because Michel had signed a clause in an agreement with the sperm bank stipulating that the sperm should only be released in his presence. In 1991, a court in Toulouse rejected Claire Gallon's request.[44] A somewhat different issue regarding the postmortem use of sperm was brought to court in Virginia and California by prisoners condemned to death who requested that their sperm be stored for possible postmortem reproduction.[45] The courts decided that such men have no right to reproduce.[46]

Since *Parpalaix* and *Hecht* were decided, a number of cases have been reported in the press involving widows who preserved the sperm of their recently dead husbands. Several used that sperm in the effort to have a child. Nancy Hart, a Louisiana widow, became pregnant several months after her husband's death with sperm that he had had preserved. After the birth of a daughter, Judith Christine, in June 1991, Hart filed a lawsuit in order to obtain Social Security survivor's benefits for the child.[47] In December 1995, a Social Security appeals council denied the child the right to receive payments. Nancy Hart plans to appeal the case in federal court.[48]

However, when *Hecht* was first heard by the California Court of Appeal in 1993, *Parpalaix* provided the only relevant legal model. The California court relied heavily on *Parpalaix* in describing the significance of a decedent's intent for determining the posthumous use of his sperm. On the basis of the *Parpalaix* precedent, the *Hecht* court constructed the concept of intent so as to reincorporate and invoke traditional family values, the values of a world in which family relations were understood as embedded in inexorable truth.

Parpalaix involved the request of Corinne Richard Parpalaix, a young widow, for her dead husband's sperm. In that request she was supported by her husband's parents. In 1981, Alain Parpalaix, ill with testicular cancer, was told that chemotherapy, the only hope for a cure, might render him sterile. Alain and Corinne were not yet married, but they were living together. Alain deposited nine vials of sperm with the Centre d'Etude et de Conservation du Sperme (CECOS), a government-run sperm bank located outside of Paris. Alain left no directions with the sperm bank about the future use of his sperm. In December 1983 Alain died, two days after marrying Corinne.

CECOS refused Corinne's request for Alain's sperm. After the French Ministry of Health declined to rule swiftly on Corinne's request, she and Alain's parents went to court.[49] There they argued that as Alain's heirs they succeeded to Alain's contractual rights as a sperm depositor with CECOS to receive his sperm upon request. The court found French civil law governing contracts of deposit inapplicable and proceeded instead to consider Alain's intent. In fact, for the *Parpalaix* court Alain's intent constituted the only important question in the case.[50]

In language quoted and relied on by the California court in *Hecht*, the *Parpalaix* court described Alain's intent in terms that almost completely separated that intent from legal agreements and the world of contractual negotiations. The court defined "[s]perm [as] the seed of life; it is connected to the fundamental liberty of a person to conceive or not to conceive."[51] The court explained that as such, sperm cannot be subject to civil rules governing contracts of deposit but must be governed by "the intent of the man from whom it emanates." The court concluded that for that reason Alain's intent regarding the use of his sperm constituted the sole issue presented.[52]

In considering Alain's intent, the court clearly separated the analysis of that intent from a world associated with market relations and embedded it firmly in a world of familial relations understood in traditional terms. For the *Parpalaix* court, Alain's intent regarding his sperm was central to his sense of self and, therefore, the fate of those sperm could not be cavalierly regulated by the rules of contract. However, the court did not hesitate to assess and delineate Alain's intent about the posthumous use of his sperm despite the fact that Alain had apparently never made that intent clearly known. Indeed, the court required Alain's widow to prove Alain's intent was "unequivocable"[53]—a proof that might not seem achievable in the absence of any clear statement left by the dead man. But the court easily found the necessary intent on Alain's part by reference to Alain's familial connections (of enduring love and loyalty) to those anxious that Alain's sperm be made available to Corinne. The court explained that,

> the testimony of Pierre and Danielle Richard, the parents of Corinne Parpalaix, the attitude of Alain Parpalaix, who in the middle of his illness, and with the agreement of [Corinne] desired to preserve his opportunity to procreate, an attitude impressively confirmed two days before his death by a religious and civil marriage, the value of the position in this proceeding of Alain Parpalaix's parents, who would have been able to know the deepest intentions of their son, provide a set of testimony and presumptions that establish, without equivocation, the express intent of Corinne Parpalaix's husband to make his wife the mother of a common child, either during his life or after his death.

For the *Parpalaix* court, Alain's intent about the fate of his sperm was not demonstrated by a contract, but by Alain's loving relations as son, husband, and potential father. Paul Lombard, Corinne Parpalaix's attorney, told the court that it could "decide to consecrate a new legal precedent where a deceased man would have the right to implant life in a woman's womb, and prove that love is more powerful than death."[54] The statement suggests the continuing significance of Alain Parpalaix's autonomy but, at the same time, defines Alain through his enduring connections of familial love to his spouse and potential child.

The intent that the court identified with Alain's "deep desire" was assumed, not demonstrated, to exist in light of Alain's familial connections. The court satisfied the search for Alain's contractual intent by substituting the desires of Alain's survivors for his intent. Thus, the court identified Alain (as family) with his widow and parents, presumed to delineate *their* deep desires, and agreed to effect those desires as if they were (and assumed them to be) Alain's "deep desire." Thus, in relying on Alain's intent and ordering release of his cryopreserved sperm to Corinne's doctor, the court presumed the dictates of traditional understandings of family at least as much as it presumed the dictates of the world of the market.

In November 1984, Corinne was inseminated with Alain's sperm. She did not become pregnant. Of the nine vials of sperm that Alain had deposited with CECOS, seven were used in the insemination and two were used in tests.[55]

The California court in *Hecht* relied heavily on *Parpalaix* in answering the arguments of Kane's children's that public policy forbid the posthumous insemination of Hecht with their father's sperm. In doing so, the court suggested that Kane's intent, as Parpalaix's, was to be understood as a "deep desire"[56] to create familial bonds, at least as much as it was to be understood as the motive for contractual negotiations.

Both courts—*Parpalaix* explicitly and *Hecht* by implication—depicted intent as an emotional and moral matter more than as a matter of contractual motivation. Each court began by considering the decedent's choice in terms resembling those typically used in interpretations of disputed and ambiguous contracts. But each court switched its ideological bearings and sought, instead, to identify the decedent's (familial) desires, thereby presuming to create for the decedent the emotional future and family constellation he would have established for himself had he lived long enough to do that.

The choice that proves conclusive for the courts in these cases (reliance on the notion of intent) is an overdetermined choice—a choice of the market and a choice of the home. Freud used the term "overdetermined" to refer to a dream symbol that actually appeared in a dream because it carried a heavy load (an overload, from the perspective of the unconscious) of meanings. Freud described an overdetermined dream-symbol as referring to many dream-thoughts.[57] Analogously, reliance on the notion of intent seemed compelling for the courts in these cases because, as constructed, the notion of intent provides at the same time for the preservation of tradition and for the acceptance of modernity. It might appear therefore that nothing is lost and a great deal is gained.

For each court, though more clearly for the court in *Hecht,* the decision to recognize the dead man's intent included recognition of that man's autonomous individuality, including his ability to design his own future contractually, as well as recognition of his connected status within the context of familial relationships. For the courts, the dead men's choice during life to procreate posthumously had to be effected because the rules of the market demand that freely bargained choices be effected by the law; and, contrastingly, because, as a moral matter, the choice to reproduce posthumously actualized each man's loving commitment and enduring connections to family, and thus preserved each man's "deep desire."

As models for future cases, *Parpalaix* and *Hecht* offer little real guidance. Both courts justified their conclusions as compelled by the dead sperm donor's intent. But neither court seriously considered how to determine the relevant intent. The two courts either rejected expressly, or avoided implicitly, exclusive reliance on principles of contract law. As a result neither court provided for a sperm donor's changing or conflicting intentions, or for a sperm donor with no conscious intentions about the posthumous use of his sperm. In the effort to preserve traditional models of family but also to incorporate forms of interaction traditionally identified with the marketplace, not the home—in the effort both to respect traditional families and to safeguard the rights of the individual to design and effect unique families—the courts in these cases failed to address the confusions underlying the disputes, confusions about the meaning and future of parents, children, and families.

III. "Intent" Becomes Contract

Cases such as *Davis, Johnson, Hecht,* and *Parpalaix* demonstrate the allure that the dictates of the marketplace hold for the law in resolving complicated disputes about the meaning and scope of family and familial relationships. These cases demonstrate as well the continuing grip on the society and the law of an ideology of family constructed during the early years of the Industrial Revolution and elaborated during the course of the subsequent decades. Within that view, families are distinguished from the world of work as enduring, stable, and deeply loyal. Moreover, within the ideology of family developed during the past two centuries, the social facts of family—the ways in which families *are* loyal and enduring, for instance—are understood as deeply embedded in a set of biological truths that generate and define the essential connections between kin. Changes in family life during the past few decades, including those occasioned by the new reproductive technologies, challenge that ideology. However, cases such as *Davis, Johnson, Hecht,* and *Parpalaix* show the ambivalence of the law about expressly reconstructing the family so that the distinctions between home and work evaporate. The law, much like the larger society, is redefining the parameters of family but is simultaneously attempting, though often not self-consciously, to mask the process of redefinition by connecting the new meanings to old understandings of family.

Thus, the law recognizes the consequences of marketplace negotiations in the construction of families and familial relationships, but attempts to modulate the consequences of unlimited choice in the creation and definition of families. That aim has led, among other things, to judicial reliance on intent in cases such as *Johnson* that ask courts to determine parentage and in cases such as *Davis, Hecht,* and *Parpalaix* that ask courts to determine the status and fate of gametic material. In all these cases, courts have reconstructed the meaning of intent so that the term appears to mediate between the world of the traditional family and the world of the marketplace. On the one hand, the intent to become a parent is taken to determine parentage because courts in these cases defined this intent to stem from, and thus to indicate, the deepest sense of self, the self that desires and thereby constitutes, motherhood or fatherhood. On the other hand, the concept of intent in these cases suggests rational negotiation and shifting bargains. The concept of intent, the apparent mediator between tradition and modernity, itself becomes another aspect of the contemporary debate about family.

In that debate, intent, however elaborately redefined, remains the firm associate of contract and choice. Allowing the family to be defined through choice—and through intention—may be the transition to families defined through contract. An essential aspect of the traditional ideology of family is the inexorability of family relationships. Understood as grounded in blood or genes, family relationships simply mirror the inevitability of natural processes. That does not gainsay that actual families have appeared in a broad assortment of forms and that actual relationships within families have varied widely from family to family during the course of the past two centuries. Yet, these variations have been understood within an encompassing ideology that defined the family in contrast with the marketplace. To some extent, judicial reliance on intent to determine parentage in recent cases represents a continuation of this process. However, in cases such as *Davis* and *Johnson* the family is not distinguished from the marketplace. Rather, intent (often evidenced by reference to actual contracts) as the ground on which familial relations are constructed, substitutes for blood and genes in constituting the parent-child relationship. In this construction, choice and bargain, essential incidents of contractual interaction, become central to the definition of family.

Some implications of this process of change emerge from the history of contract law itself which contains a similar transition. Two hundred years ago, the law refused to recognize idiosyncratic bargains. The fledgling law of contracts, seeking to preserve the last vestiges of status in the marketplace, enforced only those contracts that reflected the traditions of the old order. The law often supported only commercial exchange that reflected traditional understandings of the proper relations among people. Even as late as the eighteenth century, laws regulating contractual agreements—though not yet acknowledged as a separate domain of law—largely concerned the transfer of title and the actualization of "customary obligations." [58] Only with the start of the Industrial Revolution did the law of contracts recognize agreements that failed to reflect expected customs and tradition. Analyzing the history of contract law, Jay M. Feinman and Peter Gabel describe this transition:

> Eighteenth-century contract law would be barely recognizable to the modern lawyer. The core of eighteenth-century contract law was not the enforcement of private agreements but the implementation of customary practices and traditional norms. . . .
>
> In part, contracts was that portion of the law of property concerning the transfer of title to specific things from one person to another—the process by which "my horse" became "your horse." . . . Contract law also concerned customary obligations between people related to status, occupation, or social responsibilities. For example, a patient was "contractually" obligated by custom to pay for a physician's services whether or not he actually had promised to pay prior to the rendering of the services. In all types of contracts cases, the substantive fairness of the agreement or relation was subject to scrutiny by a lay jury applying community standards of justice. If a physician sued for his fee or a seller of goods for her price, the jury could decide that even an amount agreed to by the parties was excessive and inequitable, and so award a smaller sum instead.
>
> Thus, eighteenth-century contract law did not encourage commercial

exchange. The traditional image of the world presented by contract law regarded the enforcement of market transactions as often illegitimate, so a seller could never be guaranteed the price he or she had bargained for, and liability might be imposed in the absence of agreement when required by popular notions of fairness.[59]

With the burgeoning of capitalism at the end of the eighteenth and early part of the nineteenth centuries, courts increasingly referred to, and enforced, the will of the parties to a contract. In addition, at this time law-makers began to define contract law itself as an instrument for realizing the will of free, putatively equal, individuals. By the middle of the nineteenth century, the understanding that courts were obliged to respect and enforce bargains among negotiating parties stood at the center of contract law, replacing a view of contracts as a documentation of a relationship (such as that between a buyer and seller of property) that reflected, and that therefore was willing to seal in the particular case, some aspect of the enduring order of things.

Feinman and Gabel suggest that the ideological underpinnings of contract law shifted yet again by the middle of the twentieth century in response to new social and economic changes in the larger society. Twentieth-century law imposed constraints on the uncontrolled commercialism of the previous century.[60] Thus, courts limited the contractual freedom that defined the nineteenth-century market by exploring, for example, the fairness of a bargain and refusing to enforce bargains that seemed seriously unfair (e.g., unconscionable).

The ideology of family that developed during the nineteenth century depended upon, and encouraged, nineteenth-century commercialism by defining the family as a necessary refuge from tensions of the market. Home and work were understood as different, even as opposites, but not as antagonists. Each depended on the other. Society elaborated the ideological distinction between family and market through the 1950s. After that, the distinction began to blur even as an ideological matter. Thus, beginning in the middle of the twentieth century, within a period of three or four decades, society redefined the market in terms closer to those that earlier defined the home and the family. And the family, a few decades later but during approximately the same period, was redefined in terms closer to those that earlier defined the world of work and money. Changing understandings of the market are indicated and illustrated by the history of contract law during the last several decades. Cases such as

Davis, Johnson, Hecht, and *Parpalaix* indicate and illustrate changing understandings of the family, even as the changes are masked by the continuing invocation of nineteenth-century images of family life.

The temptation of relying on a reconstructed conception of intent in such cases is clear. The consequences may be less clear. But among the obvious consequences is the recognition of contract as an appropriate mode for creating family relationships, including those between parents and children. The courts in these cases dimmed the import of that recognition by defining intent to reflect traditional images of family as strongly as images of contractual negotiation and money exchange. But the notion that the two images can be harmoniously combined is clearly illusory.

Less clear is the kind of family image that will replace that forged during the first century following the Industrial Revolution. The law may come fully to recognize and applaud the creation, and perhaps the operation, of family relations on the basis of principles of contract. Contract principles could, for instance, determine the law's response to changed intentions.

One commentator, suggesting that the law should recognize the contractual ordering of the parent-child relationship, especially in cases occasioned by reproductive technology, would rely expressly on principles of contract law to interpret agreements about parentage. She argues, for instance, that the law can provide for changing intentions about parentage as it can provide for changing intentions about other matters:

> Enforcement of promises occurs precisely because people change their minds about performing obligations they have assumed. Indeed, a subset of contract doctrine governs when changed circumstances should excuse nonperformance. Presumably, even under existing doctrine, some changes of mind in the context of reproductive agreements might lead to excused performance. For instance, if a surrogate mother's two existing children died in a fire during her surrogate pregnancy, a court might relieve her of the obligation to perform the surrogacy agreement. . . . By contrast, if the surrogate simply mispredicted how attached she would feel to this baby, the claim of excuse would be hard to sustain under existing contract doctrine.[61]

Such an unambivalent appropriation of contract principles in establishing parentage is internally consistent. The approach openly relinquishes the preservation of traditional conceptions of family in that this approach rejects definitively the notion that families are defined through inexorable truths as nonnegotiable, hierarchically organized units of enduring relationships. People creating families through reliance on principles of contract may still *choose* to establish and sustain families that resemble those portrayed in the traditional ideology of family. But such families, because *understood* as products of culture, of self-conscious negotiation and choice, and not as products of nature, will be understood as constantly open to challenge and replacement by alternative choices.

Thus, judicial reliance on intent in cases occasioned by reproductive technology appears to represent a transitional response. The attempt to mediate between, and thus preserve, images of traditional family life and images of families created, and perhaps operated, through contract and choice will almost certainly prove self-defeating. Under pressure, courts have invoked the concept of intent to resolve specific disputes and to fashion a response to the larger confusions presented by the advent of reproductive technology. But the concept, invoked to amalgamate traditional and contemporary understandings of family, is inimical to the traditional ideology of family. The basic impulse of the concept of intent is, however, barely noticed at all. By its nature, the concept of intent entails that of choice and thus poses an essential ideological contrast to traditional understandings of family.

Thus the ideological opposition arises, not only from without, but from within. It seems likely to remain attractive to the law. If so, the law's reliance on intent in cases occasioned by reproductive technology, and in others in which courts are asked to determine parentage, may become express reliance on principles of contract.

SEVEN

Suffer the Children

Judicial reliance on intent in cases occasioned by reproductive technology represents an innovative, though ultimately unstable, approach to defining parentage and to understanding the parent-child relationship. That approach has sometimes seemed attractive insofar as it has appeared to recognize the creation of the parent-child relationship in contractual terms without expressly renouncing a traditional ideology of family that for almost two centuries has eschewed the amalgamation of contractual and familial relationships.

Ultimately, the law's reliance on intent to define parentage or custody is a temporary measure that fails to provide stable guidance to a society faced with phenomena such as frozen embryos, gestational surrogacy and posthumous insemination. This is so because intent is linked essentially to a world of autonomous individuality and choice, not to a world of fixed relations predicated on biological truth. As a result, the decision to rely on intent is a decision to rely fully on contractual agreements in resolving such cases. At present, society is not willing to do that. Moreover, intent cannot accomplish the task assigned it because intentions shift and are always complex. Only if the meaning of intent is restricted to that intent made obvious in a contract does it become possible to specify a party's intent with certainty and to effect that intent.

So, other courts have tried other approaches to the resolution of disputes engendered by reproductive technology and surrogacy. Some courts, rather than fashioning new approaches to the problems presented by these cases, have attempted to mold familiar approaches to resolve the new dilemmas. A few courts, especially in traditional surrogacy cases, have relied almost exclusively on the best-interest standard to identify the parents or custodians of a child. This approach, unlike judicial reliance on intent, makes use of a principle that has been institutionalized for almost a century for use in the resolution of family law disputes involving children's parentage or custody. As a result, reliance on the best-interest standard in cases occasioned by surrogacy or new reproductive technology often appears to integrate those cases with other, far more familiar disputes about family matters and thereby suggests that these cases are not as unsettling to traditional understandings of family as they usually appear to be.

However, this approach is not proving more satisfactory than reliance on the notion of intent. Yet, the reasons for each approach's failure are quite different. Reliance on the best-interest principle proves inadequate to resolve cases occasioned by reproductive technology and surrogacy because application of the best-interest principle depends on at least the illusion (if not the reality) of shared assumptions within society about the contours and meaning of familial relationships. The questions presented by cases involving children (or gametes) produced through the use of the new reproductive technologies are too large, too disturbing, and too unprecedented for that illusion to be easily sustained. In these cases, courts, compelled to reconstruct the meanings of maternity and paternity, are unable to assume that, however a specific dispute is resolved, family is still ultimately family, and that nothing very important is changing.

In fact, the extent of the disruption that the new reproductive technologies present to traditional views of family is indicated by the very failure of the best-interest standard generally to resolve disputes engendered by use of this technology. For over a century, the notion that a child's custody (and sometimes even a child's parentage) can be determined by examining the child's best interests has served family law faithfully. Certainly, the principle has always provided little concrete guidance to courts faced with disputes involving children. Decisions about children's custody and parentage have always depended on the wisdom, insight, and worldview of the presiding judge. Until recently, however, the very indeterminacy of the best-interest standard has proved useful. As social values have shifted over time, the law has been able to depend consistently on one standard for resolving a large set of cases involving children in families. Now, however, especially in cases occasioned by reproductive technology, almost every assumption that undergirded the traditional ideology of family is being challenged at once. In consequence, the disruption these cases pose to traditional understandings of family cannot be accommodated by a principle that demands at least some broad agreement within society about the character of familial connections.

That is, applications of the principle depend on courts' actualizing a variety of social assumptions about the families and familial relationships that they regulate. As long as those assumptions are at least broadly generalized throughout the society, the best-interest principle can serve to cement and justify particular custody determinations. This is, however, often no longer true. And it is certainly not true in cases occasioned by the new reproductive technologies.

Courts do seem able and willing to rely on the best-interest principle more often in traditional surrogacy cases than in cases involving reproductive technology, probably because traditional surrogacy, although threatening to a traditional ideology of family, does not also threaten to disrupt the biological correlates of human reproduction. So, for instance, in *Baby M.*, the most well-known legal case involving a traditional surrogacy arrangement, the New Jersey trial court determined the child's parentage by assessing her best interests. And the state supreme court, while reversing the trial court decision in almost every other regard, praised the lower court's analysis of the child's situation and welfare.

In cases occasioned by the new reproductive technologies courts have only rarely relied on the best-interest principle. However, even in these cases, courts have almost always invoked children and their interests and have justified the decisions reached with assurances that those decisions serve the interests of the children involved. So, for example, in *Johnson v. Calvert*, the California Supreme Court relied on parental intent to identify the Calverts as baby Christopher's parents, but asserted that in such cases the interests of children are very likely to be served by courts' recognizing their intending parents as their legal parents and custodians.[1] The continued invocation of children's best interests in such cases proves as significant for understanding the law's changing response to the family as does the general failure of the best-interest principle satisfactorily to resolve disputes occasioned by assisted reproduction.

For many decades the best-interest standard has enjoyed a moral superiority in family law, even though the principle has often served actual children rather poorly. For almost two centuries, society has equated children and family and has described the development of happy, protected children as the ultimate purpose of the traditional family.

A lasting nostalgia for traditional families during the course of the past two centuries has consistently been expressed by the law through reference to children and their interests. These references have provided evidence, both real and symbolic, that images associated with old-fashioned, decent families are still valued and that, in turn, such families are valued as well.

Nostalgia for old-fashioned family life is not new. As the family has obviously changed during the course of the past two centuries, each generation has shown some reverence for the lost family of the generation before. Until recently, however, the confusions and uncertainties produced by changes in the form and meaning of family could be accommodated within the broad ideology of family that developed with the Industrial Revolution. That is no longer the case. As a result, the best-interest principle seems more and more obviously inadequate as the law's primary response to custody and parentage disputes. In cases occasioned by assisted reproduction, that inadequacy is especially transparent. It is clear from cases in which the best-interest principle is obviously no more than an incidental rhetorical device as well as from cases in which courts have relied on the best-interest principle to determine a child's custody or parentage but have obviously failed to focus adequately on the best interests of the child involved in light of the changing parameters of family.

Even more, a similar invocation of children and their welfare, and a similar failure of these invocations to resolve social confusions, characterize the ongoing social debate about family that encompasses, and that is often reflected in, the law's contemporary debate about family. In general, a panoply of contradictory voices is responding to reproductive technology through a set of similar, and similarly nostalgic, references to the central role that children must play in any acceptable understanding of home and family. As the debate about families produced through assisted reproduction unfolds, social conclusions about the value reproductive technology may hold for actual families and actual children become increasingly murky.

More generally still, examination of legal cases as well as of broader social responses to surrogacy and the new reproductive technologies suggest that, despite the continued invocation of children and their interests, society is rapidly revising an understanding of childhood and children that has been central to the ideology of family for at least two centuries. Thus, reliance on the best-interest standard in surrogacy and reproductive technology cases, and invocations of children and their welfare by the law and by society in the larger social debate about assisted reproduction, seem still to reflect traditional responses to family matters. But more and more often, contradictions displace even the illusion of consensus.

I. Contradictory Social Impulses: The Best-Interest Standard

During the past century, the best-interest principle has been institutionalized everywhere in the United States either through state statutory provisions or through judicial precedent as the applicable rule for establishing a child's custody in cases of parental divorce or separation and for establishing custody, and sometimes parentage, in cases involving parental death or the termination of parental rights.

The widespread institutionalization of the standard reflects the apparent concern of the society and of the law during the past two centuries with the welfare of children. Images of children and of the value of childhood continue to play an essential role in the law's treatment and definition of families. The concern with children did not always exist, at least not as a central component in understandings of family. Recent developments in the law's response to children can be evaluated only in light of a longer history in which children's interests became important to the law.

Images of children and childhood became practically sacred within the ideology of family during the nineteenth century. Since that time, nostalgic images of children have shaped and justified the law's understanding and regulation of family matters. By the middle of the twentieth century, such images had become indispensable to the ideology of the family in the United States. A deep nostalgia for a world portrayed as having protected children—the world of the traditional family—continues to be reflected even in the decisions of courts supporting, or even more, self-consciously advocating, the development of non-traditional family structures.

Before the Industrial Revolution the welfare and interests of children were not relevant to determinations of custody and parentage. When called upon to determine a child's custody or parentage, English common law virtually ignored the child's welfare. Although peculiar and outrageous to contemporary ears, this was not a self-conscious attempt to subvert the interests of children. Inquiries into children's interests were not made and then discounted. Such inquiries were not made because almost no one expected them to have been made. Focus on children's interests in disputes about custody or parentage makes sense only to a world that frames childhood as a separate stage (beyond infancy) and that values children and childhood. Such a world did not come fully into existence until the late eighteenth, or early nineteenth, century. In the colonial period children were generally not even mentioned in divorce petitions, and when they were, it was not primarily to invoke their interests but to indicate that the marriage of their parents was long-standing.

Traditionally, the common law, reflecting Roman law before it, viewed children as belonging to their fathers who had a moral, but not a legal, obligation to support the children. A father, in this view, had "the perfect legal right . . . to the possession and controul of his child."[2] Thus fathers, but not mothers, almost invariably gained custody, even in cases in which the child's welfare would obviously be ill-served by paternal custody. In *Rex v. DeManneville*, often noted to show the tenacity of that rule, an English court gave custody of a nursing baby to its father in spite of the uncontested claim by the mother that her separation from the father was caused by his extreme cruelty.

By the mid-nineteenth century, changes in the law's treatment and understanding of children appeared in English statutory law. At that time, mothers were given a statutory right to seek custody of young children.[3] In the United States at the same time, courts began to question rigid adherence to a rule that virtually always granted custody to fathers. Although fathers' rights to custody usually remained paramount in American courts during the nineteenth century, such rights were increasingly predicated on a father's obligations, both moral and legal, to support and educate his children.

Although many United States courts preferred fathers in custody cases as late as the early twentieth century, things were changing. Preference for fathers was no longer automatic. Specifically, it began to be limited through reference to the welfare of the children involved. By this time, courts were willing to grant custody to mothers in cases in which fathers were proven unfit. And even as early as the mid-nineteenth century, some courts in the U.S. embraced the welfare of the child as the crucial principle in determining a child's custody. In 1840, a New York court, granting custody to a divorcing mother with a two-year-old child, stated clearly that "[t]he interest of the infant is deemed paramount to the claims of both parents."[4] The court explained that the interest of the child lay with maternal, rather than paternal, custody because "the law of nature" attached mothers, more strongly than fathers, to their young children. Thus, the court, though justifying its decision by reference to natural truth, inevitably suggested that that truth was itself fungible, or at least debatable. After all, other courts had long assumed that custody belonged to fathers as a matter of natural or supernatural truth.

By the end of the nineteenth century, the old rules for resolving family disputes, including those relevant to the determination of custody in cases of parental divorce or separation, were clearly being challenged by new understandings of family. New rules developed. Increasingly, courts facing custody disputes appeared to ignore the interests and rights of parents and focused instead on the welfare of the children involved. This approach, ultimately institutionalized as the best-interest principle, provided great flexibility to a legal system uncertain about what kinds of families and what sorts of parents the social order endorsed or would soon endorse.

The express focus of the best-interest principle on the welfare of children seemed to provide a moral frame within which to determine custody. However, the changing set of presumptions through which the standard has been applied to actual children suggests that the standard was never rigidly anchored in an unchanging conception of family. The reach of the best-interest standard, initially linked with, and used to support, a new reverence for motherhood in the nineteenth century, soon widened to support other interests and other understandings of family. The principle could successfully be applied to, and could make sense of, any set of presumptions about family that conformed broadly to the ideology of family developed in the nineteenth century and now described through references to "traditional" families. Indeed, the standard itself never demanded the sort of shifting, even opposing, conclusions about the welfare of children whose parents divorce that actual applications of the standard have supported over the years.

Moreover, applications of the best-interest standard have reflected a deep irony. In theory, the standard demands that some vision of children and their interests lie at the heart of every custody decision. In fact, however, courts, not always fully conscious of the implications of their own procedures, have frequently substituted the interests of contending adults for those of the children. Judicial attention to the conduct of adults seeking custody is almost always essential to the process of evaluating options for a child. However, conclusions about the moral, psychological, or social traits of adults seeking custody can easily become conclusions about custody rather than information that courts use to discern a child's best interests.

The best interests of a child can be subverted by a judge who simply fails to understand the complicated personalities and relationships involved in a custody case, as well as by a judge who does not focus carefully on the details of a particular case but instead assumes that middle-class, comparatively mainstream custodians will better serve a child's interests than poorer or more socially marginal custodians. So, for instance, in 1995 the Virginia Supreme Court in *Bottoms v. Bottoms* granted custody of a young boy to the grandmother rather than the mother, essentially on the grounds that the child's best interests would not be served by residence with his lesbian mother.

Despite its shortcomings, however, the best-interest standard has not only survived but has been invaluable to the evolution of family law in the past century. The standard has provided the illusion of sane stability in a society undergoing rapid change. More important, judicial reliance on the standard has successfully suggested in case after case that the families constructed through reference to the best interests of children are more moral and more decent than alternatives *because* moral, decent families and the best-interest standard are alike presumed to place children at the center. Thus, the best-interest standard, as much as any principle in family law today, stands for tradition. But it has also served the interests of those who, self-consciously or not, favor changes in the family and in family law.

In a society for which children and the parent-child bond have come to be understood as the surviving vestige and lasting representation of old-fashioned families, the best-interest principle affirms the continuing significance of traditional families within the social order. At the same time, the standard has masked, and thus provided a certain comfort to, departures from known and expected patterns. The standard's survival cannot be attributed to the protection of actual children. Rather, the best-interest standard has supported society's continuing nostalgia for the way families were thought once to have been.

II. Judicial Reliance on Best-Interest Standard in Surrogacy and New Reproductive Technology Cases: Contradictory Messages about Children

A similar nostalgia, and a related attempt by the law to accommodate changes in the present through comparison with constructed images of a valued past, marks social and legal responses to surrogacy and new reproductive technology. However, the challenge now presented by assisted reproduction is of a new order. Efforts to assimilate these changes, like those of earlier decades, to familiar images of family life, continue but are marked by increasing contradiction and confusion.

Society does not yet presume to fully understand the implications of surrogacy and the new reproductive technologies, even as these phenomena are generating fervent moral debate. In that debate, society and the law continue, but less insistently and less conclusively, to measure change against its consequences for children. In public presentations, both opponents and proponents of surrogacy and new reproductive technology evaluate the use of assisted reproduction against images of traditional families and images of children within such families. Advocates and adversaries of surrogacy and of new reproductive technology suggest in concert that children and the parent-child bond represent the lasting sacred core of family life and, accordingly, praise or condemn the new technologies and surrogacy through reference to the apparent results for children.

Underlying these varied claims lie other interests which serve adults more than children and which support the correlates of autonomous individuality more than those of social connection. But now, in contrast to the interplay in earlier decades between the law's invocation of children and its focus on adult interests, the contradictions and confusions cannot be as easily masked and thus ignored. The semblance of an ordered rule that characterized the law's response to disputes involving custody and parentage in earlier decades has yielded to more obvious uncertainty and bewilderment.

Contradictions between images of traditional families and the reality of creating families through reproductive technology are becoming harder to contain. Courts invoke children and their best interests in cases occasioned by reproductive technology, but more and more often these invocations fail to mediate the differences between images of traditional family life and actual families created through commercial negotiations and technological intervention. Images of childhood and the interests of children, though still often invoked, are in fact becoming less central to the regulation of family matters.

Illustrative Cases

Three cases, each of which has already been presented, as well as one other, illustrate various levels of attention to children and their interests in cases of assisted reproduction. *Davis v. Davis*, involving the Davises' divorce and their resulting dispute about the fate of their seven frozen embryos, elaborates, to the point of derailing altogether, the concern of the law with children (or potential children) and their interests. In *Davis* the familiar judicial tendency in cases about custody or parentage to disguise the satisfaction of one set of interests (those of adults) by invoking another set of interests (those of children), becomes almost a parody. Both of the decisions of the New Jersey courts in *Baby M.*, a case presenting social more than biological confusions, involved extensive and express reliance on the best-interest standard. The case illustrates the use of the best-interest principle, whether self-consciously or not, to effect the illusion that traditional families can be safeguarded despite the enormity of change. In addition, the case indicates the complexities that actually face courts seeking to discern the best interests of a child produced as a result of surrogacy and other forms of assisted reproduction. In such cases, so many expectations about the scope and meaning of family are challenged at once that it becomes almost impossibly difficult to accommodate the changes. In such cases, the best-interest principle seems hardly able to preserve the illusion of order. *Moschetta v. Moschetta*, a traditional surrogacy case, complicated by a divorce between the intending parents, reveals even more starkly than *Baby M.* the confusions created by use of the best-interest principle in cases involving assisted reproduction. Finally, in *Johnson v. Calvert*, the California case involving gestational surrogacy, the state supreme court invoked, but otherwise ignored, the best interests of the child and decided the case on grounds that referred only incidentally to the child's interests. However, the dissent in that case presents one of the few instances in which a judge recommended establishing parentage in a case occasioned by reproductive technology on the basis of a best-interest determination.

Davis did not involve children at all. Yet, the case vividly suggests how the law can rely on the best-interest standard, and other, related principles, to effect agendas that have no real concern for children or their welfare. In particular, the case reveals the power of invoking the moral status of children (or in *Davis*, itself, of embryos) to establish an apparent connection with decency and tradition.

The Tennessee trial court in *Davis* expressly defined the cryopreserved embryos, about which Mary Sue and Junior Davis were arguing, as children and expressly considered the best interests of those embryos in deciding to allow Mary Sue to gestate them and give birth to the resulting child or children. However, neither of the two higher Tennessee courts that rendered decisions in the case viewed the embryos as children.

The supreme court, relying on ethical standards promulgated by the American Fertility Society, defined the embryos (called preembryos) as neither persons nor property but as entitled to "special respect because of their potential for human life."[5] In so defining the embryos, the court situated its own ideological sympathies between the trial court's concern with the embryos as children and the intermediate appellate court's treatment of the embryos as property, or something quite like property. Such conclusions about the ontological status of frozen embryos do not automatically determine their fate in cases such as *Davis*. A conclusion, for instance, such as that of the *Davis* trial court, that the embryos were ontologically no different from children might lead to a number of different decisions about their actual fate. Presumably, however, a court's approach to questions about the embryos' actual fate would be consistent with that court's conclusions about the embryos' ontological status.

Yet, in a remarkable and ironic twist, the state supreme court defined the embryos as deserving "special respect" and then ordered that the embryos be discarded. In making this determination, the court offered no comment on the transparent contradiction between its description of the embryos' ontological status and its actual holding in the case. Finally ordering that the embryos be given to Junior's lawyer who would presumably discard them, the court apparently ignored its own insistence on the respect that must be afforded to cryopreserved embryos.

The court announced that the embryos were owed "special respect" but never explained or examined the implications of that conclusion, and in explaining its actual holding, the court did not focus on the embryos at all. Instead, the court concluded that the comparative strength of the rights claimed respectively by Mary Sue and by Junior would prove determinate. Moreover, the court expressly approved the use of contracts and contract principles in future cases involving cryopreserved embryos. Justice Daughtrey explained that the Davises' respective interests would be determinative only because the parties could not agree and had never entered into an agreement about the fate of their unused embryos.

In sum, the *Davis* court invoked the embryos, and defined them as worthy of special respect, analogous to the way that other courts faced with disputes involving custody or parentage invoke children and their best interests. But immediately the *Davis* court reached a decision that overlooked the embryos, their status, and the respect due them because of that status. Instead, similar to other courts handling routine custody cases, the *Davis* court focused only on the interests of the disputing adults.

If questioned about the apparent contradiction between its holding and its discussion of the embryos' status, the court might have noted that it invoked the progenitors' constitutional rights, not their property interests, and thus never treated the embryos as property and never confused the correlates of home with those of the marketplace. However, that explanation would be unconvincing. First, the court asserted that, although it did focus on the parties' constitutional rights, it would have preferred to focus on their interests as defined through contract law and that it would certainly have done so had the parties entered into a relevant contractual agreement. Second, the constitutional rights to which the court looked, rights concerning people's intimate relationships such as the right to autonomy in matters relating to procreation, afford protection to the *individual* in intimate matters, not to the family as such. Thus, the court's focus on Junior's and Mary Sue's respective constitutional rights does not demonstrate that the court respected the embryos, as its analysis of those embryos' status suggests it should have. In explaining its actual holding, the court made no place for the embryos, and made no effort to take account of the respect apparently owed them.

The contradictory positions of the *Davis* court with regard to the frozen embryos—its invocation of their special status and then its total disregard for them in its holding—is more transparent than similar contradictions in other cases involving custody disputes over actual children. The court, by detailing its concern for the embryos and by concluding they should be given special respect, aligned itself with a traditional ideology of family. The court's concern for the embryos, however real, was also a pretext. As pretext, the court's concern with the embryos played no part in the holding. The court could disregard the embryos so easily and openly in reaching its holding, because, in fact, there were no actual children to protect. But the more important point is that the court's express concern for the embryos' special status served only to temper the implications of the actual holding in *Davis*. In effect, conclusions in *Davis* about the embryos' status and the respect owed them due to that status became a rhetorical device that served to preserve a connection between the decision and a traditional view of family.

The ontological and moral confusions presented by gametic and embryonic cryopreservation are completely novel. Thus, it is not surprising that the discrepancies between agenda and result in *Davis* are stark. Because the contradictions underlying *Davis* are so evident, the case provides an illuminating model through which to consider the more opaque, but essentially similar, contradictions underlying more routine cases involving the resolution of custody and parentage questions. In those cases, the apparent concern of the law with the welfare of children is often belied by the treatment afforded to actual children. In these cases, however, the contradiction is generally disguised by an express judicial effort to determine and effect the children's best interests. Not even the pretense of such an effort existed in *Davis* with regard to ensuring proper "respect" for the frozen embryos.

In contrast, in a number of disputes occasioned by surrogacy contracts, courts have actually relied on the best-interest principle to resolve custody and parentage issues. Such cases differ from *Davis* and other cases that unsettle expectations about the process of human reproduction. Surrogacy disturbs social, but not biological, understandings of maternity and paternity. The creation of the parent-child relationship in contractual terms is proving troubling to society, but traditional surrogacy, which relies only on artificial insemination and not on more complicated, technological forms of assisted reproduction, does not challenge traditional notions about biological reproduction. In fact, in *Baby M.* none of the parties questioned Mary Beth Whitehead's biological maternity nor William Stern's biological paternity.

The trial court judge, apparently validating the contract into which the parties had entered, described the "primary issue" in the case as the best interests of Baby M.[6] In accordance with its best-interest analysis, the trial court granted parentage and custody to the biological father, William Stern, and his wife, Elizabeth Stern. The court's reliance on the child's best interests to determine parentage, not just custody, was unusual but not unprecedented. The state supreme court, reversing that aspect of the lower court's decision, applauded the lower court's best-interest analysis and relied on it in granting custody to William Stern. That reliance and its consequences in this case reveal the complexities and confusions that result from the application of existing family law principles, such as the best-interest principle, to cases that disrupt social expectations about the creation and incidents of familial relationships by combining family love with market negotiations.

In recognizing Mary Beth Whitehead as Baby M.'s mother and William Stern as her father, and in giving each the right to continued association with the child (though William Stern alone was given custody), the state supreme court decision created a family unlike families reconstructed following divorce or following the separation of unmarried parents. The surrogacy agreement entered into by Whitehead and Stern aimed to create a child produced from Whitehead's ovum and Stern's sperm. Yet the two had never lived together or had sexual relations with each other; they never expected to share a life together, and had not intended, and never desired, to share the parental role. Had the interests of the child been thoughtfully considered in this case, these facts would have been at the center of the judicial inquiry. In fact, this aspect of the child's interests was not considered at all.

The best-interest analysis of the trial court did not consider these matters because that court had named the Sterns as the baby's parents and terminated Whitehead's parental rights. The court thus had no reason to consider the effects on the child of having Whitehead for a mother and Stern for a father and of living at least some of the time with each of them. In relying on the lower court's best-interest analysis, the supreme court failed to consider the changed context that resulted from its having reversed most of the trial court's holding. The higher court ignored the real choices that followed from its invalidation of the surrogacy contract. Instead the court defined the issue in the case as a simple choice between "life ... for Baby M. ... with primary custody in the Whiteheads or one with primary custody in the Sterns."[7] The court then concluded that on the basis of the trial court's best-interest analysis, custody should remain with William Stern. Finally, the supreme court remanded the case to the lower court for a determination about the extent of Whitehead's visitation. In remanding the case, the court declared that the fact of Whitehead's visitation was "not open to the trial court on . . . remand."[8]

The supreme court's decision failed completely to consider the possibility that its basic determination—that Stern be named the child's legal father and Whitehead her mother—might not serve the interests of the child. The court understood state statutory law as giving it little alternative in this regard. However, the court did not relate that limitation to its best-interest analysis and, more importantly, did not instruct the trial court on remand to consider the particular and unique aspects of the dispute in determining the details of Whitehead's visitation.

The court remarked, though almost incidentally, that the case was unlike most custody disputes following divorce, and resembled other cases "in which the non-custodial spouse has had practically no relationship with the child."[9] By implication, the child's best interests would not likely be served by assuming the facts of a typical custody dispute. But that is just what the supreme court in effect did, and so the court had to justify its approach. In doing that, the court referred to Whitehead's early custody of Baby M. during the four-month period in which she lived with the child in Florida after having escaped with the baby from the Sterns and from state law.

In addition, the court dismissed as inconsequential the implications of the dispute's unique history by asserting the rights of the biological mother rather than the interests of the child. The court explained:

> [Mrs. Whitehead] is not only the natural mother, but also the legal mother, and is not to be penalized one iota because of the surrogacy contract. Mrs. Whitehead, as the mother (indeed, as a mother who nurtured her child for its first four months—unquestionably a relevant consideration), is entitled to have her own interest in visitation considered. Visitation cannot be determined without considering the parents' interests along with those of the child.[10]

At this crucial point in its analysis of the case, the court substituted the interests of the mother for those of the child, and therefore, despite its apparent focus on the child's best interests, made it impossible to decipher the actual interests of that child. That task would have required analysis of the consequences for the child of moving between two significantly different homes, between three parents and two mothers originally joined together as contract partners, and between parents whose intense animosity toward each other was expressly a consequence of the child's negotiated birth. Those determinative facts are unique to *Baby M.*, and should clearly have been central to the law's consideration of the child's interests.

On remand, the trial court was directed to decide the terms, but not the fact, of Whitehead's visitation. In response, that court provided for "unsupervised, uninterrupted, liberal visitation" between Whitehead and the child.[11] Some of the complications that follow, even in theory, from the supreme court's best-interest determination were vividly suggested in a 1994 story in *Redbook* that featured Baby M. and her family. The story, subtitled, "An Exclusive Interview with America's Most Famous Surrogate Mother about the Daughter She Fought so Hard to Keep, But Couldn't," included small, familiar pictures of Baby M., the Sterns, and Mary Beth Whitehead taken at the time of trial and other, larger pictures showing seven-year-old Baby M., now known as "Sassy" Stern, at the beach, in the park, and at her maternal grandparental home in Florida with her mother (now known publicly as Mary Beth Whitehead and privately as Mary Gould). The story also featured Mary Beth's immediate family, including her two children with Richard Whitehead from whom she was divorced, two younger children born before and during Mary Beth's second marriage, and her second husband, Richard Gould.

The story did not include pictures of the child with the Sterns, who were not interviewed by the magazine and apparently played no part in the preparation of the story. However, the contrast, especially in Mary Beth's view, between life in her home and life in that of the Sterns provides the central theme of the story. Whitehead compared her own health with what "her spies" in the Stern's New Jersey community described as Betsy Stern's worsening physical state as a result of multiple sclerosis. Whitehead complained about the child's following the "frumpy, old" model set by Betsy Stern and angrily contrasted the eating, conversation, and recreational patterns in the two homes, finding the Stern home seriously wanting.

Parts of the story present problems familiar to unfriendly divorces. In Baby M.'s case, her mother's antagonism is directed at a second mother, more than at a father, but that may happen after a divorce, following the remarriage of one parent. Far more consequentially, the child here knows clearly, and apparently hears frequently, at least from Whitehead, that her negotiated birth brought and continues to bring great sadness to her parents. Even the fact that a popular magazine, displayed in supermarkets and other stores throughout the country, featured the child in a story increases the likelihood of the child's exposure to the pain her birth brought others. Whitehead's mother, Eileen Messer, told the *Redbook* reporter, out of Whitehead's hearing: "This whole business has destroyed our family, and it's changed her [Mary Beth]."

Equally discordant consequences might well have followed had the supreme court affirmed the lower court's ruling and sanctioned the termination of Whitehead's maternity, or had the court granted maternal rights and custody to Whitehead. That notwithstanding, the supreme court was remiss in not requiring that the child's best interests be examined anew in light of its own holding which restored Whitehead's maternity and rescinded the adoption of the child by Elizabeth Stern. The decision failed to acknowledge that a child's best interests are actualized or not in concrete settings and in particular relationships and that the setting established by a commercial surrogacy arrangement is quite different from most family settings that courts consider.

The best-interest analysis in this case ultimately served interests beyond those of the child. For each court, reliance on the best-interest principle served to endorse a particular vision of family. That vision, similar for both courts, was predicated on the centrality of children and of the parent-child bond. Each decision reflected a traditional ideology of family; each court sought to preserve a family that would reflect that ideology. However, the facts of the case made that result difficult to design with certainty. That is indicated by the extent to which the best-interest principle in *Baby M.* became a term in an ongoing debate about family quite as much as a tool for resolving the particular dispute. In this, the consequences of judicial reliance on the best-interest principle in this case are similar to the consequences of judicial reliance on the concept of intent in other cases occasioned by reproductive technology.

Three years after *Baby M.*, a California trial court, asked to resolve a traditional surrogacy dispute in that state, applied the best-interest test and granted joint custody to the intending biological father and the surrogate mother (referred to as the "unintended" mother by the California appellate court).[12]

That case began in 1989 when Robert and Cynthia Moschetta, anxious to have a child but unable to do so, entered into a surrogacy contract with Elvira Jordan. Cynthia, almost fifty years old when the parties entered into the surrogacy contract, had had a tubal ligation before she married Robert in 1981. The surrogacy contract provided that Robert Moschetta would pay $10,000 to Jordan in " 'recognition' of Robert's 'obligations to support [the] child and his right to provide [Jordan] with living expenses.' "[13] Elvira became pregnant through artificial insemination by the end of that year. However, before the birth of the child, a daughter born in May 1990, the Moschettas' marriage had begun obviously to fall apart. Jordan learned of difficulties in Robert and Cynthia's marriage from Cynthia while Elvira was in labor. As a result, she hesitated to surrender the child but finally allowed the Moschettas to take the baby home from the hospital on condition that she be permitted to visit with the child during the first year. Further, she refused to agree to a termination of her own parental rights for at least one year.

About six months after the birth of the baby, named Marissa, the Moschettas' separated. Robert departed from the marital home with the child. After this, Cynthia, Robert, and Elvira all commenced actions in court. These actions were consolidated, and in the spring of 1990, Judge Nancy Weiben Stock declared Robert to be Marissa's father and Elvira, her mother. She further ordered that the two parents would share physical and legal custody of baby Marissa.

Judge Stock's custody determination is not unusual for expressly denying the importance to the court's decision of class and ethnic differences among potential custodians. However, the decision is unusual among custody cases generally, and among surrogacy cases more particularly, in reaching a conclusion that cannot in fact be easily attributed to such factors. Judge Stock explained:

> Robert . . . was Caucasian, a middle income professional and a new father. Elvira was an Hispanic middle-aged single mother with one pre-teen child at home. Elvira had a low income, was at one time on welfare and worked as a resident manager of her apartment complex. . . .
>
> The attorneys for Cynthia, Elvira and Marissa all urged the court not to base its custody decision on these socio-economic factors. The Court shared their hesitation.[14]

However, the factors upon which the court did rely in determining that the child's best interest lay in a joint-custody arrangement were poorly delineated. In deciding that Elvira and Robert should share physical and legal custody of the baby, the court contravened the recommendations of both court-appointed experts, a clinical psychologist and a marriage, family, and child counselor. The experts had opined that,

> Elvira Jordan had "difficulty in setting structure and limits as her children grow." Her two older children had dropped out of school and her eldest had "problems related to drugs." Her "attitudes, competitiveness, lack of self-awareness, and possessiveness" limited the type of custody plan that could be developed.[15]

Judge Stock explained that in this case she ordered joint custody because she was not satisfied that Robert would make a fit sole custodian. She compared Robert's "lack of sensitivity to the needs of the child as separate and apart from his own" with Elvira's constant readiness to give (her "unrefuted intent" was to "give the gift of life to an infertile couple").[16] Judge Stock further based her joint-custody order on her conclusion that "frequent and continuing contact with both biological parents was in Marissa's best interests."[17] She buttressed this decision with reference to the legislative direction that where possible parents " 'share the rights and responsibilities of child rearing.' "[18] The court rejected Robert's argument that the standard was not intended to be applied to situations such as that involved in *Moschetta*: "[W]hether the child is the product of a marital union or not, the court is not foreclosed from applying public policy considerations applicable to the child's best interests."[19]

The California Court of Appeal affirmed the lower court's decision as to parentage, despite the state supreme court's decision in *Johnson*, decided after the trial court opinion in *Moschetta*. The *Moschetta* court, refusing to extend *Johnson*'s intent-analysis to a case involving traditional, rather than gestational, surrogacy, distinguished *Johnson*, described as having involved a biological "tie" between two "mothers," from *Moschetta* (in which Elvira was the only biological mother), and concluded that in a dispute occasioned by traditional surrogacy, the biological mother of the child is the legal mother as well. However, the court remanded the case for a reconsideration of the custody issue on the ground that the trial court had "penalized" Robert for having insisted at trial that Jordan was not the child's mother and for having aggressively litigated the controversy. The court asserted: "The statement of decision [by the trial court] treats Robert Moschetta as a recalcitrant divorced parent who obstructs the legitimate visitation rights of a former spouse."[20]

In fact, Robert was a divorcing spouse though he was divorcing Cynthia, not Elvira. That divorce was central to the history that led to *Moschetta* and to the trial court opinion in the case. Elvira's initial reluctance to surrender the child after her birth stemmed from Elvira's apprehension about the child's being raised by a single father. Similarly, the trial court judge explained her joint custody decision with reference to her concerns about Robert's ability to serve adequately as sole custodian.

In another, more startling regard, the *Moschetta* divorce informed the trial court's approach to the case. Although the court certainly recognized that Robert was divorcing Cynthia and was to share custody of Marissa with Elvira, the court conflated the two women at a crucial point in its decision. For the first seven months of Marissa's life, the baby had lived together with Cynthia and Robert. In considering Robert's conclusions about the consequences for the child of his departure with the child from the marital home and from Cynthia, the court asserted that Robert showed "gross misconceptions about maternal/infant bonding."[21] Later, considering a possible role for Cynthia in the child's life, the court declared:

> At trial Robert clung to the position that Cynthia had no rights and should be terminated from Marissa as quickly as possible. All three child custody experts disagreed with this approach. Elvira, on the other hand fully endorsed a role for Cynthia that would resemble that of a beloved aunt or Godmother. Although at trial Elvira was facing an evaluation report recommending very limited access and rights with Marissa, Elvira was consistent in her offer to share with Cynthia whatever visitation time she had with the minor.[22]

Thus, in determining Marissa's best interests, the trial court implicitly assumed the parameters of a routine divorce case rather than those of a surrogacy dispute complicated by a divorce between the intending parents. The court, in effect, replaced the dimensions of the actual case with those of an easier, less disturbing case. By so redefining the case, as an unexceptional custody action in the context of a divorce, the court, without particularly considering the matter, was able to rely on a familiar family law rule, and on the basis of its best-interest determination, grant joint custody of Marissa to Elvira Jordan and Robert Moschetta. Unfortunately, however, this best-interest determination assumed a family that did not exist and in important regards ignored the family that did exist. The uncertainties that defined the actual case were disguised and replaced with a revised understanding of the underlying context. The appellate court was quite correct in concluding that the trial court's "statement of decision" treated Robert Moschetta as "a recalcitrant divorced parent who obstructs the visitation rights of a former spouse." In fact, that seems to be how the trial court actually envisioned the case.

The appellate court affirmed the finding that Elvira and Robert were the child's parents but remanded the case for a reevaluation of the trial court's decision to grant Elvira and Robert joint custody of the child. As a result, in 1995, five years after the child's birth, a state trial court reviewed the case and Judge Stock's original joint-custody decision. At that time, a court-appointed psychiatrist testified that the original decision "split ... the child in half, Solomon-like," which led to symptoms of depression and anxiety in the child, now five years old.[23] Accordingly, Judge John C. Woolley, who presided at the proceedings, reversed Judge Stock's earlier decision and granted sole custody to Robert. This decision, as did the earlier one, "brush[ed] aside the issues of surrogacy."[24] The court simply explained that the child had suffered under the earlier custody order and that therefore "the child's health, safety and welfare dictate placement with the father."[25]

Thus, the trial courts in both *Baby M.* and *Moschetta* (and to some extent the state supreme court in *Baby M.*) relied on the best-interest principle to resolve surrogacy disputes, and in doing that, reconstructed the dimensions of the two disputes. Each court molded the dimensions of the case before it to conform with assumptions underlying traditional family law principles. In doing that, each court disregarded significant aspects of the actual case before the court and replaced that case with a different and more traditional case. In effect, each court determined the best interests of the child for whose fate it was responsible almost as if the surrogacy arrangements that led to the two children's respective conceptions and births had never existed.

With disputes occasioned by gestational surrogacy, it is harder for courts to rely on traditional family law principles and harder to effect even the illusion that those cases can be encompassed by existing family law rules, formulated to handle far more traditional sorts of cases. Thus in *Johnson v. Calvert*, decided two years after the trial court originally decided *Moschetta*, the same state's supreme court relied on the notion of intent to determine the baby's parents and thereby resolve the dispute. In fact, none of the three California courts that issued decisions in *Johnson* relied on the best-interest principle. Although two of the three courts referred to the welfare of the child and declared that its holding served his advantage, neither premised its decision on his interests. Only the dissent in the state supreme court suggested that the baby's interests should be determinative.

The trial court, which held for the genetic parents on the ground that the parent-child bond is at base a genetic bond, made no independent findings about the welfare of the actual child involved in the case but did refer several times to the best interests of children in general. For instance, the court rejected the suggestion that it find three natural parents, asserting that such a finding would not serve the child's interests. Later the judge described his decision as "definitely pro child."[26] Ironically, however, in explaining that conclusion the judge referred to the interests of the Calverts rather than to those of the child. The court declared that the child "should be raised exclusively by the Calverts as natural parents. They shouldn't have to spend the next 18 years waiting for the other shoe to drop."[27]

The appellate court, anxious to avoid considerations of public policy in reaching its decision, relied on one statutory provision (which defined a mother as a woman identifiable through blood-genetic markers) and ignored another provision in California law (which defined a mother as the woman who gave birth to a child). The appellate court, seemingly anxious to avoid independent consideration of the social and moral implications of gestational surrogacy, had no need to justify its holding through invocations of children and their welfare since it presented that holding as compelled by statutory law. The court, certainly aware that, whatever its holding, an appeal would likely follow in the state supreme court, refrained almost completely from justifying its own decision. However, that decision frames dramatically the inapplicability of most existing family law statutes to cases occasioned by the new reproductive technologies.

The decisions of the California Supreme Court—particularly of Justice Panelli for the majority and of Justice Kennard in dissent—each grounded parentage on cultural, rather than natural, parameters.[28] Both the determinant selected by the majority (parental intent) and that selected by the dissent (the best interests of the child) require analysis and choice before parentage can be established; neither anchors parentage in even the illusion of inexorable truth.

Despite this important similarity, the two approaches differ significantly. The majority attempted to preserve a traditional model of family that presumes parentage to flow inevitably from the facts of the case, but substituted intent (and the world of contract implied therein) for biology as the central operating principle through which claims to parentage can be settled. The dissent, in contrast, relied on the central family law principle for resolving custody disputes (the best interests of the child), but applied that principle so as to construct a new model of parentage. In this model, a child's interests do not follow from, but rather establish, "natural" parentage. Justice Kennard noted that her procedure for determining the child's parentage was not unprecedented. That is so. However, her procedure does challenge society's general understanding of natural parentage.

The majority criticized the dissent for relying, in effect, on the best-interest standard potentially to upset, rather than to affirm, the basic order of things, an order that inexorably provides "natural" parents for each child apart from considerations of those parents' abilities to serve in the parental role. The claim, as the dissent recognized, is peculiar, given the majority's own recommendation that parentage be established through reliance on a standard (parental intent) far less often connected to the regulation of family matters than is the best-interest principle.

As described in the previous chapter, the majority blurred the potential contradictions between its own reliance on intent and its apparent preference for traditional understandings of family by reconstructing the notion of intent to conform with, and to suggest, those more traditional understandings. However, the contradictions underlying the majority's position cannot be so easily mediated. And the controversy between the dissent and the majority about the best approach to such cases illustrates starkly the inability of the society, including its courts of law, to interpret sensibly and uniformly, and to adjust easily to, contemporary changes in the creation and operation of the family.

Justice Panelli's majority opinion and Justice Kennard's dissent each depart from traditional understandings of family and parentage. However, the two opinions taken together focus attention on a long-standing, central assumption about parentage that has been essential in applications of the best-interest principle throughout the twentieth century. This assumption, that parents almost always serve their children's interests, that they "naturally care for their children and love them," is reflected in the majority decision, but in a new form, and is questioned in Justice Kennard's dissent.

The assumption was made startlingly clear more than a decade before *Johnson*, in *Parham v. J.R.* In that case, the United States Supreme Court validated a Georgia statute that provided for the commitment of children to mental institutions upon application of a parent or guardian and authorization by the superintendent of the hospital. The Court justified its holding through reference to "natural bonds" that guide parents to act in their children's best interests:

> The law's concept of the family rests on a presumption that parents possess what a child lacks in maturity, experience, and capacity for judgment required for making life's difficult decisions. More important, historically it has been recognized that natural bonds of affection lead parents to act in the best interests of their children.[29]

This assumption—that parents naturally act to serve their children's interests—routinely informs courts' applying the best-interest principle. Although the assumption obviously does not assist courts to select between two fit parents, it has usually served the interests of parents in disputes with potential nonparental custodians.

The assumption that parents serve their children's interests *because* they are parents is reflected in *Johnson* in the majority's express claim that parents, here identified through intent rather than through biological connections, will serve their children well because the interests of children will not likely "run contrary to those of adults who choose to bring them into being."[30] So, after establishing the Calverts' parentage on the basis of their parental intent, the state supreme court was able to conclude that Crispina and Mark would be "good" parents. Contrastingly, the court concluded that Johnson's initial denial of parental intent "conceded the best interests of the child [were] not with her."[31] The majority thereby presumed that its decision served the child's interests as that decision reconstructed parentage through reliance on the notion of intent. In contrast, the dissent reversed traditional assumptions about the connection between parentage and best interests, and proposed that parentage should flow from, and thereby ensure, a child's interests.

In fact, neither the majority nor the dissent in *Johnson* paid real heed to the actual interests of the child involved. The majority precluded the need to examine the child's interests by presuming expressly that, in the nature of the case, intending parents will serve their children's interests. The dissent, proposing that the child's best interests determine its parentage, left future courts without a clue about how to assess the consequences of gestational surrogacy in order really to accomplish the task of deciphering a child's best interests in a case such as *Johnson*.

Both the majority and the dissent in *Johnson* unsettle traditional understandings of family by expressly substituting choice for inexorable truth as the determinant of parentage. Each justified that substitution by invoking or relying expressly on the interests of the child. Neither, however, entertained concretely the interests of the actual child involved.

The Cases Compared

The responses of the courts that heard *Baby M.* and *Moschetta* most closely resemble those of courts handling routine custody disputes. This is not accidental. Compared with *Davis* and *Johnson*, *Baby M.* and *Moschetta* present only minimal disruption to cultural expectations about the biological processes underlying human reproduction. Artificial insemination, used in *Baby M.* and *Moschetta*, has been known for centuries, and has been used in human reproduction for well over one hundred years. The procedure, in requiring the extra-corporal transfer of sperm, disrupts the continuity of the reproductive process, but no longer seriously challenges cultural assumptions about the meanings of maternity, paternity, or the parent-child bond. As a result, *Baby M.* and *Moschetta* could be treated much as courts treat other less noteworthy disputes about children between adults contending for custody or parentage.

Baby M. and *Moschetta* did, however, threaten *social* expectations about the forms through which families should be established. Most of the contradictions and confusions presented by the opinions in these cases result from a broad social reluctance to define the parent-child bond in contractual terms. Each of the courts that heard these cases was able to rely on the best interests of the children to resolve the disputes in a manner that seems, at least at first glance, to differ only minimally from many other decisions involving custodial issues. In fact, each court's best-interest analysis, largely because each was effected *as if* these cases were no different from a thousand other custody cases, failed ultimately to take account of each child's best interests within the social contexts that led to the creation of, and that would continue to define, each child's life.

Both *Davis* and *Johnson*, in contrast with *Baby M.* and *Moschetta*, challenge the social and biological correlates of familial relationships. In each case, courts invoked children (or embryos) and justified the decisions reached with assurances that the children or potential children would be well served. Neither case was resolved through application of the best-interest principle and although the state supreme court's dissent did rely on the best-interest principle, it did so with the unusual though not unprecedented aim of establishing parentage, not custody.

In *Davis* the Tennessee supreme court determined that embryos, though not people, are owed a "special respect" as potential people, and thereby established the moral frame within which the dispute should be resolved. Then, without apparent recognition of the gap between that frame and the resolution actually reached, the court examined, and selected among, the interests of the adults whose donated gametes had produced the embryos in question. Similarly, the California supreme court in *Johnson* bypassed familiar legal responses. The court instead fashioned a novel response (reliance on parental intent) which sided with the world of contract and autonomous individuality and then described that response to benefit the children whose fate it would determine.

In all these cases, courts invoked children and their interests in order to justify a wide variety of ends not directly related to those children. For instance, children (or embryos) were invoked (by the trial court in *Baby M.*) to mitigate that court's obvious discomfort at having validated the contractualization of the parent-child bond; (by the state supreme court in *Davis*) to proclaim the potential humanity of, and consequent respect owed to, embryonic material; (by the state supreme court in *Johnson*) to mediate the contradictions between a world founded in terms of contract (intent, as generally understood) and a world founded in terms of status ("intent" as reinterpreted by the court).

III. Visions of Children:
Responses to Biotechnological Children

The same sort of contradiction that underlies the law's responses to cases occasioned by assisted reproduction is found in broader social responses to surrogacy and the new reproductive technologies as well as to the "biotechnological" children thereby produced.[32] Social and moral conclusions being voiced both in opposition to, and in favor of, assisted reproduction are being justified by references to children and their interests.

Those opposing reproductive technology, for instance, focus on children and suggest that children conceived through the assistance of such technology will suffer serious psychological, and even physical,[33] harms as a result of their technological beginnings. Those harms are connected to a larger moral order. Opponents of reproductive technology and surrogacy focus on problems in self-identity that such children may face.[34] The charge is that reproductive technology threatens to substitute for familial connections, and thereby precludes the benefits of those connections for the resulting children. Again, a focus on children furthers and disguises other interests. Reproductive technology threatens the traditional order, not just with regard to the parent-child bond but with regard to almost every aspect of family life. Thus, accepting reproductive technology may seem to suggest accepting divorce, abortion, and the sort of families within which such choices make sense. Images of children are still powerfully evocative of traditional families. To the extent that reproductive technology is presented as harming children, it can be forcefully condemned in the name of a past portrayed as having protected children and as having preserved their interests.

The Catholic church, for instance, has explained its opposition to reproductive technology by referring to the "right" of a child to be conceived only in traditional ways by a married couple.[35] Other opponents of reproductive technology refer to identity confusions likely to plague babies produced from donated gametes as well as to the negative consequences that surrogate motherhood may have for children whose social mothers cannot develop a committed relationship to the fetus as a result of the biological processes of gestation.[36]

These stories suggest that, just as reproductive technology disrupts society's understanding of family life, so it disrupts the ability of children

produced through reproductive technology to form secure personal iden-
tities. Such children are portrayed as rootless and unhappy—just as the
society has been uprooted by, and should be unhappy about, the continued development and use of reproductive technology in particular and,
in general, by broader changes in the family away from traditional forms.
One story about children produced through the use of anonymously
donated semen several decades ago describes a group of angry, confused
adults. The author acknowledged that "donor-inseminated children" who
do "take up the hunt" for their genetic fathers may be especially unhappy
and thus not representative or may be the products of neglectful homes
and thereby also not representative. Despite that disclaimer, she proceeded to describe, as if completely typical of people conceived through
artificial insemination, adults obsessed with the need to discover their
genetic fathers. One such woman, a forty five-year-old legal assistant in
California, broke off relations with her mother's husband (her legal
father) after she learned following the death of her mother that her
mother's husband was not her genetic parent. She explained her decision
to drop his last name: " 'I couldn't spend the rest of my life writing my
name as it was. It felt like a lie every time.' "[37]

Opponents of reproductive technology[38] also voice fears of broader
social consequences. As a group they fear especially the acceptance of
choice, limited only by technology's own limits, in the construction of
family bonds. That fear relates as directly to adults, and the definition
of marriage, at it relates to children and the construction of the parent-
child bond. The Catholic church, in one statement on the moral status
of assisted reproduction, declared expressly:

> [M]arriage possesses specific goods and values in its union and in procre-
> ation which cannot be likened to those existing in lower forms of life.
> Such values and meanings are of the personal order and determine from
> the moral point of view the meaning and limits of artificial interventions
> on procreation and on the origin of human life.[39]

Other contemporary theologians have similarly condemned reproductive
technology as morally objectionable because, in the words of one, the
technology "insist[s] on free choice about human relations."[40]

Much like those opposing assisted reproduction, those favoring its
development do so with references to children. They refer, for instance,
to the capacity of assisted reproduction to enable the creation of happy

families for couples who might otherwise remain childless. The children born to, or for, such couples are described as especially cared for and loved.[41] Proponents of reproductive technology focus on concrete images of normal, even privileged, children, whose happy childhoods are attributed to their unusual beginnings. The parents of such children are described as better, more caring parents because they yearned for children who were only produced after great expenditures of time, money, and emotional energy. For instance, one newspaper article concluded that "[p]arents of test tube babies are better mothers and fathers than those of normally conceived children."[42] Proponents of reproductive technology describe that technology as extending and magnifying both the sanctity of childhood and the joys that children bring. The technology provides more—not just more children, as in the multiple births that so frequently result with fertility treatment, but happier, securer, even smarter children.[43] This focus on children, however, hardly disguises other interests at stake in the development and use of reproductive technology, including the interests of couples unable to have children without assistance, the interests of a medical fertility industry with annual profits of billions of dollars, and the interests of an entire society obsessed with the availability of unending choice.

Fertility clinics depend on images of thriving children to support their work. The first of a series of articles in the *New York Times* in 1996 on "The Fertility Market,"[44] focused on the large financial stakes and inevitable competition for money and power within fertility clinics. The article featured a clinic at New York Hospital-Cornell Medical Center, where doctors earn salaries of up to one million dollars a year, and which provides the larger hospital with two million dollars in annual surplus income. The article detailed the intense antagonism among doctors and scientists in the clinic, described to have the highest pregnancy and birth rate in the country. A dozen scientists left the clinic last year for other professional homes as a result of internal antagonisms. Yet, above the article, on page one of the newspaper—in apparent contrast with the story's description of the clinic's aggressive bid for patients—sits a large picture of the clinic director, Dr. Zev Rosenwaks, posed cross-legged on the floor, holding three babies, two of them apparently neonates, and surrounded by four others. Dr. Rosenwaks smiles broadly. The children nibble crackers, stare at each other, or sleep quietly.

In recent years, many clinics have attempted to gain publicity, approval, and thus presumably increased business and funding for their efforts by hosting "reunions" for children produced through reproductive technology and for those children's grateful parents. Often, these reunions, held in parks and other public places, have welcomed the press. The stories that result[45] contrast miraculous conceptions and births with normal, everyday childhood behaviors. One such story, typical of the genre, reported on a "reunion" organized by a fertility clinic and held at a local park. The reunion brought together two hundred children conceived through the clinic's assistance, along with those children's parents.[46] The reunion-picnic was described as a celebration of the "medical advancement that, in the words of many, had miraculously changed their lives." The story reported: "While the children played ball, blew bubbles and hugged the life-size Disney characters who paraded through the park, many of their parents swapped war stories with one another, just as they had during similar picnics that have been held each of the past three years."

Particular children have also been used to portray the value of reproductive technology.[47] The fifteenth and sixteenth birthdays of Louise Brown formed the focus of an array of news stories about reproductive technology. Louise, the first person conceived in vitro, was born in Oldham, England, on July 25, 1978. Louise made the celebration of her fifteenth birthday a context for supporting the growth and development of infertility treatment. She agreed to have the day celebrated publicly and two months early in order to have it coincide with Britain's first National Fertility Week. The stories about Louise's birth and development reflect the themes of the reunion stories. One such story began: "A miracle of technology brought Louise Brown into this world, but that was 15 years ago and now she's just another teenager."[48] Another began with a description of Louise: "In her jeans, floppy rugby shirt and overpriced running shoes, Louise Brown looks like a typical teenager. Her parents complain that she likes 'loud music and stupid clothes' and much prefers the company of friends to 'us old codgers.' "[49] "But," the story continued, "if life in the Brown household in Bristol, England, is rather routine, the world's memory of Louise is anything but."

In each of these generally favorable stories, those about the fertility clinic reunions and those about Louise Brown, the miracle, as reported, is supposed to be as much the typical (and thus remarkable) childhoods of children produced through the use of reproductive technology as it is the technology itself. Each of these stories proclaims that reproductive technology is impressive *because* it allows for the creation of typical, and therefore treasured, babies for their loving parents, and that it does so even more certainly than traditional forms of human reproduction. Louise is described as being exactly what a teen-age girl should be *because* her technological origins ensured a propitious—and thus normal—childhood.

Other stories of the same sort focus less intently on children and more on the needs and frustrations, and on the successes or failures, of parents and potential parents. These stories detail the anguish—and usually (in the stories) the rewards—of infertile adults, especially women, who are treated for infertility.[50] One such story[51] reported the pain of great sadness an infertile thirty five-year-old woman felt on occasions such as Mother's Day, and upon seeing women with baby carriages. After months of treatment, described in detail, the woman and her husband had a child (born after in vitro fertilization, cryopreservation of the resulting embryos, and finally thawing and implantation of the embryos). The story concludes with the woman's proclaiming that "the good Lord knew He put us through such hell to have her [the baby]. He figured He'd give us the perfect baby."

IV. Conclusion

That advocates and opponents of reproductive technology both justify their assertions through references to children and childhood adds fuel to the suggestion that those references are a pretext that, at least, in part serves other ends. Reproductive technology is testing the meaning and parameters of the family, and the debate occasioned by use of that technology is about much more than the consequences of that technology for actual children. The developing debate about assisted reproduction broadens dramatically, yet continues, an older debate about the moral and social implications of the individualization and privatization[52] of family relationships—a debate that began to develop clearly in the mid-nineteenth century. Now, as then, images of children provide a powerful focal point around which the shifting scope of family life can be understood.

Now, however, even as the rhetoric about the consequences of assisted reproduction for children intensifies, both from adherents and from opponents, society and the law as a whole cannot rely securely on images of children and on references to children's interests in resolving disputes about family. For a long time, certain truths about children, about their importance and enduring value, stood seemingly unaffected, at the eye of the debate about family. These old truths provided a harbor within which the larger debate could be anchored. Messages about what the family is are still communicated, if less securely and less coherently, through references to children. However, the interests of actual children are almost visibly being encompassed and subsumed by the ideological debate. Nostalgic images of families of yore, symbolized by children-in-families, have served polemic interests for those who favor the preservation of tradition. Almost equally they have served those who endorse individualization and contractualization in the formation and operation of family life, but who temper the harshest implication of *that* choice with assurances about the continuing appreciation of children and childhood.

Conclusion

In the contemporary debate about the American family, political agendas and deeply felt, often passionate, responses are everywhere evident. This is understandably so, since the debate encapsulates many of the cultural conflicts and social conundrums central to our time, and demands that basic choices be made: between equality and inequality, between community and autonomy, and between freedom and constraint. In such demands, not only ideological intensities, but calls for prophecy and prescription, are immanent.

For the most part this book refrains from responding either to the intensities or to the calls. Basically a work of cultural anthropology, it is, by design, descriptive in nature. Because the law, as an institution, often reflects, clearly and accurately, the contours and evolution of social thought, the book deduces from actual law the state of mind, historical and current, of American culture as it has, for several centuries, confronted, and continues to confront, an issue of moment. On the question of the value of that state of mind the book is, by design, silent, as it is on the question of what may issue from it—on the confident assumption that the social scientist contributes to productive debate by defining issues, and by placing them in historical and intellectual context, so that they may be clearly seen, and in consequence clearly and honestly discussed.

The imperative of understanding the shifts in the conception of the American family—for a long time gradual, but more recently seismic—is increasingly self-evident. That conception reflects, in basic ways, the culture's view of its essential self. Thus, to analyze the shifts in the conception is to grasp, in some significant part at least, the rumination of America upon itself.

For the reasons stated, the analysis may be productively conducted through a study of American family law, and in particular through a study of the response of that law during the past few decades to surrogacy, and to revolutionary developments in reproductive technology.

This book has presented such a study, offering ideological support to no side in the debate occasioned by the law's response, but to each side impartially elucidation as an aid to debate.

Central to the study is its detailed focus upon assisted reproduction, which both reflects and accelerates recent changes in the scope and meaning of the American family. That children are conceived pursuant to contractual arrangements involving the exchange of money; that conception need not begin with sexual intercourse, and need not occur within the body of a woman; that the genetic makeup of a child (and of its cloned twin or triplet) can be selected from a panoply of genetic options—these factors pose a profound threat to the ideology of family as it developed in the early years of the Industrial Revolution and was elaborated and glorified in the succeeding two centuries.

Within that ideology families are understood as holistic, hierarchical, social units, that endure in the face of, and as a defense against, the tensions and contingencies of everyday life. Moreover, the endurance of familial relationships is a moral precept of fundamental significance and is understood to stem from, and to reflect, almost inevitably, the natural truths that undergird social connections among kin. Within traditional families, children love their parents, and parents their children, not because they chose one another, but because the biological bonds that connect them ensure enduring love.

That this ideology of family was never perfectly or even closely reflected in most actual relationships was largely irrelevant to the continued predominance of the ideology. In fact, to the extent that society perceived and reacted to the gap between ideology and reality, it bemoaned the reality and imagined ways to compel real families to conform more closely to preferred forms. Until recent decades, the gap between ideology and reality was far more often used to criticize the reality than self-consciously to reevaluate the ideology.

The traditional ideology of family has been consistently complemented by a deep nostalgia for families of yore. Those families, always placed a few decades before the present, and always imagined to have been precisely what families are supposed to be, convinced society during successive decades of its unique responsibility for the destruction of traditional family life. Ironically, the families so imagined never existed. But the ability to imagine them provided a constant reminder during the course of the last two centuries that families could be precisely what they were supposed to be, but were not.

The nostalgia that accompanied the development of the ideology of family during the nineteenth century relied on images associated with a much more ancient world in which relations defined through the inexorable connections of land and blood organized much of the social world. In that preindustrial world, autonomous individuality was far more limited and unrestricted choice far more suspect than they became in the following centuries. In fact, the development of the nineteenth-century market depended on, and valued without reservation, the freedom of autonomous individuals to choose their own bargains and design their own connections. It provided the social contrast against which, from the early nineteenth century, images of the family were constructed and prized.

The family that mid-twentieth-century Americans treasured could be characterized in almost every regard by reference to its differences from the world of the marketplace. And so, David Schneider in his mid-century ethnography of American kinship concluded that the "distinctive features of kinship in American culture" can be "understood in terms of the contrast between love and money which stand for home and work."[1]

Throughout the nineteenth century and the first half of the twentieth, the ideology of family responded with impressively steady opposition to demographic changes that persistently widened the gap between the ideology of family and the reality. During this period, the authority of fathers diminished, divorce rates rose, birth rates fell, and by the late nineteenth century women began to work for wages in increasing numbers. These shifts did not go unnoticed, but practically everyone agreed, specific practices and new patterns notwithstanding, that ideally, the family contrasted, and should always contrast, with the office, that affairs at home were matters of love, not money, and that the connection between kin was deeply, almost irretrievably, embedded in the very nature of things.

Only in the second half of the twentieth century were the demographic changes in the form of family that developed during the course of the previous century and a half approved by significant groups of people. With the clear emergence of competing ideologies of family by the 1960s, U.S. society as a whole became obviously perplexed and unsure about the proper range and shape of familial relationships. The change toward wider acknowledgment and acceptance of family forms that differed from those considered proper within the traditional ideology of family became startlingly clear in the responses of family law throughout the United States at that time. Not only did lawmakers recognize, and provide for, easy divorce, nonmarital cohabitation, and prenuptial contractual agreements, but, even more, courts expressly redefined the holistic, hierarchical family, valued in early decades, as a collection of autonomous individuals, connected only insofar, and only for so long, as the individuals involved chose to be connected. That redefinition was explicit, though little noted at the time, in the 1972 decision of the United States Supreme Court in *Eisenstadt v. Baird.* In that case, which invalidated a Massachusetts statute that made illegal the distribution of contraception to unmarried people, the Court presumed that family members (or at least adult family members) were essentially indistinguishable from the individuals who negotiate bargains in the marketplace. In that view, the type of bargains family members reach, as well as the world of interrelations they choose to effect through those bargains, may differ from most bargains negotiated in the market. However, the mode through which those interrelations are created differs only insignificantly from the mode through which contractual relations in the world of work are created.

Thus, by the second half of the twentieth century, the law accommodated changes in the form of familial relationships by recognizing those changes and, more important, by acknowledging a new understanding of family that undergirded changing modes of creating and living in families. But even the law was not unanimous in this new acceptance and redefinition of family. And in the society more broadly, the voices of dissent were strong.

In the last decades of the twentieth century the traditional understanding of family has been under siege, though it is still widely perceived as the best, if not the only proper, understanding of family. As a variety of new options for living in and understanding families has been gaining increasing recognition within society, the debate about the American family has grown in prominence and intensity.

In the late 1970s and early 1980s, the responses of the law and of society more generally to the changing family were challenged dramatically by the advent of the new reproductive technologies and the appearance of surrogacy arrangements. Whether these phenomena, especially those that depended on developments in science, appeared coincidentally with broad changes in the family, or appeared only after society was ready, however fitfully, to accept them, is a question for historians of science.

In considering the implications and consequences of creating families through contracts and financial exchange, and of redesigning human reproduction so that people can choose how, when, and where to conceive their children, and who those children will resemble once born, society is continuing its ongoing debate about the parameters of acceptable family life. Assisted reproduction presents a challenge of overwhelming proportions to traditional understandings of family. Whereas the traditional ideology of family depended on the separation of, and distinction between, relations at home and relations at work, assisted reproduction amalgamates the two worlds on a multitude of levels. Almost every aspect of human reproduction can, and is, being designed through bargained negotiations. Relations once described as "accidents of nature" now result from self-conscious choice. Reproductive technology and surrogacy do not simply resemble market relations. There is now a large market in infertility treatment. Consumers compare fertility clinics for price and success rates. Billions of dollars a year are exchanged. Contracts are signed; agreements are breached; damages are assessed.

Social responses to surrogacy and the new reproductive technologies reflect, but also exacerbate, the society's larger debate about family. Assisted reproduction provides a new context for that debate. But far more important, assisted reproduction alters the terms, and intensifies the tone, of the debate, by presenting an entirely new level of challenge to traditional understandings of family.

For the most part, society and the law, in accepting and approving new forms of familial connection in the decades following mid-century, refrained from interfering expressly with traditional understandings of the parent-child tie. It was especially the connection between mothers and their children that became the central, apparently lasting, representation of enduring, loving family bonds and that, as such, continues to be widely valued. Although that bond may be threatened in fact in particular cases, by redefinitions of marriage, divorce, and cohabitation, none of those changes directly implicates the parent-child bond. Assisted reproduction, in contrast, proclaims that the creation of the connection between parents and their children can be manipulated. Although Western society understood the social and biological dimensions of family as separable in theory before the advent of the new reproductive technologies, it was assumed until that phenomenon appeared that a set of biological truths undergirded, and directed, the social dimensions of familial relationships. The possibilities of separating maternity into aspects such as freezing gametic material for decades before it is used to conceive a child, creating embryos after the deaths of the embryos' progenitors, producing babies from aborted fetuses, and other possibilities similar to these, seriously unsettle social expectations about human reproduction, and as a result unsettle assumptions about the social consequences of biological reproduction.

In sum, surrogacy and the new reproductive technologies disturb traditional understandings of family in two different, but equally basic, regards. First, these phenomena challenge the long-standing notion that the parent-child tie should be founded in love, not in money. In every state of the United States, adoption laws prohibit the exchange of money for a baby. Yet, commercial surrogacy arrangements and the growing market in infertility treatment involve the exchange of money for gametes, embryos, and babies, pursuant to a variety of contractual agreements. Second, the new reproductive technologies, including gestational surrogacy (but less so traditional surrogacy), muddle assumptions about the social correlates of biological reproduction. Specifically, these phenomena disturb basic assumptions that undergirded public understandings of the parent-child relationship. Certainly, people can choose to create families through reproductive technology or surrogacy that, once formed, resemble traditional families in that their members understand one another as deeply and lastingly bonded together. But because they are founded in choice, rather than created as an inevitable consequence of natural processes, such families can always be replaced by others, attributable to other and different choices.

Assisted reproduction has transformed an evolutionary change in the family into a revolutionary change. The culture barely accommodates the challenge that assisted reproduction adds to older uncertainties and confusions about the meaning and fate of the family. When change occurs slowly, over centuries, culture has the capacity to adjust itself to the change, or to force the change to conform to existing cultural patterns. The pace of the new challenge presented almost daily by assisted reproduction is antithetical to culture's ability to respond consistently or sagely.

This challenge, and society's halting, muddled response, are reflected in the law. State legislatures have hesitated to respond to the complex, volatile questions raised by assisted reproduction. This is not surprising since legislators are often loath to tread on uncertain ground and to decide hotly debated questions. Courts, however, do not have the option of remaining silent. Particular disputes involving actual litigants with real problems demand resolution. Thus, courts have become the primary arena in which the society is forging and considering its response to assisted reproduction.

More often than not conservative, the judiciary has striven, for the most part, to preserve traditional conceptions of the family in cases occasioned by surrogacy and by the new reproductive technologies, while rendering decisions that threaten traditional understandings of family. Thus, in facing such disputes, courts support and protect definitions of family that acknowledge choice and individuality, but often do so in language that supports and protects traditional conceptions of family in which relations are understood to be anchored in fixed, unchanging truths.

Courts are thus developing a set of responses that aim to preserve traditional understandings of family—understandings of family based in the separation of home and work—and to expand definitions of family so as to provided for freedom and choice—concepts that have been associated with the marketplace, not the home, during the past century and a half.

Thus, the essential task of the courts, although it would seem often undertaken with less than full consciousness, has become that of mediating between the ideological correlates of modernity (choice, autonomous individuality, and equality) and those of tradition (connection founded in inexorable truth, holism, and hierarchy). In performing that task, courts have employed a variety of legal strategies. Some, such as reliance on the concept of parental intent in determining parentage, are unfamiliar to family law as it has existed until the present. Others, such as application of the best-interest principle, are mainstays of the existing family law system. Both sorts of approaches fail to achieve their desired ends. More-over, both, fashioned to resolve some aspect of the baffling debate about the meaning and scope of the family, complicate that debate.

So, for instance, courts have redefined the concept of intent so that parental intent signals the choice to become a parent, but also becomes substitutable for blood or genes as the essential bond that assures that parents (or at least "normal" parents) will love and care for their children. Courts are asking the concept of intent to move between conflicting understandings of family.

By relying on the concept of intent, courts have avoided clearly identifying with any particular understanding of family to the exclusion of others. As a result, the confusions that the concept of intent was introduced to resolve have intensified. Rather than resolving the debate, the apparent solution has become a term in that ongoing debate. Simi-larly, reliance on the best-interest principle in cases occasioned by as-sisted reproduction has widened the debate about family, as courts have presumed, but clearly failed to comprehend, the best interests of children conceived, for example, pursuant to commercial agreements, or from the egg of one woman but gestated by another. Reliance on the best-interest standard in such cases has been more successful at revealing the enor-mity of the questions being asked than at resolving those questions.

Not only the specific strategies on which courts have relied for settling disputes involving assisted reproduction lead to ambiguity and confusion. The arguments presented to the courts by the parties in these cases, are also, and perhaps inevitably, clouded by self-contradiction. So, for in-stance, William and Elizabeth Stern and the trial court judge who in effect decided to enforce the surrogacy contract into which they had entered, justified honoring that contract *because* it promised to create a traditional, enduring, committed old-fashioned family. Similarly, Junior Davis, in arguing that he should be allowed to determine the fate of the seven frozen embryos produced from his and his ex-wife's gametes, invoked the "ancient wellsprings of kinship" in order to safeguard his own right to autonomous choice.

How these contradictions will eventually be resolved is uncertain. Perhaps, social consensus will emerge (as it did when artificial insemina-tion appeared), and a relatively uniform statutory response from state lawmakers will preclude the need for courts to reenter the debate each time the use of assisted reproduction leads to a dispute among the participants. If so, the character of the guidance that legislatures will provide may endorse the definition of familial relationships in market terms and agree to enforce surrogacy contracts and to permit the transfer, and perhaps also the purchase and sale, of gametic and embryonic material. Even if that happens, the legislative decision to permit the creation of families and of the parent-child bond through the use of contracts and money exchange may or may not indicate the shape and tone of the resulting families. Alternatively, however, legislatures, following the model of nineteenth-century lawmakers responding to the apparent threat posed by changes in the family at that time, may react to prohibit, in the hope of suppressing, the development and use of assisted reproduction.

The nostalgia that has consistently accompanied social understandings of the family since at least the early nineteenth century indicates a strong longing for a world (in some part imagined) that no longer exists. But, whether society can ever "go back" remains unclear. Certainly, a clear, though unstable, self-contradictory and openly criticized, trend exists toward increasing recognition of autonomous individuality and choice in the creation (and termination) of familial relationships. Only history will tell whether the future that trend suggests for the family is realized.

Whatever happens, the disputes currently occasioned by surrogacy and by the new reproductive technologies, and those certain to appear, reflect a larger, continuing debate in particular between traditional and modern conceptions of the family and in general between radically different, and often perhaps irreconcilable, conceptions of society. For obvious reasons, this debate must be closely and very carefully watched.

NOTES

Notes to the Introduction

1. As used in this book, the term "ideology" may include, but does not primarily refer to, a set of political beliefs. Rather, the term refers to the pervasive forms in terms of which people understand what it means to be human. This definition is similar to that of the French anthropologist and Indologist, Louis Dumont, who wrote:

> Our definition of ideology thus rests on a distinction that is not a distinction of matter but one of point of view. We do not take as ideological what is left out when everything true, rational or scientific has been preempted. We take everything that is socially thought, believed, acted upon, on the assumption that it is a living whole, the interrelatedness and interdependence of whose parts would be blocked out by the a priori introduction of our current dichotomies. (Dumont 1977, 22)

2. Insightful analyses of the development of new images of family—and new forms of family—during the nineteenth century are found in Demos (1986); Ehrenreich and English (1978, ch. 1); Mintz (1983); and Mintz and Kellogg (1988, ch. 3).

3. Uniform Status of Children of Assisted Conception Act (1988), promulgated by the National Conference of Commissioners on Uniform State Laws and found at 9B U.L.A.152 (Supp. 1994).

4. See, e.g., Orford v. Orford, 49 Ont. L.R. 15 (1921).

5. See, e.g., Doornbos v. Doornbos, 23 U.S.L.W. 2308 (Super. Ct. Cook City., Ill., Dec. 13, 1954), appeal dismissed on procedural grounds, 12 Ill. App.2d 473, 1249 N.E.2d 844 (1956).

6. See, e.g., Strnad v. Strnad, 190 Misc. 786, 78 N.Y.S.2d 390 (N.Y. Sup. Ct. 1948).

7. See e.g., People ex rel. Abajian v. Dennet 184 N.Y.S.2d 178 (1958).

8. Ga. Code Ann. tit. 74 Sec. 101.1 (1964).

9. Stephanie Coontz (1992) provides a detailed analysis of the myth of traditional family life.

10. Coontz (1992), 15.

11. De Tocqueville ([1835] 1945); (reprinted in Bremner (1970) vol. I, 347–50).

12. See Eisenstadt v. Baird (1972); *see also* discussion of *Eisenstadt* in chapter 2.

Notes to Chapter 1

1. Fox (1993), 123.
2. Strathern (1993), 22 (citation omitted) (draft on file with author).
3. Marc Bloch describes medieval families to have had a "dual character." Maternal relations (e.g., the mother's brother) were almost as important as paternal relations. Children's names, for instance, came variously from the maternal or paternal side. Bloch (1970), 137.
4. Barnett (1976); Barnett and Silverman (1979); Dumont (1967), especially Appendix (1977).
5. For direction in the description of the feudal order I am grateful to Charles T. Wood, The Daniel Webster Professor of History at Dartmouth College, and to the works of Philippe Aries and Georges Duby, eds. (1988); Marc Bloch (1968, 1970); Georges Duby (1978, 1980); and David Herlihy (1985).
6. Duby (1980), 59.
7. Quoted in ibid.
8. Ibid., 71.
9. Capitularia Regum Francorum (A. Boretins and V. Krause, eds. [1883–97]), cited in ibid., 363 n.9.
10. Duby (1980), 70.
11. Duby (1978), at 6.
12. Shaw, *St. Joan*, Sc. 4.
13. Today, this is less true of Catholicism than of other social institutions, and to that degree Catholicism presents a contemporary counterpoint to the transformation of life in the West away from feudal forms of hierarchy and holism. Increasingly, however, feudal forms seem less and less certain even here.
14. Demos (1986), 28.
15. Mintz and Kellogg (1988), 19, 20, 108.
16. Ibid., 108.
17. For my understanding of the development of the family in the years after the late eighteenth century I am especially grateful to the following works: Coontz (1992); Demos (1986); Grossberg (1985); Mintz (1983); Mintz and Kellogg (1988); and Shanley (1994).
18. Schneider (1980), 50.
19. Ibid., 48–49.
20. May (1991), 583–87.
21. Seib (1993).
22. Strathern (1993), 22.

Notes to Chapter 2

1. Chesler (1992), 160.
2. Ibid., 66–70.

3. Mintz and Kellogg (1988), 170.

4. In the mid-1990s a number of state legislatures began to consider bills aimed at limiting the development of no-fault divorce. A Michigan bill, for instance, proposed that no-fault divorce be unavailable in both cases involving children and cases in which one party preferred not to divorce (Rhode 1996). Such restrictions on no-fault divorce suggest the continuing concern of at least some groups within the United States about the obvious transformation of the family and of family law since the middle of the twentieth century.

5. Friedman (1985), 204–7.

6. Glendon (1987), 104–5.

7. Freed and Walker (1988), 560.

8. Uniform Premarital Agreement Act, Sec. 3 and cmt., 9B U.L.A. 371, 373–74 (1987).

9. The consequences of this assumption in the Victorian world are considered by Mary Lyndon Shanley in *Feminism, Marriage, and the Law in Victorian England* (1989).

10. The trial court decision in *Kingsley* was partially reversed on appeal. A Florida court of appeal held that Gregory, because still a child, did not have legal capacity to commence the termination proceeding. The error was held to have been harmless, however, because four other parties with capacity filed petitions on the boy's behalf requesting termination of Gregory Kingsley's biological mother's parental rights. *Kingsley v. Kingsley* at 790.

11. Bartholet (1993), 55–61, 170–72.

12. Ibid., 170.

13. See generally Caplan (1990).

14. Griswold, 381 U.S. at 480.

15. Conn. Gen. Stat. Sec. 53–32 (1958) (*quoted in Griswold*, 381 U.S. at 480).

16. Griswold, 381 U.S. at 486.

17. Ibid.

18. The law's claim to protect family autonomy has not, of course, meant that, in fact, the law has refrained from defining and regulating family life. Frances Olsen makes this point clearly when she argues that both state intervention in the family and the state's refusal to intervene according to the principle of family autonomy are ideological, not analytic concepts. Olsen (1993), 281.

19. See, e.g., Allen, 72 *B.U.L. Rev.* 683, 687; Coleman, 24 *Ind. L. Rev.* 399, 404.

20. Grey, 43 *Law and Contemp. Probs.* 83, 84.

21. Schwartz (1985), 227–39. An earlier draft of *Griswold* is printed in Schwartz's book. That draft makes clear the Court's uncertainty about the constitutional theory on which to base the holding in the case.

22. Of the seven justices who joined or concurred in the *Griswold* holding, no more than three agreed upon the nature of the constitutional support for that holding.

23. Griswold, 381 U.S. at 495 (Goldberg, J., concurring).

24. Poe v. Ullman, 367 U.S. at 548 (1961) (Harlan, J., dissenting). In his concurrence in *Griswold*, Justice Harlan referred to, and relied on, his dissent in *Poe v. Ullman.*

25. Griswold, 381 U.S. at 550–51.

26. Ibid., at 502 (White, J., concurring).

27. Eisenstadt, 405 U.S. at 453.

28. Ibid., at 454–55.

29. Ibid., at 453.

30. Ellman et al., (1991), 849.

31. Lochner, 198 U.S. at 65.

32. Ibid., at 46.

33. Ibid., at 52.

34. Ibid., at 53.

35. Ibid., at 54.

36. Ibid., at 62.

37. Ibid., at 64.

38. Ibid., at 53, 64.

39. Ibid., at 56.

40. Ibid., at 57.

41. Ibid., at 75.

42. For example in *Carey v. Population Servs. Int'l*, the Court invalidated a state law that restricted advertising and distribution of contraceptives because the law infringed upon "protected individual choices." *Zablocki v. Redhail* declared that marriage is a fundamental right. In *Roe v. Wade*, the Court found a limited right to abortion.

43. In 1937 the Court decided *West Coast Hotel Co. v. Parrish*. The case is generally acknowledged to have ended the *Lochner* era.

44. Griswold, 381 U.S. at 482.

45. Ibid.

46. Poe v. Ullman, 367 U.S. at 539 (Harlan, J., dissenting) (referred to, and relied on, in Justice Harlan's concurrence in *Griswold*, 381 U.S. at 500).

47. Poe, 367 U.S. at 542 (relied on in Justice Harlan's concurrence in *Griswold*).

48. Poe, 367 U.S. at 542 (relied on in Justice Harlan's concurrence in *Griswold*).

49. An earlier, unused draft for *Griswold* prepared by Justice Douglas premised the holding on a First Amendment right of spouses to associate freely. Schwartz (1985), 227–39.

50. Lochner, 198 U.S. at 61.

51. Eisenstadt, 405 U.S. at 453.

52. Ibid.

53. Dumont (1977), 4.

54. Robertson (1994a), 235.

55. Perrot (1990), 341, citing Littré, *Dictionnaire* (1863–1872).

56. 59 N.W.2d at 342.

Notes to Chapter 3

1. Genesis 16:2.

2. Maine ([1861] 1917), 179.

3. Ibid.

4. Ibid., 99.

5. MacPherson (1962), 3.

6. Maine ([1861] 1917), 99.

7. Ibid., 100 (emphasis in original).

8. My use of Maine's description of the contrasts between a world defined in status terms and a world defined in contractual terms differs in tone from earlier uses I have made of the contrast. I am grateful to Burton Agata, Jana B. Singer, and Marilyn Strathern for showing me how careful one must be in using Maine's distinction. The distinction between families defined in terms of status and families defined in terms of contract is most important to the history of ideas. As a description of a continuous historical process, the distinction is less useful and, if relied on, should be used only with great caution.

9. Hyde (1979), xi.

10. Ibid., 56–60.

11. Ibid., 61.

12. Ibid., 70.

13. Gordon (1987), 25.

14. Ragoné (1994), 80.

15. Ibid., 55.

16. Statutes regulating at least one aspect of surrogacy arrangements include: Ala. Code § 26–10–34 (1996); Ariz. Rev. Stat. Ann. § 25–218. A (1995); Ark. Code Ann. § 9–10–201 (Michie Supp. 1995); Ind. Code Ann. §§ 31–8–1–5, 38–8–2–1 (Burns Supp. 1996); Iowa Code Ann. § 710.11 (West Supp. 1995); Ky. Rev. Stat. Ann § 199–590; La. Rev. Stat. Ann. § 9.2173 (Supp. 1996); Mich. Comp. Laws Ann. §§ 722.853, 722.855(5), 722.859 (1996); Nev. Rev. Stat. § 126.045 (Michie 1995); N.H. Rev. Stat. Ann. §§ 168–B:16–25 (Supp. 1996); N.Y. Dom. Rel. Law §§ 121–24 (McKinney Supp. 1996); N.D. Cent. Code § 134–18–05 (1991); Utah Code Ann. § 76–7–204 (1996); Va. Code Ann. §§ 20–156 to 20–165 (Michie 1996); Wash. Rev. Code § 26.26.210 (1995); W. Va. Code § 48–4–16 (1996); Wis. Stat. § 69.14 (1994).

17. Stanley v. Illinois, 405 U.S. at 651.

18. Michael H., at 124.

19. Ibid., at 124 (footnote omitted).

20. See, e.g., Brady v. U.S., at 748 (waiver of constitutional right must be

voluntary to be effective in criminal cases) and Pierce v. Somerset Railway, at 648 (act or omission to act can be grounds for waiving constitutional right).

21. Brookhart v. Janis, at 4 (quoting Johnson v. Zerbst, at 464).

22. Matter of Baby M., 525 A.2d at 1170.

23. Ibid.

24. Ibid., at 1172.

25. Ibid.

26. Ibid., at 1151–52.

27. Ibid., at 1172.

28. Ibid., 537 A.2d at 1234.

29. Ibid., 525 A.2d at 1157–58.

30. Ibid., 537 A.2d at 1242.

31. Ibid., at 1246.

32. Ibid., at 1246–47.

33. Ibid., 225 N.J. Super. 267, 542 A.2d 52 (1988).

34. Ibid. M., 537 A.2d at 1264.

35. Brief on Behalf of Mary Beth and Richard Whitehead at 34–55 (hereinafter Whitehead Brief).

36. Whitehead Brief, at 34–55.

37. Ibid. at 37.

38. Ibid., at 38–39.

39. Brief on Behalf of Respondent at 99–106 (hereinafter Stern Brief).

40. Stern Brief, at 80.

41. Ibid.

42. Ibid. at 82.

Notes to Chapter 4

1. Of the Supreme Court's unwed father decisions, one (*Michael H. v. Gerald D.*) has generally been treated as representing a break with the position asserted and suggested in the other unwed father decisions, all of which were decided before *Michael H. Michael H.*, unlike the other unwed father cases, has not been analyzed as a harbinger of a new social order regarding paternal rights and relationships.

2. See Czapansky (1991), 1420, in which Czapansky describes choices involved in a father's parental role.

3. Hill (1991), 381 (footnotes omitted).

4. Stanley v. Illinois (1972); Quilloin v. Walcott (1978); Caban v. Mohammed (1979); Lehr v. Robertson (1983); Michael H. v. Gerald D. (1989).

5. See, e.g., Zinman (1992), 980.

6. Stanley, 405 U.S. at 651.

7. Ibid., at 657 n.9.

8. See, Batty (1990), 1181; DeMarco (1985), 301–3.

9. Stanley, 405 U.S. at 665–66 (Burger, J., dissenting).

10. It is not entirely clear from Justice Burger's language whether he predicated these conclusions on a natural, and thus presumably inexorable, propensity of females to bond strongly with their children and a natural absence of such a propensity in males, or whether Justice Burger would have allowed that the condition he described is cultural, and thus presumably more easily mutable.

11. See Hubbard (1990), 114–17 especially, for a good discussion of some of the complexities involved in sorting out the consequences of nature and nurture for people.

12. Ga. Code Sec. 74–101 (1975); Ga. Code Sec. 74–103 (1975). Quilloin, 434 U.S. at 249.

13. Quilloin, 434 U.S. at 251.

14. Ibid., at 256.

15. Ibid., at 255.

16. Ibid., at 256.

17. Ibid., at 255.

18. Ibid., at 253 n.14. For procedural reasons, the Court refused to consider Quilloin's equal protection claim based on his gender.

19. The version of Section 111 of the New York Domestic Relations Law in effect at the time provided that " 'consent to adoption shall be required as follows: 1. Of the adoptive child. . . . ; 2. of the parents or surviving parent, whether adult or infant, of a child born in wedlock; 3. Of the mother, whether adult or infant, of a child born out of wedlock; 4. Of any person or authorized agency having lawful custody of the adoptive child.' " N.Y. Dom. Rel. Law § 111 (quoted at Caban 441 U.S., at 385 n.4).

20. Ibid., at 391.

21. Ibid., at 388 (quoting Transcript of Oral Argument at 41).

22. Caban, 441 U.S. at 389.

23. Ibid.

24. See, e.g., Eveleigh (1989), 1062; Perry (1984), 1511; Wintjen (1990), 1075.

25. Caban, 441 U.S. at 389.

26. Barthes (1967), 76. The distinction between marked and unmarked terms, recognized in linguistics, has proved useful in the study of other social phenomena. In this derivative use, marked terms refer to people and groups of people who are in some sense considered peripheral. Thus, using the example of gender, "male" is the unmarked term, and "female" is the marked term. Marked categories (e.g., women) will frequently be identified as such. Thus, a female politician or a female doctor will more often be referred to through use of the gender designation than will a male politician or a male doctor. Male politicians or male doctors will simply be referred to as politicians or doctors. Unless otherwise informed, the culture still *assumes* politicians and doctors are male.

27. Caban, 441 U.S. at 397 (Stewart, J., dissenting).

28. This appears to be the case in which maternity is invoked per se and in which maternity is compared with paternity. In other cases (which will be considered later in this chapter), cases in which one kind of maternity is opposed to other kinds of maternity, the comparative significance of genetics and gestation may be reversed.

29. Caban, 441 U.S. at 397 (Stewart, J., dissenting).

30. Ibid., at 405 n.10 (Stevens, J., dissenting). Justice Stevens asserted that sociological and anthropological research indicated the presence and importance of the bond to which he referred.

31. Lehr, 463 U.S. at 256.

32. Ibid., at 259–60.

33. Ibid., at 260 (quoting Caban, 441 U.S. at 397 [Stewart, J., dissenting]).

34. Lehr, 463 U.S. at 262.

35. In this sense, the unwed father cases further limit mother's choices. See, e.g., Czapansky (1991), 1416, 1456–63 (describing mothers as "draftee" parents and fathers as "volunteer" parents).

36. Justice Stewart seemed to restrict his use of the term "biological ties" to ties with a genetic base. Caban, 441 U.S. at 397 (Stewart, J., dissenting). However, the mother's "more enduring" connection with the child in the form of her having gestated and born the child, to which Justice Stewart referred as establishing her parenthood, is clearly *biological*, though not genetic.

37. Lehr, 463 U.S. at 267.

38. Ibid. (quoting Caban, 441 U.S. at 392).

39. Ibid., at 269 (White J., dissenting).

40. Ibid., at 267 (quoting Caban, 441 U.S. at 392).

41. See Gomez v. Perez (1973). (Texas violated the equal protection clause by not allowing children of unmarried parents the right to paternal support, although children of married parents were given this right.)

42. See Strathern (1992), 148–49.

43. The holding in *Michael H.* was based on a plurality opinion written by Justice Scalia, joined by a concurrence written by Justice Stevens.

44. Lehr, 463 U.S. at 261.

45. Michael H., 491 U.S. at 124 n.3.

46. Joint Appendix at 44, Michael H..

47. California Evidence Code Sec. 621 (quoted at 491 U.S. at 115). The statute allowed rebuttal of its presumption within two years of the child's birth by the husband or, if the biological father filed an affidavit of paternity, by the wife. The biological father was given no right to rebut the section's presumption. Michael H., 491 U.S. at 115.

48. Michael H., 236 Cal. Rptr. 810, 818 (Ct. App. [1987]).

49. The California Supreme Court denied certiorari. That judgment is reported at 23 California Official Reports, Minutes of the Supreme Court 9 (1987); Brief for Appellant Victoria D. at 1, Michael H. v. Gerald D., 491 U.S. 110 (1989)

(No. 87–746). Thus, Michael and Victoria were able to appeal directly to the United States Supreme Court. Michael H., 485 U.S. 903 (1988).

50. Michael H., 491 U.S. at 119.

51. Ibid., at 123. Justice Brennan pointed out in dissent that in *Quilloin*, *Caban*, and *Lehr* "the putative father's demands would have disrupted a 'unitary family' as the plurality defines it." 491 U.S. at 144 (Brennan, J., dissenting).

52. Michael H., 491 U.S. at 123.

53. See, e.g., Hinnan (1990), 623; Ibid., at 157–58 (Brennan, J., dissenting).

54. Michael H., 491 U.S. at 160 (White J., concurring) (quoting Lehr, 463 U.S. at 261 [quoting Caban, 441 U.S. at 392 n.7]).

55. Michael H., 491 U.S. at 123.

56. Ibid., n.3.

57. Ibid., (Brennan, J., dissenting).

58. Following the Court's decision in *Michael H.*, the California legislature amended the statute at issue in the case. The amendment allowed a "presumed father" to rebut the presumption of the mother's husband's paternity if a motion is brought within two years of the child's birth. 16 Fam. L. Rep. 1520 (1990). The sections' definition of "presumed father" would have covered the biological father in *Michael H.*

59. See, e.g., Barnett and Silverman (1979), 46; Schneider (1980), 107–10, 114–17.

60. Michael H., 491 U.S. at 118 (emphasis in original).

61. See e.g., Ibid., at 130 n.6, n.7.

62. Ibid., at 124.

63. See, e.g., Note, *Michael H. v. Gerald D.: The Constitutional Rights of Putative Fathers and A Proposal for Reform* 1990, 1201; Note, *Tradition and the Liberty Interest: Circumscribing the Rights of the Natural Father* 1990, 314.

64. 463 U.S. at 272 (White, J., dissenting) (footnote omitted).

65. In 1990, in *In re Raquel Marie X*, New York's highest court declared unconstitutional a statute that gave only certain unwed fathers the right to veto the adoptions of their children. The court referred expressly to the statutes' focus on the relationship between the two parents as a basis for paternal rights and declared that focus inappropriate as a measure of a father's commitment to his children. The case thus affirms the direct importance of the father-child relationship to protecting legal paternity. However, the facts in *Raquel Marie* involved a father who did establish a relationship with his child's mother. Indeed, the father in the case married his child's mother, but only after the child had been placed for adoption pursuant to the mother's consent. In *In re Baby Girl S.*, consolidated and decided by the New York Court of Appeals with *Raquel Marie*, the father, upon learning of his lover's pregnancy, responded, "I love you and want to marry you." 535 N.Y.S. 2d at 678. The two did not marry because the mother refused. Thus, both fathers involved in *Raquel Marie* demonstrated a fitting commitment, not just to their children, but to the mothers of those children as well.

66. Obviously, some unwed fathers can now obtain constitutional protection for their relation to their children despite the absence of an appropriate relation between the father and the child's mother. Such cases include, for instance, a case in which the children's mother is deceased. There are, that is, other ways for the father to establish the requisite "family" unit than by establishing a home with the children's mother, but they are not thought of as prototypical.

67. Strathern (1992), 148–49.

68. Lehr, 463 U.S. at 260 (quoting Caban, 441 U.S. at 397 [Stewart, J., dissenting]).

69. Caban, 441 U.S. at 397 (Stewart, J., dissenting).

70. Baby M., 525 A.2d at 1132 (emphasis added).

71. Ibid., at 1170.

72. Ibid., at 1168.

73. Ibid., at 1160.

74. Ibid., at 1157 (emphasis added).

75. Rothenberg (1990), 345.

76. Johnson, No. X-633190, slip op. at 18.

77. Ibid., slip op. at 10.

78. Ibid., slip op. at 18.

79. Lehr, 463 U.S. at 260 (quoting Caban, 441 U.S. at 397 [Stewart, J., dissenting]).

80. Johnson, No. X-633190, slip op. at 21.

81. Ibid. (emphasis in original).

82. Healy (1991), 95.

83. Ibid. 97 n.39.

84. Johnson v. Calvert, *sub nom.* Anna J. v. Mark C., 286 Cal. Rptr. at 380–81.

85. Rothenberg (1990), 346.

Notes to Chapter 5

1. Collins (1995).

2. Clifton and Schneider (1992), 463 n.2.

3. The first pregnancy in a human resulting from the implantation of an embryo that had been frozen and then thawed occurred in 1983. That pregnancy did not result in a birth, but other pregnancies and births (begun with embryos that had been frozen) soon followed. Trounson and Mohr (1983), 707–9.

4. Marrs et al. (1986), 1503.

5. Fox (1993), 122, 123–24.

6. Jenkins (1994).

7. Petitioner's Opening Brief at 8, Johnson v. Calvert.

8. Respondents' Brief at 23, Johnson v. Calvert (*sub nom.* Anna J. v. Mark C.).

9. Appellant's Reply Brief at 8, ibid.

10. Johnson v. Calvert, No. X-633190, slip op. at 5.

11. Respondents' Brief at 22–26, Johnson v. Calvert (*sub nom.* Anna J. v. Mark C.).

12. Respondents' Brief at 23, ibid.

13. Respondents' Brief at 26, ibid.

14. Appellant's Opening Brief at 27, ibid.

15. Petitioner's Opening Brief at 8, Johnson v. Calvert, 851 P.2d 776.

16. Appellant's Opening Brief at 5–xii (quoting transcript of testimony offered at trial, R.T. vol. III 579), Johnson v. Calvert (*sub nom.* Anna J. v. Mark C.).

17. Appellant's Opening Brief at 5–ii (quoting from transcript of testimony offered at trial, R.T. vol. III 483), ibid.

18. Appellant's Opening Brief at 5–iv (quoting transcript of testimony offered at trial, R.T. vol. III 491), ibid.

19. Appellant's Opening Brief at 5–v, ibid.

20. Appellant's Opening Brief at 5–vi (quoting transcript of testimony offered at trial, R.T. Vol. III 496), ibid.

21. Appellant's Opening Brief at 5–vi (quoting transcript of testimony offered at trial, R.T. vol. III 497), ibid.

22. Respondents' Brief at 45, ibid.

23. Respondents' Brief at 49, ibid.

24. Respondents' Brief at 51, ibid. In response to Johnson's claim that her partial Indian heritage made the Indian Child Welfare Act applicable to the case, the Calverts asserted that the baby "has no blood relationship to Anna Johnson," Ibid. That act requires notification to the relevant tribe should an Indian child be made available for adoption. 25 U.S.C. Sec. 1903–1919.

25. Appellant's Reply Brief at 8, Johnson v. Calvert (*sub nom.* Anna C. v. Mark C.).

26. Appellant's Reply Brief at 6–7 (quoting transcript of testimony offered at trial, R.T. Vol. III 621), ibid.

27. Drs. Klaus, Chamberlain, and Harrison testified at trial as experts for Anna Johnson; Dr. Call testified as an expert for Crispina and Mark Calvert.

28. Appellant's Reply Brief at 8 (citations to transcript omitted), Johnson v. Calvert (*sub nom.* Anna J. v. Mark C.).

29. Appellant's Opening Brief at 5–xi (quoting transcript of testimony offered at trial, R.T. Vol. III 565), ibid.

30. Appellant's Opening Brief at 46, Johnson v. Calvert (*sub nom.* Anna J. v. Mark C.).

31. Johnson v. Calvert, 19 Cal. Rptr.2d at 499 n.8.

32. Johnson v. Calvert, 851 P.2d at 781.

33. Michael H., 491 U.S. at 118.

34. Respondents' Answer to Amicus Curiae Brief by ACLU at 16, Johnson v. Calvert (*sub nom.* Anna J. v. Mark C.).

35. Robert J. McDonald provided a very different story of the case, both in his

briefs and supporting papers and during two telephone interviews (July 7 and 8, 1994). According to Robert, the case involved massive fraud on the part of his wife Olga and the infertility clinic. McDonald asserted that he had been told originally that the babies were produced from donor sperm and that his own sperm were probably inadequate to fertilize an egg. Brief for Plaintiff-Appellant, Robert J. McDonald at 8–9, McDonald v. McDonald. Moreover, Robert asserted that Olga had initially informed him that her pregnancy had resulted from the fertilization of her own eggs. In fact, the pregnancy resulted from the fertilization of donor eggs. Ibid. at 6. At least until late 1994, Robert continued his efforts to discover the identity of the ova donor, whose eggs, once fertilized with his sperm, resulted in the conception of the twin girls involved in the case. The appellate division denied Robert's request that the medical records pertaining to the in vitro fertilization and implantation be made available to him. The court declared: "Clearly, resolution of the custody issue in the instant case does not require revelation of the wife's medical records concerning her in-vitro fertilization. . . . Since any information regarding the egg donor is not relevant to the issue of custody in this case, that branch of the husband's motion was properly denied." McDonald v. McDonald, 608 N.Y.S.2d at 481.

36. Brief for Plaintiff-Appellant Robert J. McDonald at 3, McDonald v. McDonald. I am grateful to Dr. Robert McDonald for providing me with the briefs in this case.

37. Johnson v. Calvert, 851 P.2d at 762 n.10.

38. McDonald, 608 N.Y.S.2d at 480 (citation and footnote omitted).

39. Brief for Plaintiff-Appellant, Robert J. McDonald at 18–19, McDonald v. McDonald. At the center of Robert's arguments to the court was the "fraudulent conduct" allegedly committed by Olga and the fertility clinic, in which she was treated and which performed the IVF that led to the conception of the babies. Ibid. at 27; Letter from Robert J. McDonald to Office of Professional Medical Conduct, N.Y.S. Dept. of Health (July 25, 1991).

40. Brief for Defendant-Respondent, Olga B. McDonald at 24, McDonald v. McDonald.

41. Ibid.

42. Ibid. at 7.

43. Ibid. at 8.

44. Ibid. at 10.

45. Ibid. at 11.

46. Ibid. at 12 (citation omitted).

47. Ibid. at 16.

48. Ibid. at 17.

49. Strathern (1995), at 6.

50. Brief for Defendant-Respondent, Olga B. McDonald at 21–22, McDonald v. McDonald.

51. Ibid. at 21.

52. Brief for Plaintiff-Appellant, Robert J. McDonald at 18–19, McDonald v. McDonald.

53. York v. Jones, 717 F. Supp. at 427.

54. Roe, 410 U.S. at 159.

55. Roe, 410 U.S. at 160 and n.59 (relying on L. Hellman and J. Pritchard 1971, p. 493).

56. Akron, 462 U.S. at 458 (O'Connor, J., dissenting). In *Akron*, the Court declared second trimester hospitalization requirements for abortion unconstitutional.

57. Roe, 410 U.S. at 163.

58. Probably, the most well-known and forceful institutional advocate of the position that a human being exists at conception is the Catholic church which holds that:

[T]he fruit of human generation from the first moment of its existence, that is to say, from the moment the zygote has formed, demands the unconditional respect that is morally due to the human being in his bodily and spiritual totality. The human being is to be respected and treated as a person from the moment of conception and therefore from that same moment his rights as a person must be recognized, among which in the first place is the inviolable right of every innocent human being to life. ("Sacred Congregation for the Doctrine of Faith," Instruction on Respect for Human Life in Its Origin and on the Dignity of Procreation, in *Donum Vitae* 1990, app. at 211)

59. Smith (1985–86).

60. Davis, 1989 Tenn. App. LEXIS 641, at *36.

61. Ibid., at *13.

62. Ibid., at *31.

63. Ibid., at *37.

64. Davis, (1990) Tenn. App. LEXIS 642, at *1 (emphasis added).

65. Ibid., at *8–9.

66. Davis, 842 S.W.2d at 596.

67. Ibid., at 597.

68. Ibid., at 604.

69. Ibid.

70. Curriden (1993), A2.

71. Ragoné (1994), 125.

72. Transcript of Proceedings, Davis, at 41.

73. In *Diamond v. Chakrabarty*, for instance, the U.S. Supreme Court concluded that living things can be patented under federal patent law.

74. Davis, 842 S.W.2d at 597.

75. Professor Jerome Lejeune (obituary), *The Times* (London), April 7, 1994.

76. Transcript of Proceedings, Davis, at 23.

77. Ibid., at 48.

78. Ibid., at 78. The term "zygote" generally refers to the fertilized ovum immediately after fertilization occurs.

79. Ibid., at 79.

80. Ibid., at 51.

81. Davis, 1989 Tenn. App. LEXIS, at *10.

82. The other experts who testified at trial included: Prof. John A. Robertson, Baker and Botts Professor of Law at the University of Texas at Austin, Texas; Dr. Irving Ray King, director of the Fertility Center of East Tennessee in Knoxville; Dr. Charles A. Shivers, head of the Department of Zoology at the University of Tennessee in Knoxville; and Deborah Cooper McCarter, RN, primary patient coordinator at Dr. King's IVF Clinic. The court summarized the testimony of these, and other witnesses in Appendix B to its opinion. Davis, 1989 Tenn. App. LEXIS 642, at *75–84.

83. Ibid., at *24–25.

84. Brief for Appellee at 18, Davis, 842 S.W.2d 588. I am grateful to Mr. Charles M. Clifford, Esq. (lawyer for Junior Davis) for providing me with the briefs in this case.

85. Ibid. at 7, Davis, 842 S.W.2d 588 (citing John A. Robertson [1986], 974).

86. Davis, (1990) Tenn. App. LEXIS 642, at *2 (footnote omitted).

87. Davis, 842 S.W.2d, at 593.

88. Ibid., at 594.

89. Ibid.

90. Brief for Appellee at 18, Davis, 842 S.W.2d 588.

91. Ibid., at 9.

92. Ibid., at 9–11.

93. Ibid., 11.

94. Ibid., at 10.

95. Ibid., at 11.

96. Davis, 842 S.W.2d at 593–94.

97. Ibid., at 598.

98. Ibid., at 600.

99. Ibid., at 601.

100. Ibid., at 603–4.

101. Ibid., 596–97.

102. Strathern (1995) 31 (footnote omitted).

Notes to Chapter 6

1. Strathern (1990), 10 (emphasis in original).

2. Barnett and Silverman (1979), 69.

3. Strathern (1990), 8.

4. See, e.g., Trespalacios (1992).

5. Shultz (1990).

6. Andrews (1986), 20.

7. Davis v. Davis, 842 S.W.2d at 597.

8. Ibid., at 604.

9. Ibid., at 601.

10. Ibid., at 601, 604.

11. Johnson v. Calvert, 851 P.2d at 799 (Kennard, J., dissenting).

12. Ibid., at 782, n.10.

13. Ibid., at 782.

14. Ibid., n.10.

15. Johnson v. Calvert, 872 P.2d at 799 (Kennard J., dissenting).

16. Johnson v. Calvert, 851 P.2d at 782 (quoting Hill [1991], 441) (emphasis omitted).

17. Ibid., at 783 (quoting Stumpf [1968], 196) (emphasis omitted).

18. Ibid., at 796 (Kennard, J., dissenting).

19. Ibid., at 783 (quoting Shultz [1990], 323) (footnote omitted).

20. Ibid., at 796–97 (Kennard, J., dissenting).

21. Ibid., at 783 (quoting Shultz [1990], 397).

22. Ibid., at 799 (Kennard, J., dissenting).

23. Ibid., at 782.

24. People v. Sorensen, 437 P.2d at 499.

25. Ibid., at 498.

26. Ibid., at 501.

27. Orford, 49 Ont. L.R. at 23.

28. See Harris, Comment 1981, 924 (citing Ga. Code Ann. § 101.1 [1964]).

29. See, e.g., *In re* Baby Doe; Byers v. Byers.

30. See, e.g., People v. Dennett.

31. Donovan (1982–83), 194, 216–22.

32. Jhordan, 224 Cal. Rptr. at 531.

33. Hecht, 20 Cal. Rptr. 2d at 276.

34. Ibid., n.1.

35. Ibid., at 276 (quoting agreement between Kane and California Cryobank, Inc.).

36. Ibid., at 276.

37. Ibid., at 279, n.3.

38. Ibid., at 281.

39. Answer of Real Parties in Interest William Everett Kane, Jr., Katharine E. Kane and Robert L. Greene, Administrator CTA of the Estate of William E. Kane to Petition for Writ of Mandate/Prohibition in the First Instance and/or Other Extraordinary Relief at 9, Hecht, 20 Cal. Rptr.2d 275 (1993).

40. Hecht, 20 Cal. Rptr.2d at 283–84.

41. Hecht, 44 Cal. Rptr.2d 578, 1995 Cal. App. 842, 1995 Cal. App. Lexis 842, at *6.

42. Hecht, 20 Cal. Rptr.2d at 288.

43. Ibid., at 287.

44. Reuters Library Report, "French Court Rejects AIDS Widow's Insemination Plea" (1991).

45. Robertson (1994b).

46. See Goodwin v. Turner (1990).

47. See, Rick Bragg, "Cheating Death, and Testing a Reproductive Law," (1994).

48. "High-Tech Mom Vows to Fight for Federal Benefits," (1995)

49. Dionne (1984).

50. Parpalaix, at 561–62.

51. Ibid., at 561.

52. Hecht, 20 Cal. Rptr.2d at 288 (describing conclusions of *Parpalaix* court).

53. Parpalaix, at 562.

54. "Court Awards Young Widow Sperm of Late Husband," (1984).

55. "Woman Fails to Conceive from Dead Husband's Sperm" (1985).

56. Hecht, 20 Cal. Rptr.2d at 288–89.

57. Freud ([1900] 1950), 343–43.

58. Feinman and Gabel (1990), 375.

59. Ibid.

60. Ibid., at 379–81.

61. Shultz (1990), 349.

Notes to Chapter 7

1. Johnson v. Calvert, 851 P.2d at 783.

2. In the Matter of Kottman, 2 Hill at 364.

3. Infants Custody Act, 1873, 36 and 37 Vict. c. 12.

4. Mercein v. The People, 25 Wend. at 102.

5. Davis, 842 S.W.2d at 597.

6. Mattter of Baby M., 525 A.2d at 1143.

7. Matter of Baby M., 537 A.2d at 1257.

8. Ibid., 537 A.2d at 1263.

9. Ibid.

10. Ibid.

11. Matter of Baby M., 542 A.2d at 55.

12. Moschetta, 30 Cal. Rptr.2d at 894.

13. Ibid., at 895.

14. Moschetta, D324349 at 17.

15. Moschetta, 30 Cal. Rptr.2d at 901.

16. Moschetta, D 324349 at 14.

17. Ibid., at 13.

18. Ibid.

19. Ibid.

20. Moschetta, 30 Cal. Rptr.2d at 902.

21. Moschetta, D324349 at 15.

22. Ibid., at 16.

23. Boucher (1995).

24. Ellingwood (1995).

25. Ibid. (quoting Orange County Superior Court Judge John C. Woolley's oral opinion of November 17, 1995).

26. Johnson v. Calvert, No. X-633190 at 14.

27. Ibid.

28. Justice Arabian wrote another, concurring, opinion in the case. He wrote to voice his disagreement with the court's conclusion that surrogacy contracts are " 'not inconsistent with public policy.' " Johnson, 851 P.2d at 788.

29. Parham, at 602.

30. Johnson, 851 P.2d at 783 (quoting Shultz [1990] at 397).

31. Johnson, 851 P.2d at 782, n.10.

32. I am grateful to Professor Larry I. Palmer of Cornell Law School for the term "biotechnological children." Professor Palmer was not the first to use the term. However, his use is especially instructive because it clearly suggests both the descriptive *and* ironic appeal of the term. See Palmer (1994).

33. See e.g., Horne (1994); Winslow (1994).

34. See e.g., "Moral Torpor Spawns Designer Babies" (1994); "Donum Vitae" (1990), Appendix.

35. "Donum Vitae" (1990), Appendix, at 216.

36. See e.g., "Moral Torpor Spawns Designer Babies" (1994).

37. Orenstein (1995).

38. This discussion does not refer to feminist opponents of reproductive technology. Feminist opposition to reproductive technology focuses as much on physical and psychological harms that befall women as a result of being treated for infertility as on the harms that befall the resulting children.

39. "Donum Vitae" (1990), Appendix, at 208.

40. See, e.g., Cahill (1990).

41. See, e.g., Baurac (1992); Williams (1992); Laboy (1993); Lawson (1993).

42. Mihill (1994).

43. Pallot (1993).

44. Gabriel (1996).

45. See e.g., Hopkins (1995); Clancy and Tropiano (1994).

46. Steinberg (1993).

47. See, e.g., Pearce (1994); Ratcliffe (1994); Lawson (1993); Midgley (1993); Wells (1993).

48. Wells (1993).

49. Lawson (1993).

50. See e.g., Rochell (1995); Shaver (1995); Lane and Szabo (1992); Doten (1991).

51. Loose (1993).

52. See Singer (1992).

Notes to the Conclusion

1. Schneider (1977), 66.

BIBLIOGRAPHY

Books and Articles

Allen, Anita L. 1992. "Autonomy's Magic Wand: Abortion and Constitutional Interpretations." 72 *B.U.L.Rev.* 683.

Andrews, Lori B. 1986. "Legal and Ethical Aspects of New Reproductive Technologies." 29 *Clin. Obstet. & Gyn* 190.

Aries, Philippe, and Georges Duby, eds. 1988. *A History of Private Life,* vol. 2.

Barnett, Steven A. 1976. "Approaches to Changes in Caste Ideology in South India." In *Essays on South India.* Ed. Burton Stein.

———. 1977. "Identity Choice and Caste Ideology." In *Symbolic Anthropology: A Reader in the Study of Symbols and Meanings.* Ed. Janet L. Dolgin et al.

Barnett, Steven A., and Martin G. Silverman. 1979. *Ideology and Everyday Life.*

Barthes, Roland. 1967. *Elements of Semiology.*

Bartholet, Elizabeth. 1993. *Family Bonds: Adoption and the Politics of Parenting.*

Batty, David L. 1990. Note, "Michael H. v. Gerald D.: The Constitutional Rights of Putative Fathers and a Proposal for Reform." 31 *B.C.L. Rev.* 1173.

Baurac, Deborah Rissing. 1992. "On the Infertility Front the Weapons Are Many. *Chig. Trib.,* May 3, at 1, available in LEXIS, News Library.

Bloch, Marc. 1968. *Feudal Society,* vol 2. Trans. L. A. Manyon.

———. 1970. *Feudal Society,* vol. 1. Trans. L. A. Manyon.

Boucher, Geoff. 1995. "Doctor: Surrogate Deal Stresses Child." *L.A. Times,* Nov. 2, at B4.

Bragg, Rick. 1994. "Cheating Death, and Testing a Reproductive Law." *N.Y. Times,* Dec. 22, at A16.

Bremner, Robert H., ed. 1970. *Children and Youth in America.*

Cahill, Lisa Stowle. 1990. "The Ethics of Surrogate Motherhood: Biology, Freedom, and Moral Obligations." In *Surrogate Motherhood: Politics and Privacy.* Ed. Larry Gostin.

Caplan, Lincoln. 1990. *An Open Adoption.*

Chesler, Ellen. 1992. *Woman of Valor: Margaret Sanger and the Birth Control Movement in America.*

Clancy, Michael A., and Dolores Tropiano. 1994. "Mom's the Word at Reunion with Fertility Doctor." *Ariz. Rep.,* May 11, at B6.

Clifton, Perry, and L. Kristen Schneider. 1992. "Cryopreserved Embryos: Who Shall Decide Their Fate?" 13 *J. Legal Med.* 463.

Coleman, Phyllis. 1981. "Who's Been Sleeping in My Bed? You and Me, and the State Makes Three." 24 *Ind. L. Rev.* 399.

Collins, J. A., et al. 1995. "An Estimate of the Cost of In Vitro Fertilization Services in the United States in 1995." 64 *Fert. & Steril.* 538.

Comment. 1935. "Custody and Control of Children." 5 *Ford. L. Rev.* 460.

Comment. 1985. "Delineation of the Boundaries of Putative Fathers' Rights: A Psychological Parenthood Perspective." 15 *Seton Hall L. Rev.* 290.

Comment. 1928. 42 *Harv. L. Rev.* 112.

Coontz, Stephanie. 1992. *The Way We Never Were: American Families and the Nostalgia Trap.*

Corea, Gena. 1985. *The Mother Machine.*

"Court Awards Young Widow Sperm of Late Husband." 1984. UPI, Aug. 1, available in LEXIS, News Library.

Curriden, Mark. 1993. "Embryo Fight Yields Few Answers: Disposal Disclosed: Embryos Are Discarded in a Tennessee Case, but Legal and Ethical Questions Remain." *Atlanta J. & Const.*, June 14, available in LEXIS, News Library.

Czapansky, Karen. 1991. "Volunteers and Draftees: The Struggle for Parental Equality." 38 *UCLA L. Rev.* 1415.

de La Rouciere, Charles. 1988. "Tuscan Notables on the Eve of the Renaissance." In *A History of Private Life,* vol. 2. Eds. Philippe Aries and Georges Duby.

Demos, John. 1986. *Past, Present, Personal: The Family and the Life Course in American History.*

De Tocqueville, Alexis. [1835] 1945. *Democracy in America.* Trans. Henry Reeve. Ed. Phillips Bradley II.

Dianelli, Diane M. 1995. "Fraud Scandal Closes California Fertility Clinic." 38 *Amer. Med. News,* June 19, at 1.

Dionne, E. J., Jr. 1984. "A French Widow Sues Over Sperm." *N.Y. Times,* July 2, at A7.

Donovan, Carol. 1982–83. "The Uniform Parentage Act and Nonmarital Motherhood-by-Choice." 11 *N.Y.U. Rev. L. & Soc. Change* 193.

Donum Vitae (The Gift of Life): The Proceedings of a National Conference on the Vatican Instruction on Reproductive Ethics and Technology. 1990. Eds. Marilyn Wallace and Thomas W. Hilgers.

Doten, Patti. 1991. "In Vitro: Testing the Limits." *Boston Globe,* Nov. 26, available in LEXIS, News Library.

Duby, Georges. 1978. *Medieval Marriage.* Trans. Elborg Forster.

———. 1980. *The Three Orders.* Trans. Arthur Goldhammer.

———. 1988. "The Aristocratic Households of Feudal France." In *A History of Private Life,* vol. 2. Eds. Philippe Aries and George Duby.

Dumont, Louis. 1967. *Homo Hierarchicus.*

————. 1977. *From Mandeville to Marx: The Genesis and Triumph of Economic Ideology.*

Ehrenreich, Barbara, and Deidre English. 1978. *For Her Own Good: 150 Years of the Experts' Advice to Women.*

Ellingwood, Ken. 1995. "Surrogate Loses Custody of O.C. Girl." *L.A. Times,* Nov. 18, at A1.

Ellman, Ira Mark, et al. 1991. *Family Law: Cases, Text, Problems.*

"Ethical Consideration of the New Reproductive Technologies." 1990. 53 *Fert. & Steril.* (Supp.)

Eveleigh, Laurel J. 1989. Note, "Certainty Not Child's Play: A Serious Game of Hide and Seek with The Rights of Unwed Fathers." 40 *Syracuse L. Rev.* 1055.

Fashing, Felicia R. 1984. Note, "Artificial Conception: A Legislative Proposal." 5 *Cardozo L. Rev.* 713.

Feinman, Jay, and Peter Gabel. 1990. "Contract Law as Ideology." In *The Politics of Law: A Progressive Critique,* rev. ed. Ed. David Kairys.

Fitzgerald, Wendy Anton. 1994. "Maturity, Difference and Mystery: Children's Perspectives and the Law." 36 *Ariz. L. Rev.* 11.

Fox, Robin. 1993. *Reproduction and Succession.*

Freed, Doris J., and Timothy B. Walker. 1988. "Family Law in the Fifty States: An Overview." 22 *Fam. L.Q.* 417.

Freud, Sigmund. [1900] 1950. *The Interpretation of Dreams.* Trans. A. A. Brill.

Friedan, Betty. 1963. *The Feminine Mystique.*

Friedman, Lawrence M. 1985. *A History of American Law,* 2d ed.

Gabriel, Trip. 1996. "The Fertility Market: High-Tech Pregnancies Test Hopes Limit." *N.Y. Times,* Jan. 7, at A1.

Glendon, Mary Ann. 1987. *Abortion and Divorce in Western Law: American Failures, European Challenges.*

Gordon, Mary. 1987. "Baby M': New Questions about Biology and Destiny." *MS,* June.

Grey, Thomas. 1980. "Eros, Civilization and the Burger Court." 43 *Law & Contemp. Probs.* 83.

Grossberg, Michael. 1985. *Governing the Hearth: Law and Family in Nineteenth-Century America.*

Hadad, Elizabeth A. 1990. Note, "Tradition and the Liberty Interest: Circumscribing the Rights of the Natural Father." 56 *Brook. L. Rev.* 291.

Hafen, Bruce. 1983. "The Constitutional Status of Marriage, Kinship, and Sexual Privacy—Balancing the Individual and Social Interests." 81 *Mich. L. Rev.* 463.

Harris, Lindsey E. 1981. Comment, "Artificial Insemination and Surrogate Motherhood—A Nursery Full of Unresolved Questions." 17 *Willamette L. Rev.* 913.

Healy, Nicole M. 1991. "Beyond Surrogacy: Gestational Parenting Agreements under California Law." 1 *UCLA Women's L.J.* 89.

Hellman, L., and J. Pritchard. 1971. *Williams Obstetrics,* 14th ed.

Henkin, Louis. 1974. "Privacy and Autonomy." 74 *Colum. L. Rev.* 1410.

Herlihy, David. 1985. *Medieval Households.*

"High-Tech Mom Vows to Fight for Federal Benefits." 1995. *L.A. Times,* Dec. 3, at A43.

Hill, John L. 1991. "What Does It Mean to Be a Parent? The Claims of Biology as a Basis for Parental Rights." 66 *N.Y.U.L. Rev.* 353.

Hinnan, Tina M. 1990. Note, "Lovers' Triangle Turns Bermuda Triangle: The Natural Father's Right to Rebut the Marital Presumption." 25 *Wake Forest L. Rev.* 617.

Hochheimer, Lewis. 1908. "The Law in Its Relation to the Child." 67 *Central L. J.* 395.

Hopkins, Mary Ellen. 1995. "Fertility Funfare: In Vitro Program Celebrates Successes with Reunion." *Sun-Sentinel,* Jan. 1, at 3.

Horne, Terry. 1994. "Couples Take the Risk to Conceive a Child." *Indianapolis News,* Sept. 6, at A1.

Hubbard, Ruth. 1990. *The Politics of Women's Biology.*

Hyde, Lewis. 1979. *The Gift.*

Jenkins, Simon. 1994. "A Plot against the Family." *The Times,* July 6, available in LEXIS, News Library.

Laboy, Julio. 1993. "State-of-the-Art Stock." *Newsday,* Dec. 12.

Lane, Ellen, and Liz Szabo. 1992. "Using Technology to Conceive." Gannett News Service, August 18, available in WESTLAW, 1992 WL 9387463.

Lawson, Carol. 1993. "Celebrated Birth Aside, Teen-Ager Is Typical Now." N.Y. *Times,* Oct. 4, at A18.

Loose, Cindy. 1993. "A Holiday Comes to Life." *Wash. Post,* May 9, at A1.

MacPherson, C. B. 1962. *The Political Theory of Possessive Individualism.*

Maine, Sir Henry. [1861] 1917. *Ancient Law.*

Marrs, Richard P., et al. 1986. "Successful Pregnancies from Cryopreserved Human Embryos Produced by In Vitro Fertilization." 156 *Am. J. Obstet. & Gyn.* 1503.

Marx, Karl. [1867] 1967. *Das Kapital.* Trans. Samuel Moore and Edward Aveling.

Mason, Mary Ann. 1994. *From Father's Property to Children's Rights: The History of Child Custody in the United States.*

May, Elaine Tyler. 1991. "Myths and Realities of the American Families." In *A History of Private Life,* vol. 5. Trans. Arthur Goldhammer. Eds. Antoine Prost and Gerard Vincent.

Midgley, Carol. 1993. "The Bubbly Louise." *Daily Mail* (Eng.), March 27, at 3.

Mihill, Chris. 1994. "IVF Couples: Better Parents." The Guardian, Jan. 10, at 8.

Mintz, Steven. 1983. *A Prison of Expectations: The Family in Victorian Culture.*

Mintz, Steven, and Susan Kellogg. 1988. *Domestic Revolutions: A Social History of American Family Life.*

"Moral Torpor Spawns Designer Babies" (Observer Lead Page). 1994. *Observer* (Eng.), Jan. 9, available in LEXIS, News Library.

Note, "Certainly Not Child's Play: A Serious Game of Hide and Seek with the Rights of Unwed Fathers." 1989. 40 *Syracuse L. Rev.* 1055.

Obituary, Professor Jerome Lejeune. 1994. *Times* (London), April 7, available in LEXIS, News Library.

Olsen, Frances. 1993. "The Myth of State Intervention in the Family." In *Family Matters: Readings on Family Lives and the Law*. Ed. Martha Minow.

Orenstein, Peggy. 1995. "Are You My Father?" N.Y. *Times Mag.*, June 18, Sec. 6, at 28.

Pallot, Peter. 1993. "Intelligence Test for the Time Warp Twins." *Daily Telegraph* (Eng.), Jan. 2, at 3, available in LEXIS, News Library.

Palmer, Larry I. 1994. "Who Are the Parents of Biotechnological Children?" 35 *Jurimetrics J.L. & Sci. Tech.* 17.

Pearce, Kelly. 1994. " 'My Parents Tell Me I'm Special': Test-Tube 'Miracles' Celebrate Life." *Ariz. Rep.*, Nov. 15, at B1.

Perrot, Michelle. 1990. "At Home." In A *History of Private Life*, vol. 4. Eds. Phillipe Aries and George Duby.

Perry, Jane P. 1984. Note, "Lehr v. Robertson: Putting The Genie Back in the Bottle: The Supreme Court Limits the Scope of the Putative Father's Right to Notice, Hearing, and Consent in the Adoption of His Illegitimate Child." 15 *U. Tol. L. Rev.* 1501.

Ragoné, Helena. 1994. *Surrogate Motherhood: Conception in the Heart.*

Ratcliffe, Sandra. 1994. "Louise Brown Talks about Life under the Microscope from Day 1." *Scottish Daily Rec.*, Jan. 17, at 2/21, available in LEXIS, News Library.

Regan, Milton C. 1993. *Family Law and the Pursuit of Intimacy.*

Reuters Library Report. 1991. "French Court Rejects AIDS Widow's Insemination Plea." March 26, available in LEXIS, News Library.

Rhode, Deborah L. 1996. "Equal Rights: To Fault or Not to Fault." *National Law Journal*, May 13, at A19, col. 1.

Robertson, John A. 1986. "Embryos, Families, and Procreative Liberty: The Legal Structure of the New Reproduction." 59 *S. Cal. L. Rev.* 939.

———. 1994a. *Children of Choice: Freedom and the New Reproductive Technologies.*

———. 1994b. "Posthumous Reproduction." 69 *Ind. L.J.* 1027.

Rochell, Anne. 1995. "Four Bundles of Joy." *Atlanta J. & Constit.*, April 25, at C3.

Rothenberg, Karen H. 1990. "Gestational Surrogacy and the Health Care Provider: Put Part of the 'IVF Genie' Back into the Bottle." 18 *Law Med. & Health Care* 345.

Schneider, David M. 1977. "Kinship, Nationality, and Religion in American Culture: Toward a Definition of Kinship." In *Symbolic Anthropology: A Reader in the Study of Symbols and Meanings*. Ed. Janet L. Dolgin et al.

———. 1980. *American Kinship: A Cultural Account*, 2d ed.

Schwartz, Bernard. 1985. *The Unpublished Opinions of the Warren Court.*

Seib, Gerald F. 1993. "New Ideas Enter Standard Debate on Social Decline." *Wall St. J.,* Mar. 17, at A16.

Shanley, Mary Lyndon. 1989. *Feminism, Marriage, and the Law in Victorian England.*

Shaver, Katherine. 1995. "Three Birthdays and an Anniversary." *St. Petersburg Times,* March 4, available in LEXIS, News Library.

Shaw, George Bernard. [1924] 1971. *St. Joan.* Ed. Stanley Weintraub.

Shultz, Marjorie. 1990. "Reproductive Technology and Intent-Based Parenthood: An Opportunity for Gender Neutrality." *Wis. L. Rev.* 297.

Singer, Jana B. 1992. "The Privatization of Family Law." *Wis. L. Rev.* 1443.

Smith, George P. II. 1985–86. "Australia's Frozen 'Orphan' Embryos: A Medical, Legal and Ethical Dilemma." 24 *J. Fam. L.* 27.

Squire, Susan. 1994. "Whatever Happened to Baby M?" *Redbook,* Jan., at 60.

Steinberg, Jacques. 1993. "Gathering Shows Growing Acceptance of In Vitro Fertilization: Parents of Test Tube Babies Hold Picnic to Celebrate Medical Advancement." *Dallas Morning News,* May 29, at A49.

Strathern, Marilyn. 1990. *Disembodied Choice.* Draft.

―――. 1992. *Reproducing the Future: Essays on Anthropology, Kinship, and the New Reproductive Technologies.*

―――. 1993. *New Knowledge for Old: Reflections Following Fox's Reproduction and Succession.* Draft.

Stumpf, Andrea E. 1986. Note, "Redefining Mother: A Legal Matrix for New Reproductive Technologies." 96 *Yale L.J.* 187.

Tawney, R. H. 1964. *Equality.*

Teitelbaum, Lee E. 1985. "Family History and Family Law." *Wis. L. Rev.* 1135.

Trespalacios, Mario J. 1992. "Frozen Embryos: Toward an Equitable Solution." 46 *U. Miami L. Rev.* 803.

Trounson, Alan, and Linda Mohr. 1983. "Human Pregnancy Following Cryopreservation, Thawing and Transfer of an Eight-Cell Embryo." 305 *Nature* 707.

Uniform Premarital Agreement Act. 1987. 9B U.L.A. 371 (promulgated by National Conference of Commissioners on Uniform State Laws).

Wells, Paul. 1993. "World's First Test-Tube Baby—or, Teenager Visits In Vitro Clinic." *Gazette* (Montreal), Oct. 10, at A3, available in LEXIS, News Library.

Weston, Kath. 1991. *Families We Choose.*

Wintjen, Gayle. 1990. Note, "Make Room for Daddy: Putative Father's Rights to His Children." 24 *New Eng. L. Rev.* 1059.

Williams, Linda S. 1992. "Biology or Society? Parenthood Motivation in a Sample of Canadian Women Seeking In Vitro Fertilization." In *Issues in Reproductive Technology: An Anthology.* Ed. Helen Bequaert Holmes.

Winslow, Ron. 1994. "Trouble Plagues Premies Who Are Saved." *Wall St. J.,* Sept. 22, at B1, col. 3.

"Woman Fails to Conceive from Dead Husband's Sperm." 1985. Reuters Northern Europe Service, Jan. 11, available in LEXIS, News Library.

Zainaldin, Jamil S. 1979. "The Emergence of Modern American Family Law: Child Custody, Adoption, and the Courts, 1796–1861." 73 *N.W.U.L. Rev.* 1038.

Zinman, Daniel C. 1992. Note, "Father Knows Best: The Unwed Fathers Right to Raise His Infant Surrendered for Adoption." 60 *Ford. L. Rev.* 971.

Cases

In re Adoption of Anonymous, 345 N.Y.S.2d 430 (N.Y. Sup. Ct. 1973).

Akron v. Akron Center for Reproductive Health, Inc., 462 U.S. 416 (1983).

In re Baby Doe, 353 S.E.2d 877 (S.C. 1987).

In re Baby Girl S., 535 N.Y.S.2d 676 (Sup. Ct. 1988), *aff'd sub nom. In re* Raquel Marie X, 559 N.E.2d 418 (N.Y. 1990).

Baehr v. Lewin, 852 P.2d 44 (Hawaii 1993).

Blisset's Case, Lofft 748, 98 Eng. Rep. 899 (K.B. 1774).

Bottoms v. Bottoms, 444 S.E.2d 276 (1994) *rev'd*, 457 S.E.2d 102 (S. Ct. Va. 1995).

Bowers v. Hardwick, 478 U.S. 186 (1986).

Bradwell v. Illinois, 83 U.S. 130 (1872).

Brady v. U.S., 397 U.S. 742 (1970).

Brookhart v. Janis, 384 U.S. 1 (1966).

Byers v. Byers, 618 P.2d 930 (Okla. 1980).

Caban v. Mohammed, 441 U.S. 380 (1979).

Carey v. Population Servs. Int'l et al., 431 U.S. 678 (1977).

Davis v. Davis, No. E-11496, 1989 Tenn. App. LEXIS 641 (Tenn. Cir. Ct. Sept. 21, 1989), *rev'd* No. 180, 1990 Tenn. App. LEXIS 642 (Tenn. Ct. App. Sept. 13, 1990), *aff'd*, 842 S.W.2d 588 (Tenn. 1992), *cert. denied sub nom.* Stowe v. Davis, 507 U.S. 911 (1993).

Diamond v. Chakrabarty, 447 U.S. 303 (1980).

Doornbos v. Doornbos, 23 U.S.L.W. 2308 (Super. Ct. Cook Cnty., Ill., Dec. 13, 1954) *appeal dismissed on procedural grounds*, 12 Ill. App.2d 473, 1249 N.E.2d 844 (1956).

Eisenstadt v. Baird, 405 U.S. 438 (1972).

Foster v. Alston, 7 Miss. (6 How.) 406 (1842).

Gomez v. Perez, 409 U.S. 535 (1973).

Goodwin v. Turner, 908 F.2d 1395 (8th Cir. 1990).

In re Gregg, 6 Pa. L.J. 528 (N.Y. City Super. Ct. 1847).

Griswold v. Connecticut, 381 U.S. 479 (1965).

Gursky v. Gursky, 242 N.Y.S. 2d 406 (N.Y. Sup. Ct. 1963).

Hecht v. Superior Court, 20 Cal. Rptr.2d 275 (Cal. Ct. App. 1993).

Jhordan C. v. Mary K., 224 Cal. Rptr. 530 (Cal. Ct. App. 1986).

Johnson v. Calvert, No. X-633190 (Cal. App. Dep't Super. Ct. Oct. 22, 1990) slip.

op., *aff'd sub nom.* Anna J. v. Mark C., 286 Cal. Rptr. 369 (Cal. Ct. App. 1991), *aff'd sub nom.* Johnson v. Calvert, 851 P.2d 776 (Cal. 1993), *cert. denied*, 114 S.Ct. 206 (1993).

Johnson v. Zerbst, 304 U.S. 458 (1938).

Jones v. Jones, 91 S.E. 960 (1917).

Kane v. Superior Court, 44 Cal. Rptr.2d 578 (Cal. Ct. App. 1995).

Kass v. Kass, N.Y.L.J., Jan. 23, 1995, at 34 (N.Y. Sup. Ct.).

In re Kingsley, 1992 WL 551484 (Fla. Cir. Ct. Oct. 21, 1992), *aff'd in part and rev'd in part sub nom.* Kingsley v. Kingsley, 623 So.2d 780 (Fla. Dist. Ct. App. 1993).

In re Knoll Guardianship, 167 N.W. 744 (1918).

In the Matter of Kottman, 2 Hill (S.C. Law) 363 (1833).

Lehr v. Robertson, 463 U.S. 248 (1983).

Lindsey v. Lindsey, 14 GA. 657 (1853).

Lochner v. New York, 198 U.S. 45 (1905).

Marvin v. Marvin, 557 P.2d 106 (Cal. 1976).

Matter of Baby M, 217 N.J. Super. 313, 525 A.2d 1128 (1987), *aff'd in part and rev'd in part*, 109 N.J. 396, 537 A.2d 1227 (1988).

McDonald v. McDonald, 608 N.Y.S.2d 477 (1994).

McGuire v. McGuire, 157 Neb. 226, 59 N.W.2d 336 (1953).

Mercein v. The People, *ex. rel.* Barry, 25 Wend. (N.Y. Ct. Err.) 64 (1840), *rev'd*, People *ex rel.* Barry v. Mercein, 3 Hill (N.Y. Sup. Ct.) 399 (1842).

Michael H. v. Gerald D., 485 U.S. 903 (1988) (noting probable jurisdiction), 491 U.S. 110 (1989), *aff'g*, 236 Cal. Rptr. 810 (Ct. App. 1987).

Moschetta v. Moschetta, No. D 324349 (Sup. Ct. Orange Cnty. March 9, 1993) (written statement of decisions rendered orally on April 18, 1991 and Sept. 26, 1991), *aff'd in part and rev'd in part*, 30 Cal. Rptr.2d 893 (App. 4 Dist. 1994), *review denied* (Oct. 13, 1994).

Olmstead v. United States, 277 U.S. 478 (1928).

Orford v. Orford, 49 Ont. L.R. 15 (1921).

Parham v. J.R., 442 U.S. 584 (1979).

Parpalaix v. CECOS, Trib. Gr. Inst. Creteil, Gazette du Palais [G.P.], Sept. 15, 1984.

People v. Abajian v. Dennett, 15 Misc.2d 260, 184 N.Y.S.2d 178 (1958).

People v. Dennett, 184 N.Y.S. 178 (N.Y. Sup. Ct. 1958).

People v. Sorensen, 437 P.2d 495 (Cal. 1968).

Pierce v. Somerset Railway, 171 U.S. 641 (1898).

Poe v. Ullman, 367 U.S. 497 (1961).

Posner v. Posner, 233 So.2d 381 (Fla. 1970).

Quilloin v. Walcott, 434 U.S. 246 (1978).

In re Raquel Marie X, 559 N.E.2d 418 (N.Y.), *cert denied sub nom.* Robert C. v. Miguel T., 498 U.S. 984 (1990).

Regenvetter v. Regenvetter, 213 Pac. 917 (1923).

Rex v. DeManneville, 5 East 221, 102 Eng. Rep. 1054 (K.B. 1804).

Roe v. Wade, 410 U.S. 113 (1973).

Schnuk v. Schnuk, 173 S.W. 347 (1915).

Stanley v. Illinois, 405 U.S. 645 (1972).

State *ex rel.* J.R. v. Mendoza, 481 N.W.2d 165 (Neb. 1992).

Strnad v. Strnad, 190 Misc. 786, 78 N.Y.S.2d 390 (N.Y. Sup. Ct. 1948).

Webster v. Missouri Reproductive Health Services, 492 U.S. 490 (1989).

West Coast Hotel v. Parrish, 300 U.S. 379 (1937), *rev'g* Adkins v. Children's Hosp., 361 U.S. 525 (1923).

York v. Jones, 717 F. Supp. 421 (E.D. Va. 1989).

Zablocki v. Redhail, 434 U.S. 374 (1978).

INDEX